# NORTH CAROLINA SLAVE NARRATIVES, Vol 2 J-Z

*A Folk History of Slavery in the United States
From Interviews with Former Slaves*

**TYPEWRITTEN RECORDS PREPARED BY THE FEDERAL WRITERS' PROJECT**

**1936-1938**

**Volume III in the *We The People Series***

**Edited By**

**Stephen Payseur**

**NORTH CAROLINA SLAVE NARRATIVES, Vol 2 J-Z**

Volume III in the *We the People Series*

Copyright 2017

By Creekside Publishing Company

Po Box 1848

Lincolnton NC 28093

ISBN 13  978-0-9656697-5-7

Cover Design by Shannon Vernitsky

All of the photos on the cover and in the interior of the book are of actual freed slaves taken by the Writers Project of the WPA from 1936 to 1938

For additional copies or public appearances contact

Steve Payseur, PO Box 1848, Lincolnton NC 28093

Email: creekside@charter.net

## Table of Contents

| | |
|---|---|
| **Editor's Preface** | Page 5 |
| **Introduction** | Page 7 |
| **Informants** | Page 10 |
| **Illustrations** | Page 10 |
| **The Narratives** | Page 11 - 202 |

# Editor's Preface

This is the second volume of the Slave Narratives of North Carolina, letters J though Z.

I had mixed emotions as I was putting together this book. Though I felt that the subject matter was very important, there was still an element of uneasiness.

The words of these former slaves resonated. Their nobility and humility was very apparent in the words that they chose. Through it all they all demonstrated the best of the human spirit. Though their lives were extremely hard, they persevered.

All of these people suffered through hardships we can only imagine. Few, if any of us have ever had to endure anything approaching the magnitude of what these people experienced. I hope none of us ever have to. There were beating, families separated when one or more of them were sold, even deaths. No personal possessions to speak of, yet they found a way to cope and survive.

Those things were encouraging and uplifting.

However fascinating I found these narratives, there was always something that was unsettling about them. I was never really comfortable reading them. It was as if there was a dull ache that I couldn't identify, but I knew it was there. The fact that there were people in the United States of America who told these stories from their lives here was disturbing.

When the WPA started the Writers Project, their thrust was to collect the oral histories of a diverse population. Their goal was to put people to work. They succeeded; I am sure, beyond their expectations. Through the interviews they conducted, we can all get a much clearer picture of the horrors of slavery.

I appreciate the fact that they tried to write as the respondents spoke, using phonetic spellings for the dialect. In today's world, it would be considered politically incorrect to do the same thing. It would be considered to be degrading to those who spoke the words. However, I'm glad they did. It gives us an insight that we would have most likely missed. It makes the words come alive, as if someone is actually speaking to us. I think they are.

Some of the words and phrases used in this book are offensive to our modern sensibilities. But as you read, keep in mind that these stories are a reflection not only of the times in which these people lived, but a caution to our own time.

The persons interviewed in this book are all dead now, but their story lives own. I firmly believe that we should all read them with the interest, respect and fascination that they deserve. The reader should feel blessed to have met these people if only through the printed word. Finally, I hope that the reader will be unsettled and feel that nagging ache that simply won't subside.

Stephen Payseur, Editor

# Introduction

In 1935, as part of the WPA, President Roosevelt created the Federal Writers Project. This was a very ambitious program designed to put unemployed writers, editors, teachers and others to work. They were paid between $20 and $25 per week on average.

Over 6000 people were employed by the Federal Writers Project. Some later on became quite famous in the literary world. Among those were Conrad Aiken, Nelson Algren, Saul Bellow, Arna Bontemps, John Cheever, Malcolm Cowley, Edward Dahlberg, Ralph Ellison, Zora Neale Hurston, Claude McKay, Kenneth Patchen, Philip Rahv, Kenneth Rexroth, Harold Rosenberg, John Steinbeck, Studs Terkel, Margaret Walker, Richard Wright and Frank Yerby.

One of the Writers Project most well known projects was the Oral History Project. Interviewers went out all over the country talking to the "common" people to document their lives. Thousands of people in hundreds of groups were interviewed. One of these groups was former slaves.

This book is a compilation of some of these interviews conducted in North Carolina. As you read through them, you will quickly notice that the interviewers tried to write as their subjects spoke, in dialect. The former slaves used words and terms that not politically correct in today's world. They may be offensive to some, but I hope not. It is how the subjects of the interview actually spoke.

In this book, the interviews are presented exactly as they were written during the years 1936-1938. They have not been edited. The writers at that time were instructed to stick the exact words used by the subjects. Editing, it was feared, would change the tone and the meaning of the interview.

So here they are. If they give anyone offense, I sincerely apologize. I feel that these documents are far too important to be languishing in some collection, that most people will never see.

It is my hope that you will find these stories compelling, fascinating, disturbing, interesting, and an essential chronicle of an unpleasant and embarrassing period in our national history.

# SLAVE NARRATIVES

*A Folk History of Slavery in the United States
From Interviews with Former Slaves*

TYPEWRITTEN RECORDS PREPARED BY
THE FEDERAL WRITERS' PROJECT
1936-1938
ASSEMBLED BY
THE LIBRARY OF CONGRESS PROJECT
WORK PROJECTS ADMINISTRATION
FOR THE DISTRICT OF COLUMBIA
SPONSORED BY THE LIBRARY OF CONGRESS

*Illustrated with Photographs*

WASHINGTON 1941

## VOLUME XI

## NORTH CAROLINA NARRATIVES

## PART 2

Prepared by
the Federal Writers' Project of
the Works Progress Administration
for the State of North Carolina

# INFORMANTS

| | | |
|---|---|---|
| Jackson, John H. | Johnson, Ben | Johnson, Isaac |
| Johnson, Tina | Jones, Bob | Jones, Clara |
| Jordon, Abner | Lassiter, Jane | Lawson, Dave |
| Lee, Jane | Littlejohn, Chana | McAllister, Charity |
| McCoy, Clara Cotton | McCullers, Henrietta | McCullough, Willie |
| McLean, James Turner | Magwood, Frank | Manson, Jacob |
| Manson, Roberta | Markham, Millie | Mials, Maggie |
| Mitchel, Anna | Mitchner, Patsy | Moore, Emeline |
| Moore, Fannie | Moring, Richard C. | Nelson, Julius |
| Nichols, Lila | Organ, Martha | Parker, Ann |
| Penny, Amy | Perry, Lily | Perry, Valley | Pitts, Tempe |
| Plummer, Hannah | Pool, Parker | Raines, Rena |
| Ransome, Anthony | Richardson, Caroline | Riddick, Charity |
| Riddick, Simuel | Rienshaw, Adora | Robinson, Celia |
| Rogers, George | Rogers, Hattie | Rountree, Henry |
| Scales, Anderson | Scales, Catherine | Scales, Porter |
| Scott, William | Shaw, Tiney | Smith, John |
| Smith, John | Smith, Josephine | Smith, Nellie |
| Smith, Sarah Ann | Smith, William | Sorrell, Laura |
| Sorrell, Ria | Spell, Chaney | Spikes, Tanner |
| Stephenson, Annie | Stewart, Sam T. | Stone, Emma |
| Sykes, William | Taylor, Annie | Taylor, R.S. |
| Thomas, Elias | Thomas, Jacob | Thornton, Margaret |
| TillieTrell, | Ellen Trentham, | Henry James |
| Upperman, Jane Anne Privette | | Whitley, Ophelia |
| Wilcox, Tom | Williams, Catharine | Williams, Rev. Handy |
| Williams, John Thomas | Williams, Lizzie | Williams, Penny |
| Williams, Plaz | Williamson, Melissa | Woods, Alex |
| Wright, Anna | Yellady, Dilly | Yellerday, Hilliard |

# ILLUSTRATIONS

| | | |
|---|---|---|
| Tina Johnson | Fannie Moore | Julius Nelson |
| Lila Nichols | Tempe Pitts | Adora Rienshaw |
| William Scott | Tiney Shaw | John Smith |
| Josephine Smith | Sam T. Stewart | William Sykes |

N.C. District:

Worker: **Mrs. W.N. Harriss**

No. Words: **1363**

Subject: **Memories of Uncle Jackson**

Interviewed: **John H. Jackson**
**309 S. Sixth St.**
**Wilmington, N.C.**

[TR: Date stamp: JUN 26 1937]

# MEMORIES OF UNCLE JACKSON

"I was born in 1851, in the yard where my owner lived next door to the City Hall. I remember when they was finishin' up the City Hall. I also remember the foreman, Mr. James Walker, he was general manager. The overseen (overseer) was Mr. Keen. I remember all the bricklayers; they all was colored. The man that plastered the City Hall was named George Price, he plastered it inside. The men that plastered the City Hall outside and put those colum's up in the front, their names was Robert Finey and William Finey, they both was colored. Jim Artis now was a contractor an' builder. He done a lot of work 'round Wilmin'ton.

"Yes'm, they was slaves, mos' all the fine work 'round Wilmin'ton was done by slaves. They called 'em artisans. None of 'em could read, but give 'em any plan an' they could foller it to the las' line."

Interviewer: "Did the owner collect the pay for the labor, Uncle Jackson?"

"No, ma'm. That they did'n. We had a lot of them artisans 'mongst our folks. They all lived on our place with they fam'lies. They hired theyselves where they pleased. They colle'ted they pay, an' the onliest thing the owner took was enough to support they fam'lies. They all lived in our yard, it was a great big place, an' they wimmen cooked for 'em and raised the chilluns.

"You know, they lays a heap o' stress on edication these days. But edication is one thing an' fireside trainin' is another. We had fireside trainin'.

"We went to church regular. All our people marched behind our owners, an' sat up in the galle'y of the white folks church. Now, them that went to St. James Church behind their white folks didn' dare look at nobody else. 'Twant allowed. They were taught they were better than anybody else. That was called the 'silk stockin' church. Nobody else was fitten to look at.

"My mother was the laund'ess for the white folks. In those days ladies wore clo'es, an' plenty of 'em. My daddy was one of the part Indian folks. My mammy was brought here from Washin'ton City, an' when her owner went back home he sold her to my folks. You know, round Washin'ton an' up that way they was Ginny (Guinea) niggers, an' that's what my mammy was. We had a lot of these malatto negroes round here, they was called 'Shuffer Tonies', they was free issues and part Indian. The leader of 'em was James Sampson. We child'en was told to play in our own yard and not have nothin' to do with free issue chil'en or the common chil'en 'cross the street, white or colored, because they was'nt fitten to 'sociate with us. You see our owners was rich folks. Our big house is the one where the ladies of Sokosis (Sorosis) has their Club House, an' our yard spread all round there, an' our house servants, an' some of the bes' artisans in Wilmin'ton lived in our yard.

"You know, I'm not tellin' you things what have been told me, but I'm tellin' you things I knows.

"I remember when the Zoabbes company came from Georgia here to Wilmin'ton an' they had all ladies as officers.[1]

"I remember when the Confederates captured part of the Union Army at Fort Sumter, S.C., and they brought them here to Wilmin'ton and put them out under Fourth Street bridge, and the white ladies of Wilmin'ton, N.C. cooked food and carried it by baskets full to them. We all had plenty of food. A warehouse full of everything down there by the river nigh Red Cross Street, an' none of us ever went hungry 'till the war was over.

"I remember when Gen'ral Grant's Army came to the river. They mounted guns to boombar the city. Mr. John Dawson an' Mr. Silas Martin, they went on the corner of Second an' Nun Streets on the top of Ben Berry's house an' run up a white sheet for a flag, an' the Yankees did'n' boombar us. An' Mr. Martin gave his house up to the Progro Marshells, and my mother cleaned up the house an' washed for them. Her name was Caroline West.

"I remember when that Provo Marshell told the colored people that any house in Wilmin'ton they liked, that was empty, they could go take it, an' the first one they took was the fine Bellamy Mansion on Market an' Fifth Street."

"Uncle Jackson", asked the interviewer, "don't you remember that house was headquarters of the Federal Army? How could colored people occupy it?"

Uncle Jackson: "I don't remember nothin' about Federal soldiers bein' in that house, but I'm tellin' you I knows a lot of common colored folks was in it because I seen 'em sittin' on the piazza an' all up an' down those big front steps. I seen 'em. Nice colored people wouldn't 'a gone there. They had respec' for theirselves an' their white folks. But Dr. Bellamy came home soon with his fam'ly an' those colored people got out. They wan't there long.

"Endurin' of slavery I toted water for the fam'ly to drink. I remember when there was springs under where the new Court House is now, and all the white folks livin' 'round there drank water from those springs. They called it Jacob Spring. There was also a spring on Market Street between Second and Third Streets, that was called McCrayer (McCrary) spring. They didn't 'low nobody but rich folks to get water from that spring. Of co'se I got mine there whenever I chose to tote it that far. We did'n' work so hard in those days. I don't know nothin' about field han's an' workmen on the river, but so far as I knows the carpenters an' people like that started work at 8 o'clock A.M. and stopped at 5 o'clock P.M. Of course 'round the house it was different. Our folks done pretty much what the white folks did because we was all pretty much one an' other.

"Did I ever know of any slaves bein' whipped? I seen plenty of 'em whipped over at the jail, but them was bad niggers, (this with a grimace of disgust, and shaking of the head), they needed whippin'. But (with a chuckle) I sho' would have hated to see anybody put they han's on one of my owner's people. We was all 'spectable an' did'n know nothin' about whippen. Our mammy's spanked us aplenty, yes mam they did.

"I remember when they didn't have no trussels 'cross either river, an' they had a passages boat by the name of Walker Moore, an' the warf was up there by the Charlotte railroad (S.A.L.) The Boat would take you from there to the bluff an' then you would have to catch the train to go to Greensboro, and other places in No'th Carolina.

"I remember when the Fourth Street Fire Department bell was in front of the City Hall. An' Mr. Maginny had his school right back of the City Hall.

"I believe we was all happy as slaves because we had the best of kere (care). I don't believe none of us was sold off because I never heard tell of it. I have always served nice folks an' never 'sociated with any other kind. I brought up Mis ——'s chil'ren an' now she gives me a life intrust in this place I lives in. I hav'nt never to say really wanted for anything. I hav'nt never bothered with wimmen, an' had nothin' to bother me.

"I mus' tell you' bout Gov'ner Dudley's election, an' the free issue niggers. They say Mr. Dudley told 'em if they'd vote for him he'd do more for 'em than any man ever had. So they voted for him an' he was elected. Then he ups an' calls a const'utional convention in Raleigh an' had all the voting taken away from 'em. An' that the big thing he done for em."[2]

## FOOTNOTES:

[1] Note: Have not been able to verify this memory, and think perhaps the unusual uniforms of the Zoaves caused the small boy to think they were women, or some adult may have amused themselves by telling him so.

[2] Note: Governor Dudley was elected before Uncle Jackson was born, but he enjoyed thoroughly telling this joke on the 'free issue niggers'.

N.C. District: No. 2
Worker: Mary A. Hicks
No. Words: 920
Subject: EX-SLAVE STORY
Story teller: Ben Johnson
Editor: Daisy Bailey Waitt

[TR: Date stamp: JUN 1 1937]

# EX-SLAVE STORY
# An interview with Ben Johnson

### 85 of Hecktown, Durham, Durham County, May 20, 1937.

Uncle Ben, who is nearly blind and who walks with a stick, was assisted to the porch by his wife who sat down near him in a protecting attitude. He is much less striking than his wife who is small and dainty with perfect features and snow white hair worn in two long braids down her back. She wore enormous heart shaped earrings, apparently of heavy gold; while Uncle Ben talked she occasionally prompted him in a soft voice.

"I wuz borned in Orange County and I belonged ter Mr. Gilbert Gregg near Hillsboro. I doan know nothin' 'bout my mammy an' daddy, but I had a brother Jim who wuz sold ter dress young missus fer her weddin'. De tree am still standin' whar I set under an' watch 'em sell Jim. I set dar an' I cry an' cry, 'specially when dey puts de chains on him an' carries him off, an' I ain't neber felt so lonesome in my whole life. I ain't neber hyar from Jim since an' I wonder now sometimes if'en he's still livin'.

"I knows dat de marster wuz good ter us an' he fed an' clothed us good. We had our own gyarden an' we wuz gittin' long all right.

"I seed a whole heap of Yankees when dey comed ter Hillsboro an' most of 'em ain't got no respeck fer God, man, nor de debil. I can't 'member so much 'bout 'em do' cause we lives in town an' we has a gyard.

"De most dat I can tell yo' 'bout am de Ku Klux. I neber will fergit when dey hung Cy Guy. Dey hung him fer a scandelous insult ter a white 'oman an' dey comed atter him a hundert strong.

"Dey tries him dar in de woods, an' dey scratches Cy's arm ter git some blood, an' wid dat blood dey writes dat he shall hang 'tween de heavens an' de yearth till he am daid, daid, daid, an' dat any nigger what takes down de body shall be hunged too.

"Well sar, de nex' mornin' dar he hung, right ober de road an' de sentence hangin' ober his haid. Nobody'ud bother wid dat body fer four days an' dar hit hung, swingin' in de wind, but de fou'th day de sheriff comes an' takes hit down.

"Dar wuz Ed an' Cindy, who 'fore de war belonged ter Mr. Lynch an' atter de war he told 'em ter move. He gives 'em a month an' dey ain't gone, so de Ku Kluxes gits 'em.

"Hit wuz on a cold night when dey comed an' drugged de niggers out'n bed. Dey carried 'em down in de woods an' whup dem, den dey throws 'em in de pond, dere bodies breakin' de ice. Ed come out an' come ter our house, but Cindy ain't been seed since.

"Sam Allen in Caswell County wuz tol' ter move an' atter a month de hundret Ku Klux come a-totin' his casket an' dey tells him dat his time has come an' if'en he want ter tell his wife good bye an' say his prayers hurry up.

"Dey set de coffin on two cheers an' Sam kisses his ole oman who am a-cryin', den he kneels down side of his bed wid his haid on de piller an' his arms throwed out front of him.

"He sets dar fer a minute an' when he riz he had a long knife in his hand. 'Fore he could be grabbed he done kill two of de Ku Kluxes wid de knife, an' he done gone out'n de do'. Dey ain't ketch him nother, an' de nex' night when dey comed back, 'termined ter git him dey shot ano'her nigger by accident.

"I members [TR: 'members] seein' Joe Turner, another nigger hung at Hillsboro in '69 but I plumb fergot why it wuz.

"I know one time Miss Hendon inherits a thousand dollars from her pappy's 'state an' dat night she goes wid her sweetheart ter de gate, an' on her way back ter de house she gits knocked in de haid wid a axe. She screams an' her two nigger sarvants, Jim an' Sam runs an' saves her but she am robbed.

"Den she tells de folkses dat Jim an' Sam am de guilty parties, but her little sister swears dat dey ain't so dey gits out of it.

"Atter dat dey fin's out dat it am five mens, Atwater, Edwards, Andrews, Davis an' Markham. De preacher comes down to whar dey am hangin' ter preach dar funeral an' he stan's dar while lightnin' plays roun' de dead mens haids an' de win' blows de trees, an he preaches sich a sermon as I ain't neber hyard before.

"Bob Boylan falls in love wid another oman so he burns his wife an' four youngins up in dere house.

"De Ku Kluxes gits him, of course, an' dey hangs him high on de old red oak on de Hillsboro Road. Atter dey hunged him his lawyer says ter us boys, 'Bury him good, boys, jist as good as you'd bury me if'en I wuz daid.'

"I shuck han's wid Bob 'fore dey hunged him an' I he'ped ter bury him too an' we bury him nice an' we all hopes dat he done gone ter glory."

N.C. District: No. 2
Worker: T. Pat Matthews
No. Words: 991
Subject: ISAAC JOHNSON
Story teller: Isaac Johnson
Editor: Daisy Bailey Waitt

# ISAAC JOHNSON

**Lillington, North Carolina, Route 1, Harnett County.**

"I am feelin' very well this mornin', while I don't feel like I used to. I done so much hard work, I'm 'bout all in. Dey didn't have all dese new fangled things to do work an' go 'bout on when I wus a boy. No, no, you jes' had to git out an' do all de work, most all de work by hand. I wus ten years old when de Yankees come through. I wus born Feb. 12, 1855.

"I belonged to Jack Johnson. My missus' name wus Nancy. My father wus Bunch Matthews; he belonged to old man Drew Matthews, a slave owner. My mother wus named Tilla Johnson. She belonged to Jack Johnson, my marster. De plantation wus near Lillington, on the north side o' de Cape Fear River and ran down to near de Lillington Cross roads one mile from de river. I had one brother and six sisters. My brother wus named Phil and my sisters name Mary, Caroline, Francis and I don't remember de others names right now. Been so long since I saw any of 'em. Dey are all dead. Yes sir, dey are all dead. I do not remember my grandpa and grandma. No sir, I don't.

"I wus too small to work, dey had me to do little things like feedin' de chickens, an' mindin' de table sometimes; but I wus too small to work. Dey didn't let children work much in dem days till dey were thirteen or fourteen years old. I had plenty to eat, good clothes, a nice place to sleep an' a good time. Marster loved his slaves an' other white folks said he loved a nigger more den he did white folks. Our food wus fixed up fine. It wus fixed by a regular cook who didn't do anything but cook. We had gardens, a plenty o' meat, a plenty, an' mo' biscuit den a lot o' white folks had. I kin remember de biscuit. I never hunted any, but I went bird blindin' an' set bird traps. I caught lots o' birds.

"Jack Johnson, my marster never had no children of his own. He had a boy with him by the name of Stephen, a nephew of his, from one of his brothers. Marster Jack had three brothers Willis, Billy, and Matthew. I don' remember any of his sisters. There was 'bout four thousand acres in de plantation an' 'bout 25 slaves. Marster would not have an overseer.

"No sir, de slaves worked very much as they pleased. He whupped a slave now an' then, but not much. I have seen him whup 'em. He had some unruly niggers. Some of 'em were part Indian, an' mean. Dey all loved him doe. I never saw a slave sold. He kept his slaves together. He didn't want to git rid of any of 'em. We went to de white folks church at Neill's Creek a missionary Baptis' Church.

"We played during the Christmas holidays, an' we got 'bout two weeks 4th of July, and lay by time, which wus 'bout the fourth. We had great times at corn shuckin's, log rollin's and cotton pickin's. We had dances. Marster lowed his slaves lots o' freedom. My mother used to say he wus better den other folks. Yes, she said her marster wus better than other folks.

"The white folks didn't teach us to read an' write. I cannot read an' write, but de white folks, only 'bout half or less den half, could read an' write den. Dere were very few pore white folks who could read an' write. I remember de baptizin's at de Reuben Matthews Mill Pond. Sometimes after a big meeting dey would baptize twenty four at one time. No slaves run away from Marster. Dey didn't have any scuse to do so, cause whites and colored fared alike at Marster's. We played base, cat, rolly hole, and a kind of base ball called 'round town.

"Dr. John McNeill looked after us when we were sick. We used a lot of herbs an' things. Drank sassafras tea an' mullen tea. We also used sheep tea for measles, you knows dat. You know how it wus made. Called sheep pill tea. It shore would cuore de measles. 'Bout all dat would cuore measles den. Dey were bad den. Wus den dey is now.

"I saw Wheeler's Cavalry. Dey come through ahead of de Yankees. I saw colored people in de Yankee uniforms. Dey wore blue and had brass buttons on 'em. De Yankees an' Wheeler's Cavalry took everything dey wanted, meat, chickens, an' stock. We stayed on wid Marster after de war. I've never lived out of de state. We lived in de same place ontill old Marster an' Missus died. Den we lived wid deir relations right on an' here. I am now on a place deir heirs own.

"Ole Marster loved his dram, an' he gave it to all his slaves. It sold for ten cents a quart. He made brandy by de barrels, an' at holidays all drank together an' had a good time. I never saw any of 'em drunk. People wan't mean when dey were drinking den. It wus so plentiful nobody notices it much. Marster would tell de children 'bout Raw Head and Bloody Bones an' other things to skeer us. He would call us to de barn to git apples an' run an'hide, an' we would have a time findin' him. He give de one who found him a apple. Sometimes he didn't give de others no apple.

"I married Ellen Johnson May 22, 1865 de year de war went up, an' my wife is livin' as you see, an' able to be about. I'm not able to work, not able to go out anywhere by myself. I know I cain't las' much longer but I'm thankful to de Lord for sparin' me dis long."

AC

N.C. District: No. 2
Worker: Mary A. Hicks
No. Words: 346
Subject: TINA JOHNSON
Story teller: Tina Johnson
Editor: Daisy Bailey Waitt

Tina Johnson [TR: Man named Tina, or wrong photo.]

# TINA JOHNSON
## Ex-Slave Story

**An interview with Tina Johnson 85, S. Bloodworth Street, Raleigh.**

"I wuz bawned in Richmon', Georgia 'round eighty-five years ago. My mammy wuz named Cass an' my father, dat is my step-father wuz named John Curtis. I got de name of Johnson frum Gen'l Johnson, I doan know who my real daddy wuz.

"My mammy belonged ter a Mis' Berry who wuz pretty good ter her, but we ain't had nothin' but de coarsest food an' clothes. I had one brother name Dennis an' me an' him wucked wid de others in de cotton patch.

"We had done moved nigh Augusta when Sherman come, an' Sherman's sister wuz a-livin' in Augusta. Dat's de reason dat Sherman missed us, case he ain't wantin' ter 'sturb his sister none.

"I ain't seed nary a Yankee, but fer two days an' nights I hyard de guns roarin' an' felt de earth shakin' lak a earthquake wuz hittin' it. De air wuz dark an' de clouds hunged low, de whole earth seemed ter be full of powder an' yo' nostrils seemed lak dey would bust wid de sting of it.

"Atter de surrender we stayed on an' went through de Ku Klux scare. I know dat de Ku Kluxes went ter a nigger dance one night an' whupped all of de dancers. Ole Marster Berry wuz mad, case he ain't sont fer' em at all an' he doan want dem.

"Seberal year's atter de war mammy married John Curtis in de Baptist church at Augusta, an' me an' Dennis seed de ceremony. I pulled a good one on a white feller 'bout dat onct. He axed me if I knowed dat my pappy an' mammy wuz married 'fore I wuz borned. I sez ter him dat I wonder if he knows whar his mammy an' pappy wuz married when he wuz borned.

"We comed ter Raleigh 'fore things wuz settled atter de war, an' I watches de niggers livin' on kush, co'nbread, 'lasses an' what dey can beg an' steal frum de white folkses. Dem days shore wuz bad."

N.C. District: No. 2
Worker: Mary Hicks
No. Words: 450
Subject: EX-SLAVE STORY
Story Teller: BOB JONES
Editor: George L. Andrews

[TR: Date stamp: AUG 17 1937]

# EX-SLAVE STORY
# BOB JONES

**An interview with Bob Jones, 86 years of age, County Home, Raleigh, North Carolina.**

"I wus borned in Warren County on de plantation 'longin' ter Mister Logie Rudd. My mammy wus Frankie. My pappy wus named [TR: illegible] [H]arry Jones. Him an' my oldes' brother Burton 'longed ter a Mister Jones dar in de neighborhood.

"Marster Logie an' young Marster Joe wus nice as dey could be, but Mis' Betsy wus crabbed an' hard ter git along wid. She whupped de servants what done de house work an' she fussed so bad dat she moughty nigh run all us crazy. Hit wus her what sold my Aunt Sissy Ann an' hit wus her what whupped my sister Mary so bad. Dar warn't but six of us slaves but dem six run a race ter see who can stay outen her sight.

"Young Marster Joe wus one of de fust ter go ter de war an' I wanted ter go wid him but I bein' only fourteen dey 'cided ter sen' Sidney instead. I hated dat, 'case I shorely wanted ter go.

"We neber seed Marse Joe but twice atter he left, de time when his daddy wus buried an' when dey brung his body home frum de war

"One day about seben or eight Yankees comed 'roun' our place lookin' fer Reb. scouts, dey said, but dey ain't fin' none so dey goes on 'bout dere business. De nex' day a few of our soldiers brings Marse Joe's body home frum de war.

"I doan 'member whar he wus killed but he had been dead so long dat he had turned dark, an' Sambo, a little nigger, sez ter me, 'I thought, Bob, dat I'ud turn white when I went ter heaben but hit 'pears ter me lak de white folkses am gwine ter turn black.'

"We buried young Marse Joe under de trees in de family buryin' groun' an' we niggers sung Swing Low Sweet Chariot an' Nearer My God to Thee an' some others. De ole missus wus right nice ter ever'body dat day an' she let de young missus take charge of all de business frum dat time.

"We stayed on de Rudd plantation fer two years atter de war, den we moves ter Method whar I met Edna Crowder. We courted fer seberal months an' at las' I jist puts my arm 'roun' her waist an' I axes her ter have me. She ain't got no mammy ter ax so she kisses me an' tells me dat she will.

"Durin' de course of our married life we had five chilluns but only one of dem lived ter be named, dat wus Hyacinth, an' he died 'fore he was a month old.

"Edna died too, six years ago, an' lef' me ter de mercies of de worl'. All my brudders an' sisters dead, my parents dead, my chilluns dead, an' my wife dead, but I has got a niece.

"Till lately I been livin' at de Wake County Home, but my niece what lives on Person Street says dat iffen I can git de pension dat she can afford ter let me stay ter her house. I hope I does, 'case I doan want ter go back ter de County Home."

EH

N.C. District: No. 2
Worker: T. Pat Matthews
No. Words: 333
Subject: CLARA JONES
Story teller: Clara Jones
Editor: Daisy Bailey Waitt

# CLARA JONES

**408 Cannon Street**

"I been unable ter work fer 10 years; I am blind. I been in bed helpless fer four years. I eats all I can get, and takes what I am told ter take. De Lord helps me, I am depending on him. He put me into de world and he can take me out. I was 17 years old at de surrender. My missus wus Dillie Scott. I wus a Scott before I married William Jones. My marster wus Aaron Scott. I loved my white folks. Hain't got no word ter say against 'em. Don't think de Government goin' to help me any; I have been fooled so many times. We all should fix our salvation right that's the thing that counts now. My time is 'bout spent here.

"De white folks went off to de war; dey said dey could whup, but de Lord said, 'No', and dey didn't whup. Dey went off laffin', an' many were soon cryin', and many did not come back. De Yankees come through, dey took what dey wanted; killed de stock; stole de horses; poured out de lasses and cut up a lot of meaness, but most of 'em is dead and gone now. No matter whether dey were Southern white folks, or Northern white folks, dey is dead now.

"I am helpless, my son, de baby, who is de only livin'chile I has, takes care o' me. My son is a Baptis' Minister, but he has no Church. He stays here, and looks after me. He is forty years old. He has heart disease, and his lungs are bad. He has no regular job, so some times we have very little ter eat. Our water is cut off now. We never have money to buy any ice. We have had only one ten cent piece of ice this summer. Sometimes my son sets up wid me all night.

"Maybe de Lawd will help us sometime. I trusts him anyway. Yes, I trusts de Lawd."

AC

N.C. District: No. 2
Worker: Mary A. Hicks
No. Words: 554
Subject: CLARA JONES
Story teller: Clara Jones
Editor: Geo. L. Andrews

[TR: Date stamp: AUG 6 1937]

# CLARA JONES

**An interview with Clara Jones of 408 Cannon Street, Raleigh, North Carolina.**

"I doan know how old I is but I wus borned long time ago case I wus a married 'oman way 'fore de war. We lived on Mr. Felton McGee's place hear in Wake County. I wurked lak a man dar an' de hours wus from sunup till dark mostly. He ain't had but about fifty slaves but he makes dem do de wurk of a hundret an' fifty. We ain't had no fun dar, case hit takes all of our strength ter do our daily task. Yes'um we had our tasks set out ever' day.

"One day, right atter my fifth chile wus borned, I fell out in de fiel'. Marster come out an' looked at me, den he kicks me an' 'lows, 'a youngin' ever' ten months an' never able ter wurk, I'll sell her'. "A few days atter dat he tuck me an' my two younges' chilluns ter Raleigh an' he sells us ter Marse Rufus Jones.

"Marse Rufus am a good man in ever' way. He fed us good an' he give us good clothes an' we ain't had much wurk ter do, dat is, not much side of what we had ter do on McGee's plantation.

"We had some fun on Marse Rufus' plantation, watermillion slicin's, candy pullin's, dances, prayer meetin's an' sich. Yes mam, we had er heap of fun an' in dat time I had eleben chilluns.

"My husband, William, still stayed on ter Mister McGee's. We got married in 1860, de year 'fore de war started, I think. I can't tell yo' much 'bout our courtin' case hit went on fer years an' de Marster wanted us ter git married so's dat I'd have chilluns. When de slaves on de McGee place got married de marster always said dat dere duty wus ter have a houseful of chilluns fer him.

"When de Yankees come Mis' Sally, Marse Rufus' wife cried an' ordered de scalawags outen de house but dey jist laughs at her an' takes all we got. Dey eben takes de stand of lard dat we has got buried in de ole fiel' an' de hams hangin' up in de trees in de pasture. Atter dey is gone we fin's a sick Yankee in de barn an' Mis' Sally nurses him. Way atter de war Mis' Sally gits a letter an' a gol' ring from him.

"When de news of de surrender comes Mis' Sally cries an' sez dat she can't do widout her niggers, so Marse Rufus comes in an' tells us dat we can stay on

"William moves ober dar, takes de name of Jones an' goes ter farmin' wid a purpose an' believe me we makes our livin'. We stay dar through all of de construction days an' through de time when de Ku Kluxes wus goin' wild an' whuppin's all de niggers. We raise our eleben chilluns dar an' dar's whar my husban' died in 1898 an' den I comes ter Raleigh.

"I wurked till four years ago when I had a stroke now I ain't able ter wurk an' I sho' does want my pension. Will yo' tell dem ter sen' hit in de nex' mail."

N.C. District: No. 3  
Writer: Daisy Whaley  
No. Words: 250  
Subject: Abner Jordan, Ex-slave Of Durham County.  
Interviewed: Abner Jordan, Durham County Home.

# ABNER JORDAN

**Ex-slave, 95 years.**

"I wus bawn about 1832 an' I wus bawn at Staggsville, Marse Paul Cameron's place. I belonged to Marse Paul. My pappy's name wus Obed an' my mammy wus Ella Jordan an' dey wus thirteen chillun on our family.

"I wus de same age of Young Marse Benehan, I played wid him an' wus his body guard. Yes, suh, Whare ever young Marse Benehan went I went too. I waited on him. Young Marse Benny run away an' 'listed in de war, but Marse Paul done went an' brung him back kaze he wus too young to go and fight de Yankees.

"Marse Paul had a heap of niggahs; he had five thousan'. When he meet dem in de road he wouldn' know dem an' when he azed dem who dey wus an' who dey belonged to, dey' tell him dey belonged to Marse Paul Cameron an' den he would say dat wus all right for dem to go right on.

"My pappy wus de blacksmith an' foreman for Marse Paul, an' he blew de horn for de other niggahs to come in from de fiel' at night. Dey couldn' leave de plantation without Marse say dey could.

"When de war come de Yankees come to de house an' axed my mammy whare de folks done hid de silver an' gol', an' dey say dey gwine to kill mammy if she didn' tell dem. But mammy say she didn' know whare dey put it, an' dey would jus' have to kill her for she didn' know an' wouldn' lie to keep dem from hurting her

"De sojers stole seven or eight of de ho'ses an' foun' de meat an' stole dat, but dey didn' burn none of de buildin's nor hurt any of us slaves.

"My pappy an' his family stayed wid Marse Paul five years after de surrender den we moved to Hillsboro an' I's always lived 'roun' dese parts. I ain' never been out of North Carolina eighteen months in my life. North Carolina is good enough for me."

N.C. District: No. 2
Worker: T. Pat Matthews
No. Words: 1044
Subject: JANE LASSITER
Story teller: Jane Lassiter
Editor: Geo. L. Andrews

[TR: Date stamp: AUG 6 1937]

# JANE LASSITER

**About 80 years old.**
**324 Battle Street**
**Raleigh, N.C.**

"I am 'bout 80 years old. I am somewhere in my seventies, don't zackly know my age. I wus here when de Yankees come an' I 'member seein' dem dressed in blue. I wus a nurse at dat time not big enough to hold a baby but dey let me set by de cradle an' rock it.

"All my white folks dead an' all my people am dead an' I haint got no one to ax 'bout my age. Dey had my age an' my mother's age in de Bible but dey am all dead out now an' I don't know whur it is.

"My mother an' me belonged to the Councils. Dr. Kit Council who lived on a plantation in de lower edge of Chatham County, 'bout three miles from New Hill. My father belonged to de Lamberts. Their plantation wus near Pittsboro in Chatham County. My father wus named Macon Lambert an' his marster wus named At Lambert. Our missus wus named Caroline an' father's missus wus named Beckie. My grandfather wus Phil Bell. He belonged to the Bells. They lived in Chatham County. My grandmother wus named Peggy an' she belonged to de same family

"We lived in little ole log houses. We called 'em cabins. They had stick an' dirt chimleys wid one door to de house an' one window. It shet to lak a door.

"We did not have any gardens an' we never had any money of our own. We jest wurked fer de white folks.

"We had plenty sumptin to eat an' it wus cooked good. My mother wus de cook an' she done it right. Our clothes wus homemade but we had plenty shiftin' clothes. Course our shoes wus given out at Christmas. We got one pair a year an' when dey wore out we got no more an' had to go barefooted de rest of de time. You had to take care of dat pair uv shoes bekase dey wus all you got a year. The slaves caught game sometime an' et it in de cabins, but dere wus not much time fer huntin' dere wus so much wurk to do.

"Dere wus 'bout fifty slaves on de plantation, an' dey wurked from light till dark. I 'member dey wurkin' till dark. Course I wus too small to 'member all 'bout it an' I don't 'member 'bout de overseers. I never seen a slave whupped, but I 'members seein' dem carryin' slaves in droves like cows. De white men who wus guardin' 'em walked in front an' some behind. I did not see any chains. I never seen a slave sold an' I don't 'member ever seein' a jail fer slaves.

"Dere wus no books, or larnin' uv any kind allowed. You better not be ketched wid a book in yore han's. Dat wus sumptin dey would git you fer. I ken read an' write a little but I learned since de surrender. My mother tole me 'bout dat bein' 'ginst de rules of de white folks. I 'members it while I wus only a little gal. When de Yankees come thro'.

"Dere wus no churches on de plantation an' we wus not 'lowed to have prayer meetings in de cabins, but we went to preachin' at de white folks church. I 'member dat. We set on de back seat. I 'member dat.

"No slaves ever run away from our plantation cause marster wus good to us. I never heard of him bein' 'bout to whup any of his niggers. Mother loved her white folks as long as she lived an' I loved 'em too. No mister, we wus not mistreated. Mother tole me a lot 'bout Raw Head an' Bloody Bones an' when I done mean, she say, 'Better not do dat any more Raw Head an' Bloody Bones gwine ter git yo'.' Ha! ha! dey jest talked 'bout ghosts till I could hardly sleep at nite, but de biggest thing in ghosts is somebody 'guised up tryin' to skeer you. Ain't no sich thing as ghosts. Lot of niggers believe dere is do'

"We stayed on at marsters when de surrender come cause when we wus freed we had nothin' an' nowhere to go. Dats de truth. Mister, dats de truth. We stayed with marster a long time an' den jest moved from one plantation to another. It wus like dis, a crowd of tenants would get dissatisfied on a certain plantation, dey would move, an' another gang of niggers move in. Dat wus all any of us could do. We wus free but we had nothin' 'cept what de marsters give us.

"When we got sick, you sees we stayed wid a doctor, he looked after us, but we had our herbs too. We took sassafras tea, catnip an' horehound tea an' flag. Flag wus good to ease pain. Jest make a tea of de flagroots an' drink it hot.

"I married Kit Lassiter in Chatham County an' I had seven chilluns. Three boys an' four girls. All am dead but two. Two girls are livin'. One named Louie Finch, her husband dead. She stays wid me an' supports me. She cooks an' supports me. My other livin' daughter is Venira McLean. She lives across de street wid her husband. Her husband had a stroke an' ain't able to wurk no more. Dey live on five dollars a week. Dey ain't able to help me now. I moved ter Raleigh 20 years ago. My husband died here.

"I heard 'bout de Ku Klux but dey never give our family no trouble cause we didn't give 'em no cause to bother us. I don't know all 'bout slavery but I 'members dere wus a lot of big fat greasy niggers goin' around, an' I reckin dey fared good or dey wouldn't a been so fat. Dey got plenty to eat even if dey did wurk 'em.

"I believe slavery wus all rite whur slaves wus treated right. I haint got nuff edication to tell you nothin' 'bout Lincoln an' dem udder men. Heard 'em say he come thro', reckon he did too. I belong to the 'United Holiness Church'."

N.C. District: No. 3  
Worker: Travis Jordan  
Subject: **Dave Lawson**  
**Ex-Slave Story**  
**Lived at Blue Wing, N.C.**

[TR: Date stamp: AUG 8 1937]

# DAVE LAWSON
# EX-SLAVE

### MY FATHER WHO KNEW THE PRINCIPLE CHARACTERS TOLD ME THIS STORY YEARS AGO

"Yes, suh, de wus' I knows 'bout slavery times is what dey tols me 'bout how come dey hung my gran'mammy an' gran'pappy. Dey hung dem bof at de same time an' from de same lim' of de tree, but dat was way back yonder befo' Mistah Lincoln come down here to set de niggers free. My mammy wuzn' but six months ole den an' I wuzn' even bawn, but Aunt Becky tole me 'bout it when I was ole enough to lissen.

"Dis ain' no nice tale you gwine hear. It's de truf, but 'tain't nice. De fus' time I heard it I didn' sleep none for a week. Everytime I shut my eyes I seed Marse Drew Norwood wid dat funnel in his mouf an' de hot steam blowin' up like a cloud 'roun' his wicked face an' skeered eyes.

"Dey say my gran'pappy's Ole Marse was de meanes' white man de Lawd ever let breath de breaf of life. His name was Marse Drew Norwood. He was de riches' lan' owner anywhere 'roun'. He owned more lan' an' more niggers den anybody in Person or Granville counties. But he didn' make his money wid no farm, no suh, he sho didn', he made his money buyin' an' sellin' niggers. He bought dem cheap an' sold dem high. He would catch all de niggers dat run away from other plantations an' keep dem in his lockup 'twell he fatten dem, den he would take dem way off down in Georgia, Alabama or some place like dat an' sell dem for a big price. He would come back wid his pockets runnin' over wid money. Some folks say he stold niggers to sell, but nobody never could catch him.

"Marse Drew lived over here on de Virginia line 'tween Red Bank an' Blue Wing. He owned lan' 'cross de No'th Carolina line too an' lived close to Blue Wing. He treated his niggers so mean dey was all de time runnin' off. If he caught dem he beat dem near 'bout to death. He did beat Cindy Norwood to death one time kaze she run off to Marse Reuben Jones place an' axed him to keep her. She got pizen in de cut places on her back an' had fits three days befo' de Lawd took her. But Marse Drew jus' laugh an' say he didn' keer; dat she wuzn' no 'count nohow.

"I ain't never seed Marse Drew kaze I was bawn way after de niggers was freed, but dey tole me he looked like a mad bull. He was short wid a big head set forward on his big shoulders. His neck was so short dat he couldn' wear no collar; he jus' kept de neck bindin' of his shirt pinned wid a diaper pin. De debil done lit a lamp an' set it burnin' in his eyes; his mouf was a wicked slash cut 'cross his face, an' when he got mad his lips curled back from his teef like a mad dog's. When he cracked his whip de niggers swinged an' de chillun screamed wid pain when dat plaited thong bit in dey flesh. He beat Mistis too. Mis' Cary wuzn' no bigger den a minute an' she skeered as a kildee of Marse Drew. She didn' live long dey say kaze Marse Drew whipped her jus' befo' dey fus' baby wuz bawn.

"Marse Drew done whip Luzanne kaze she burnt de biscuits, an' Mis' Cary give her some salve to rub on de cut places on her back. When Marse Drew foun' it out he got so mad dat he come back to de big house an' tole Mis' Cary dat he gwine touch her up wid his whip kaze she give Luzanne de salve, dat when he want his niggers doctored he gwine doctor dem hese'f, so he got to use his lash a little bit to make her remember.

"Mis' Cary got so skeered dat she run 'roun' an' 'roun' de house, but Marse Drew run after her, an' every now an' den he th'ow out dat plaited whip an' curl it 'roun' her shoulders. Every time it hit it cut clean through her clothes. Mis' Cary got so skeered dat de baby come dat night befo' 'twuz time. De baby wuz bawn dead an' Mis' Cary went on to glory wid it. Dey say she was glad to go. Yes, suh, everything on dat plantation, animal an' man was skeered of dat whip—dat whip dat never lef' Marse Drew's wris'. It was made of home-tanned leather plaited in a roun' cord big as a man's thum'. All day it swung from a leather strop tied to his wris' an' at night it lay on a chair 'side de bed whare he could reach it easy.

"It was jus' befo' de Yankees come over here to fight dat Marse Drew bought Cleve an' Lissa Lawson. Dey was my gran'mammy an' gran'pappy. My mammy den was a baby. Marse Drew bought dem for fo' hundred an' fifty dollars. Dat was cheap kaze de niggers was young wid hard farm trainin'. Ole Marse didn' buy mammy. He said a nigger brat wuzn' no good, dey wouldn' sell an' dey might die befo' dey growed up, 'sides dey was a strain on de mammy what breas' nussed it. Lissa cut up powerful kaze he made her leave de baby behin', but Marse Drew jus' laughed an' tole her dat he would give her a puppy; dat dey was plenty of houn's on de plantation. Den he snapped de chains on dey wris' an' led dem off. Lissa an' Cleve never seed dat baby no more. Aunt Beck Lawson took an' raised her an' when she got grown she was my mammy.

"Yes, suh, Marse Drew bought dem niggers like he was buyin' a pair of mules. Dey wuzn' no more den mules to him. It was early summer when he brung dem to de plantation, but when wheat cuttin' time come Lissa an' Cleve was sent to de wheat fiel's. Dey was smart niggers, dey worked hard—too hard for dey own good. In dem times 'twuz de smart, hard workin' niggers dat brought de bes' price, an' nobody didn' know dat better den Marse Drew.

"One day Cleve seed Marse Drew watchin' Lissa. She was gleamin' de wheat. Her skin was de color of warm brown velvet; her eyes was dark an' bright an' shinin' like muscadines under de frosty sun, an' her body was slender like a young tree dat bends easy. As she stooped an' picked up de wheat, flingin' it 'cross her arm, she swayed back an' fo'th jus' like dem saplins down yonder by de creek sways in de win'.

"Cleve watched Marse Drew on de sly. He seed him watchin' Lissa. He seed de lustful look in his eyes, but 'twuzn' Lissa he lustin' after; 'twuz money he seed in her slender swayin' body, in de smooth warm brown skin, an' de quick, clean way she gleam de wheat. Stripped to de wais' on de Alabama auction block she would bring near 'bout a thousan' dollars. Cleve 'gun to sweat. He turned so sick an' skeered dat he could hardly swing de scythe through de wheat. Marse Drew done took his baby away, an' now sumpin' way down in his heart told him dat he was gwine take Lissa. He didn' keer if he parted dem, 'twuz dollars he seed swingin' 'roun' his head—gol' dollars shinin' brighter den stars.

"'Twuz de nex' day dat Marse Drew went to Cleve's cabin. He walk up whistlin' an' knock on de door wid de butt of his whip.

"Cleve opened de door.

"Ole Marse tole him to pack Lissa's clothes, dat he was takin' her to Souf Boston de nex' day to sell her on de block.

"Cleve fell on his knees an' 'gun to plead. He knew Ole Marse wuzn' gwine take Lissa to no Souf Boston; he was gwine take her way off an' he wouldn' never see her no more. He beg an' promise Marse Drew to be good an' do anything he say [HW: to] do if he jus' leave him Lissa, dat she was his wife an' he love her. But Marse Drew hit him 'cross de face wid his whip, cuttin' his lip in half, den he went over an' felt of Lissa's arms an' legs like she might have been a hoss.

"When he done gone Cleve went over an' set down by Lissa an' took her han'. Lissa 'gun to cry, den she jumped up an' 'menced to take down her clothes hangin' on de wall.

"Cleve watched her for a while, den he made up his min' he gwine do sumpin', dat she ain't gwine be took away from him. He say: 'Quit dat, Lissa, leave dem clothes alone. You ain't gwine leave me, you ain't gwine nowhare, hear me?' Den he tole her to make up a hot fire while he brung in de wash pot. He brung in de big iron pot an' set it on de hearth an' raked de' red coals all 'roun' it, den he filled it wid water. While it was heatin' he went to de door an' looked out. De sun done gone down an' night was crowdin' de hills, pushin' dem out of sight. By daylight dat white man would be comin' after Lissa.

"Cleve turned 'roun' an' looked at Lissa. She was standin' by de wash pot lookin' down in de water, an' de firelight from de burnin' lightwood knots showed de tears droppin' off her cheeks. Cleve went outside. 'Bout dat time a scritch owl come an' set on de roof an' scritched. Lissa run out to skeer it away, but Cleve caught her arm. He say, 'Don't do dat, Lissa, leave him alone. Dat's death bird, he knows what he's doin'. So Lissa didn' do nothin', she let de bird keep on scritchin'.

"When 'twuz good an' dark Cleve took a long rope an' went out, tellin' Lissa to keep de water boilin'. When, he come back he had Marse Drew all tied up wid de rope an gagged so he couldn' holler; he had him th'owed over his shoulder like a sack of meal. He brung him in de cabin an' laid him on de floor, den he tole him if he wouldn' sell Lissa dat he wouldn' hurt him. But Marse Drew shook his head an' cussed in his th'oat. Den Cleve took off de gag, but befo' de white man could holler out, Cleve stuffed de spout of a funnel in his big mouf way down his th'oat, holdin' down his tongue. He ax him one more time to save Lissa from de block, but Marse Drew look at him wid hate in his eyes shook his head again. Cleve didn' say nothin' else to him; he call Lissa an' tole her to bring him a pitcher of boilin' water.

"By den Lissa seed what Cleve was gwine do. She didn' tell Cleve not to do it nor nothin'; she jus' filled de pitcher wid hot water, den she went over an' set down on de floor an' hol' Marse Drew's head so he couldn' move.

"When Ole Marse seed what dey was fixin' to do to him, his eyes near 'bout busted out of his head, but when dey ax him again 'bout Lissa he wouldn' promise nothin', so Cleve set on him to hol' him down, den took de pitcher an' 'gun to pour dat boilin' water right in dat funnel stickin' in Marse Drew's mouf.

"Dat man kicked an' struggled, but dat water scalded its way down his th'oat, burnin' up his insides. Lissa brung another pitcher full an' dey wuzn' no pity in her eyes as she watched Marse Drew fightin' his way to torment, cussin' all niggers an' Abraham Lincoln.

"After dat Lissa an' Cleve set down to wait for de sheriff. Dey knew 'twuzn' no use to run, dey couldn' get nowhare. 'Bout sunup de folks come an' foun' Marse Drew, an' dey foun' Lissa an' Cleve settin' by de door han' in han' waitin'. When dem niggers tole what dey done an' how come dey done it dem white folks was hard. De sheriff took de rope from' roun' Marse Drew an' cut it in two pieces. He tied one rope 'roun' Cleve's neck an' one rope 'roun' Lissa's neck an' hung dem up in de big oak tree in de yard.

"Yes, suh, dat's what happened to my gran'mammy an' gran'pappy in slavery times. Dis here cabin we's settin' in is de same cabin whare Cleve an' Lissa scalded Marse Drew, an' dat oak tree 'side de paf is de same tree dey was hung on. Sometimes now in de fall of de year when I'se settin' in de door after de sun done gone down; an' de wheat am ripe an' bendin' in de win', an' de moon am roun' an' yeller like a mush melon, seems like I sees two shadows swingin' from de big lim' of dat tree—I sees dem swingin' low side by side wid dey feets near 'bout touchin' de groun'."

| | |
|---|---|
| N.C. District: | No. 2 |
| Worker: | Mary A. Hicks |
| No. Words: | 390 |
| Subject: | JANE LEE |
| Person Interviewed: | Jane Lee |
| Editor: | G.L. Andrews |

[TR: Date stamp: SEP 10 1937]

# JANE LEE

**An interview with Jane Lee, 81 years old, Selma, North Carolina.**

"I wus borned de slave of Marse Henry McCullers down here at Clayton on de Wake an' Johnston line. My daddy wus named Addison an' my mammy wus named Caroline. Daddy 'longed to Mr. John Ellington who also lived near Clayton. I doan know de number of Mr. Ellington's slaves, but I know dat Marse Henry had six or seben.

"Marse Henry ain't had no oberseer ner no patterollers nother. He managed his business hisself an' ain't needed nobody. He whupped dem when dey needed hit but dat ain't often, not dat he ain't put de whuppin' on dem what did need hit.

"I 'members de Yankees comin' good as iffen hit wus yesterday. Dey comed wid a big noise, chasin' our white folks what wus in de army clean away. Dey chase dem to Raleigh an' den dey kotch 'em, but dey ain't had much time, ter do us any damage case dey wus too busy atter de Rebs.

"De woods wus full of runaway slaves an' Rebs who deserted de army so hit wus dangerous to walk out. Marse Henry give us a speech about hit an' atter I seed one rag-a-muffin nigger man dat wus so hongry dat his eyes pop out, I ain't took no more walks.

"Atter de war we moved on Mr. Ellington's place wid daddy an' dar I stayed till I married Wyatt Lee. Wyatt wus a bad proposition an' he got shot in Fayetteville atter we had five chilluns. Wyatt tuck a woman to Fayetteville an' a man named Frank Mattiner killed him about her. Den my oldest boy went to wurk in Virginia an' a man named Rudolphus killed him 'bout a yaller gal. Both of de murderers runaway an' ain't never been ketched.

"All five of my chilluns am daid now, an' fer de past ten years I'se done ever'thing but cut cord wood.

"How does I live? Well I lives now an' den. De county gives me two dollars a month an' de house am mine durin' my life time. Mr. Parrish sold hit to Judge Brooks wid de understandin' dat hit am mine long as I live. I don't know why, none of us never 'longed ter de Parrish's ner nothin' dat I knows of."

N.C. District:      No. 2
Worker:             T. Pat Matthews
No. Words:          1138
Subject:            CHANA LITTLEJOHN
Person Interviewed: Chana Littlejohn
Editor:             Daisy Bailey Waitt

[TR: Date stamp: JUN 26 1937]

# CHANA LITTLEJOHN

**215 State Street**

[HW marginal note: To P. 2] "I remember when de Yankees come. I remember when de soldiers come an' had tents in Marster's yard before dey went off to de breastworks. My mother wus hired out before de surrender an' had to leave her two chilluns at home on Marster's plantation. When she come home Christmas he told her she would not have to go back any more. She could stay at home. This wus de las' year o' de war and he tol' her she would soon be free.

"My eyes are mighty bad. De doctor said he would work on 'em if somebody in de Agriculture Building would pay it.[4] I can't see at all out of one eye and the other is bad.

"I doan reckon I wus ten years old when de Yankees come, but I wus runnin' around an' can remember all dis. Guess I wus 'bout eight years old. I wus born in Warren County, near Warrenton. I belonged to Peter Mitchell, a long, tall man. There were 'bout a hundred slaves on de plantation. My missus wus named Laura. Mother always called me 'ole Betsy' when she wus mad at me. Betsy wus Marster Peter's mother. I remember seein' her. She wus a big fat 'oman wid white hair. She give biscuits to all de chillun on Saturdays. She also looked out for de slave chilluns on Sunday. My father wus named Marcillus Littlejohn and my mother wus named Susan Littlejohn.

"We had gardens and patches and plenty to eat. We also got de holidays. Marster bought charcoal from de men which dey burnt at night an' on holidays. Dey worked an' made de stuff, an' marster would let dem have de steer-carts an' wagons to carry deir corn an' charcoal to sell it in town. Yes sir, dis wus mighty nice. We had plank houses. Dere wus not but one log house on de plantation. Marster lived in de big house. It had eight porches on it.

"Dere wus no churches on de plantation, an' I doan remember any prayer meetin's. When we sang we turned de wash-pots an' tubs in de doors, so dey would take up de noise so de white folks could not hear us. I do remember de gatherin's at our home to pray fur de Yankees to come. All de niggers thought de Yankees had blue bellies. The old house cook got so happy at one of dese meetin's she run out in de yard an' called, 'Blue bellies come on, blue bellies come on.' Dey caught her an' carried her back into de house.

"When de overseer whupped one o' de niggers he made all de slaves sing, 'Sho' pity Lawd, Oh! Lawd forgive!. When dey sang awhile he would call out one an' whup him. He had a sing fur everyone he whupped. Marster growed up wid de niggers an' he did not like to whup 'em. If dey sassed him he would put spit in their eyes and say 'now I recon you will mind how you sass me.'

"We had a lot o' game and 'possums. When we had game marster left de big house, and come down an' et wid us. When marster wan't off drunk on a spree he spent a lot of time wid de slaves. He treated all alike. His slaves were all niggers. Dere were no half-white chilluns dere.

"Marster would not let us work until we were thirteen years old. Den he put us to plowin' in soft lan', an' de men in rough lan'. Some of de women played off sick an' went home an' washed an' ironed an' got by wid it. De oberseer tried to make two of 'em go back to work. Dey flew at him an' whupped him. He told de marster when he come home, marster said, 'Did you 'low dem women to whup you?' 'Yes', he replied, den marster tole him if women could whup him he didn't want him. But he let him stay on. His name wus Jack Rivers. He wus hired by marster. Marster Rivers did not have any slaves. Dere wus no jail on de plantation, case when er overseer whupped er nigger he did not need any jail.

"De black folks better not be caught wid a book but one o' de chilluns at our plantation, Marster Peter Mitchell's[Pg 58] sister had taught Aunt Isabella to read and write, an' durin' de war she would read, an' tell us how everythin' wus goin'. Tom Mitchell, a slave, sassed marster. Marster tole him he would not whup him, but he would sell him. Tom's brother, Henry, tol' him if he wus left he would run away, so marster sold both. He carried 'em to Richmond to sell 'em. He sold 'em on de auction block dere way down on Broad Street. When dey put Tom on de auction block dey found Tom had a broken leg and marster didn't git much fer him. He wanted to git enough fer these two grown settled men to buy two young men. Tom wus married. He wus sold from his wife and chilluns. Marster did not git enough fer 'em to pay for dese two young boys. He had to pay de difference in money. De boys were 'bout 21 or 22 years ole. When marster got back wid 'em de overseer tole him he had ruined his plantation. De boys soon become sick wid yeller fever an' both died. Dey strowed it 'round, an' many died. Marster shore made a mess o' things dat time.

"Dr. Ben Wilson, of Warren County wus Marster Mitchell's brother-in-law. He 'tended de sick folks an' he made many trips. Sometimes as soon as he got home dey sent fer him again.

"We played mumble-peg an' hop-scotch when I wus a child, we played jumpin' de rope a lot.

"I have never been married. I had only one brother. He has been dead six years. Since he died I have had a hard time makin' a livin'. Brother John lived wid me until he died. I had only one sister. She died many years ago. I think slavery wus mighty hard an' wrong. I joined de church 'cause I had religion an' de church would help me to keep it. People should be religious so dey will have a place in de beyond.

"Abraham Lincoln wus a good man. I have his picture. I think Mr. Roosevelt is a good God-fearin' man. When he gits sick I prays fer him. When he is sick I is jist as scared as I kin be. I prays fer him ter stay well."

LE

## FOOTNOTES:

[4] The office of the State Board of Welfare is in the Agriculture Building.

N.C. District: No. 2
Worker: T. Pat Matthews
No. Words: 625
Subject: CHARITY McALLISTER
Story teller: Charity McAllister
Editor: Daisy Bailey Waitt

# CHARITY McALLISTER

**602 South Street**

"My name is Charity McAllister. I wus here a long time before de Yankees come here. I wus 'bout grown when dey come through. I ain't hardly able to cook my little sumptin' to eat now. I ain't able to work out. No sir, not able to work. Done and worked my time out. I wus a grown gal when de Yankees come. I wus 'bout 18 years old. I loves to give you de truth and I knows I wus dat old. I wus a grown gal.

"My father wus named Robert Blalock. He 'longed to de Blalocks o' Harnett County. My mother wus Annie McAllister. She 'longed to Jennett McAllister in Harnett County. I 'longed to John Greene at Lillington, Harnett County. My mother first 'longed to John Greene. She got in de family way by a white man, and John Greene sold her to a speculator named Bill Avery of Raleigh, a speculator. Dey sold my brother. He wus as white as you is. When de surrender come mother went back to Miss Jennett McAllister in Harnett County. Dat's how dey got back dere. I wants to tell de truth and dats what I is goin' to do.

"I tell you I wus whupped durin' slavery time. Dey whupped us wid horsehair whups. Dey put a stick under our legs an' tied our hands to de stick and we could not do nuthin' but turn and twist. Dey would sure work on your back end. Every time you turned dey would hit it. I been whupped dat way and scarred up. We slept on mattresses made o' tow sacks. Our clothes were poor. One-piece-dress made o' carpet stuff, part of de time. One pair o' shoes a year after Christmas. Dey give 'em to us on January first; no shoes till after Christmas. Dey did not give us any holidays Christmas in Harnett County. Dat wus 'ginst de rules. No prayer nor nuthin' on de plantation in our houses. Dey did not 'low us to go to de white folks church. Dey did not 'low de slaves to hunt, so we did not have any game. Dey did not 'low us any patches. No sirree, we did not have any money.

"De slaves slep' a lot on pallets durin' slavery days. A pallet wus a quilt or tow carpet spread on de floor. We used a cotton pillow sometimes. Dere wus about 50 slaves on de plantation. We had no overseer on master's plantation, and no books and schools o' any kind for niggers. I cannot read and write. No sir, I wish I could read and write.

"I split rails and worked in de Cape Fear River Low Grounds. We fenced de fields wid rails split from trees, pine trees. Dey were eleven feet long.

"Yes sir, I seed de patterollers. I seed a plenty of dem scoundrels. Oh! ho, de Ku Klux, Ha!, Ha! Dey were real scandals, and I jest caint tell you all de mean things dey done right after de war. Reubin Matthew's slave, George Matthews, killed two Ku Klux. Dey double teamed him and shot him, and he cut 'em wid de ax, and dey died.

"I wus married right after de war. De second year after de war, I married Richard Rogers, but I kep' de name o' McAllister right on. My husband been dead a good long time. Lawd, I don't know how long. I been married one time, and dat wus one time too much. I have two sons, one name Clarence, and one named John, two daughters, one in Newport News, one in Washington, D.C., one named Lovie, and one named Lula."

BN

District No.: 3
Worker: Travis Jordan
Subject: Clara Cotton McCoy
Ex-slave 82 years
Durham, N.C. RFD #7

# CLARA COTTON MC-COY

## EX-SLAVE 82 YEARS

"Yes'm, I was bawn eighty-two years ago. My mammy died den an' my gran'mammy raised me. I sho do 'member when dat man Sherman an' his mens marched through Orange County, but, it didn' take no army of Yankees to ruin my white folks home, it took jus' one Yankee, but even dat didn' bow my Mistis' head.

"I ain't never seed nobody as proud as my Mis' 'Riah Cotton. She never bowed her head to trouble nor nobody; she never even bowed her head in chu'ch. When de preacher prayed she jus' folded her hands an' set up straight, facin' de Lawd wid no fear. No, suh, my Mistis ain't gwine bow her head no time. Young Mis' Laughter broke her mammy's heart, but she ain't make her bend her head.

"Mis' Laughter's sho nuff name was Mis' Clorena Cotton. She wasn' tall an' dark like Mis' 'Riah; she was little an' roun' an' pretty as a thorn flower, all pink an' gol'. She was jus' like a butterfly, never still a minute, skippin' here an' yonder, laughin' wid everybody. Dat's whare she got her name. Us niggers 'gun to call her Mis' Laughter kaze she was so happy. She was de only one dat could make Mis' 'Riah smile. She would run up to Mis' 'Riah an' ruffle her hair dat she done comb back so slick an' smooth, den she would stick a red rose behin' her ear, an' say: 'Now, pretty Mammy, you look like you did when Pappy come cou'tin'.' Marse Ned would lay down his paper an' look fus' at Mis' 'Riah den at Mis' Laughter, an' for a minute Mis' 'Riah would smile, den she would look firm an' say to Mis' Laughter, 'Don't you know dat rightousness an' virtue am more 'ceptable to de Lawd den beauty? You's worldly, Clorena, you's too worldly.'

"Mis' Laughter would throw back her head an' laugh, an' her eyes would shine bright as blue glass marbles. She tole Mis' 'Riah dat she 'specs dat when her man come he gwine see her face befo' he seed her rightousness, so she gwine wear roses an' curls den he would know her when he seed her. Den befo' Mis' 'Riah could speak her mind, Mis' Laughter done gone skippin' down de hall, her little feets in de gol' slippers twinklin' from de ruffles of her pantalets. Everybody on de place love dat chile an' de house wasn' never de same after she done gone away.

"My gran'mammy, Rowena, say dat Mis' 'Riah was bawn for trouble. She was bawn de las' day of March 'tween midnight an' day. De moon was on de wane, an' jus 'as Mistis was bawn de wind come down de chimbley an' blew de ashes out on de hearth. Gran'mammy say dat mean trouble an' death; dat new bawn baby ain't never gwine keep long de things she love de mos', an' she better never love nobody too well, if she do dey gwine be took away from her, an' trouble sho did follow Mis' 'Riah after she growed up.

"When de war come Marse Ned went off to fight. He was Marse General Cotton den. Dat didn't leave nobody at home 'cept Mis' 'Riah, her mammy, Mis' Roberta Davis, but we called her ole Mistis, den dare was Mis' Laughter an' young Marse Jerome. Young Marse wasn' but fifteen when de war started, but dey got him in de las' call an' he didn' never come back no more.

"De plantation was big, but Mis' 'Riah 'tended to things an' handled de niggers same as a man. De fus' year of de war she rode a hoss 'bout de fields like an overseer, seein' after de cotton an' cawn an' taters. But de Yankees come an' set fire to de cotton; dey took de cawn to dey camp for dey hosses, an' dey toted off de taters to eat. De nex year Mis' 'Riah didn' plant no cotton a tall kaze de seeds an' gin done been burned up, but she had de niggers plant cawn, taters an' a good garden. Dat fall de wind blew de hickory leaves to de no'th an' by spring trouble done come sho nuff. Dey was a drouth an' de cawn didn' come up; de garden burned to pa'chment, but de taters done all right. Wid all dat Mis' 'Riah held up her head an' kep' goin'. Den one day a buzzard flew over de house top an' his wings spread a shadow out on de roof. Dat night death come an' got Ole Mistis. She passed on to glory in her sleep. ''Twas de lawd's will,' Mis' 'Riah tole gran'mammy, an' she still held up her head. But Gran'mammy said dat if somebody had shot dat buzzard an' wiped his shadow off de roof Ole Mistis wouldn' have gone nowhare.

"De nex' spring dey wasn' much to plant. De Yankees done kep' totin' off everything, hosses an' all, 'twell dey wasn' much lef'. But de niggers, gran'mammy an' pappy along wid dem, dug up de garden wid de grubbin hoe an' planted what seeds dey had. Mis' 'Riah's an' Mis' Laughter's clothes 'gun to look ole, but gran'mammy kep' dem washed an' sta'ched stiff. 'Twas Mis' Laughter dat kep' us from frettin' too much. She would look at Mis' Riah an' say, 'We'll be all right, Mammy, when Marse Ned comes home.' Sometime she call her pappy Marse Ned jus' like dat. One day Marse Ned did come home. Dey brung him home. 'Twas 'bout sunset. I 'members kaze 'twas de same day dat my ole black hen hatched de duck eggs I done set her on, an' de apple trees wus bloomin'. De blooms look jus' like droves of pink butterflies flyin' on de sky. Dey brought Marse Ned in de house an' laid him out in de parlor. Mis' 'Riah stood straight 'side him wid her head up. 'Twas de Lawd's will, she tole Gran'mammy, but Gran'mammy shook her head an 'gun to cry, an' say: 'You can't put dat on de Lawd, Mis' 'Riah, you sho can't. 'Twasn' de Lawd's will a tall, 'twas de will of de cussed Yankees.' Den she turn 'roun' an' took Mis' Laughter's hand an' led her up stairs an' put her to bed.

"After dat things got worse. Dat wind dat blew trouble down de chimbley for Mis' 'Riah when she was bawn 'gun to blow harder. De war got young Marse Jerome an' shot him down. Dey won't much to eat, de coffee was made out of parched cawn an' de sweetnin' was cane lasses, an' de ham an' white bread done been gone a long time. Dey won't no eggs an' chickens, an' dey won't but one fresh cow, but nobody ain't never seed Mis' 'Riah bow her head nor shed a tear.

"When de surrender come dey was Yankees camped all 'roun' de plantation an' Hillsboro was full of dem. One day a Yankee mans come to de house. He was young. He come to see if Mis' 'Riah didn' want to sell her place. Mis' 'Riah stood in de door an' talked to him, she wouldn' let him come on de po'ch. She tole him she would starve befo' she would sell one foot of her lan' to a Yankee, an' dat he shouldn' darken de door of her house.

"'Bout dat time Mis' Laughter come down de hall an' stood behin' her mammy. Her hair curled 'bout her head yellow as a dandylion an' she had on a blue dress. When dat sojer seed her he stopped an' dey looked an' looked at each other 'twell Mis' 'Riah turned 'roun'. When she done dat Mis' Laughter turned an' run up de stairs.

"After dat Mis' 'Riah wouldn' let dat chile go no place by hersef. I was her bodyguard, everywhare she went I had to go too. We would go to walk down in de pine woods back of de paster, an' somehow dat Yankee would go to walk in dem woods too. Every time we seed him he would give me a piece of money, an' when I got back to de house I didn' tell nothin'. Den one day I heard dat sojer tell Mis'

Laughter dat he was gwine away. Mis' Laughter 'gun to cry an' I didn' hear what else dey said kaze dey sent me down de path. But dat night Mis' Laughter put her clothes in her box an' made me tote it down to de paster an' hide it in de blackberry patch. Den she give me a note an' tole me to go to bed an' go to sleep, but when mornin' come to give de note to Mis' 'Riah.

"De nex' mornin' I give de note to Mis' 'Riah, but by den Mis' Laughter done gone off wid dat Yankee. Mis' 'Riah called all us niggers in de big room. She took down de family Bible from de stand an' marked out Mis' Laughter's name. 'I ain't got no daughter,' she say. "Member, de chile dat I had am dead an' her name mustn' never be called in dis house no more.'

"We all went out 'cept Gran'mammy, but Mis' 'Riah wouldn' let her talk to her 'bout forgivin' Mis' Laughter, an' when de letters 'gun to come dey was sent back unopened.

"Mis' 'Riah's niece, Mis' Betty an' Marse John Davis, hur husban', come to live wid Mis' 'Riah to help her 'ten' to things, but nobody was 'lowed to call Mis' Laughter's name. Even though dey was free, gran'mammy an' pappy an' some more of us niggers stayed on at de plantation helpin' on de farm, but in 'bout a year Mis' 'Riah took sick. Mis' Betty wanted to sen' for Mis' Laughter, but Mis' 'Riah wouldn' even answer, but Mis' Betty sent for her anyhow an' kept her down stairs. Den one day de sun turned black an' de chickens went to roost in de day time. Gran'mammy flung her apron over her face an' 'gun to pray kase she knew de death angel was comin' after Mis' 'Riah. Mis' Betty got Mis' Laughter an' when she come up de stairs all us house niggers stood in de hall watchin' her go in to see Mis' 'Riah. She was layin' on de bed wid her eyes shut like she was sleep.

"Mis' Laughter went in an' kneel down by de bed. 'Mammy, Mammy,' she say soft jus' like dat.

"Mis' 'Riah's hands caught hold of de quilt tight, but she ain't opened her eyes. Gran'mammy went up an' laid her hand on her head, but she shook it off.

"De tears was runnin' down Mis' Laughter's cheeks. 'Mammy,' she say, 'I'se sorry—I loves you, Mammy.'

"Mis' 'Riah turned her face to de wall an' her back on Mis' Laughter. She ain't never opened her eyes. 'Bout dat time de sun come out from behin' dem black wings of shadow an' Mis' 'Riah's soul went on to glory to meet Marse Ned.

"Yes'm, Mis' 'Riah sho was proud, but Gran'mammy say 'twon' no war dat brung all dat trouble on her, she say 'twas de wind dat come down de chimbley de night she was bawn—de no'th wind dat blowed de ashes 'bout de hearth."

N.C. District: No. 2  
Worker: Mary Hicks  
No. Words: 535  
Subject: A GOOD MISTRESS  
Teller: Henrietta McCullers  
Editor: Daisy Bailey Waitt  

# A GOOD MISTRESS

**An interview with Henrietta McCullers, eighty-seven years old, of 531 E. Davie Street, Raleigh, North Carolina.**

"I wus borned roun' eighty-seben years ago in Wake County. Me an' my mammy 'longed ter Mis' Betsy Adams an' my pappy 'longed ter Mr. Nat Jones. I think dat Marse Nat had a whole passel o' slaves, but Mis' Betsy ain't had more'n six or seben.

"Yo' ax me iffen Mis' Betsy was good ter us? She wus so good dat I loved her all her life an' now dat she's daid I loves her in her grave.

"We et de same rations what she et an' we slept in de same kind o' bed she slept in. I knows dat sometimes she'd have company an' she'd do a heap o' extra fixin'; but she ain't neber fix better fer de company dan fer us.

"She'd let us have a co'n shuckin' onct a year, an' of course, we had a heap of prayer meetin's an' a few socials. She ain't wanted her niggers ter dance case she am such a good Christian, but she let us have candy pullin's an' sich.

"When de wuck warn't pushin' she'd let us go fishin' an' swimmin' an' all, only we jist waded, case we ain't used enough ter de water. Yo' know dat niggers am natu'lly skeerd o' water anyhow.

"Iffen de wuck wus pushin' we wucked from sunup till dark an' Mis' Betsy wucked too. Man, she wus a wuckin' woman, an' she made us wuck too; but I loves her better dan I does my own chilluns now, an' dat's one reason dat I wants ter go ter heaben. All my life when I done a bad thing I think 'bout Mis' Betsy's teachin's an' I repents.

"I plowed an' dug ditches an' cleaned new groun'; an' hard wuck ain't neber hurted me yit. De master wus too puny to wuck, an' I often thinks dat maybe he married Mis' Betsy to look atter him. Dey only had one man, Uncle Mose, an' so, of course, he had to have some help ter ten' 'bout a hundert acres.

"Most of our lan' wus planted in feed stuff fer us an' de cattle. An' so we raised ever'thing but de coffee. Sometimes we drunk Japonica tea, an' done without de coffee.

"On Sunday's yo' should o' seen us in our Sunday bes' goin' ter church 'hind de missus coach, wid ole Uncle Mose high on de box. We can't read de hymns eben iffen we had a book 'cause we ain't 'lowed ter have no books, but we sung jist de same.

"At Christmas time we had a party at de big house. Mis' Betsy had sabed a bushel er so o' de lates' apples an' she made a big dish of lasses candy an' we popped pop corn an' wus happy. Mis' Betsy always give us some clothes an' we had a feas' all through de week of holidays.

"When de Yankees comed dey jist about cleaned us out. Dey kills pigs, turkeys, calves an' hens all over de place, dey gits de beserves an' a heap o' de lasses an' dey sass Mis' Betsy. All dis wus dem bad-mannered soldiers' fault, case Abraham Lincoln ain't mean't fer it ter be dis way, I know. I reckon dat most o' dem soldiers wus pore white trash. Dey doan keer 'bout de niggers, but dey ain't wanted our white folks ter be rich.

"De Yankees ain't stayed long in our neighborhood case dey am a-lookin' fer our soldiers, so dey goes away.

"Did I leave atter de war wus ober? Naw sir, I ain't, an' all de rest stayed on too. Uncle Mose stayed on too. Uncle Mose stayed de rest o' his life, but I left two years atterwards when I got married.

"My memory am gittin' so short dat I doan 'member my daddy's name, ner my brothers an' sisters names. I 'member dat my mammy wus named Piety do' an' I 'members my fust lesson from Mis' Betsy, 'Doan lie, an' doan steal, ax fer what you needs, needs, mind you, not what you wants.'"

"Niggers ort ter be back in slavery now, dey'd be better an' happier dan dey is. I ain't neber had a whuppin' in my life an' dat's more dan most of dese free niggers can say."

EH

| | |
|---|---|
| N.C. District: | No. 2 |
| Worker: | T. Pat Matthews |
| No. Words: | 1050 |
| Subject: | WILLIE McCULLOUGH |
| Person Interviewed: | Willie McCullough |
| Editor: | G.L. Andrews |

[TR: Date stamp: OCT 23 1937 (unclear)]

# WILLIE McCULLOUGH

**8 McKee Street, Raleigh, North Carolina. Age 68 years.**

"I was born in Darlington County, South Carolina, the 14th of June 1869. My mother was named Rilla McCullough and my father was named Marion McCullough. I remember them very well and many things they told me that happened during the Civil War. They belonged to a slave owner named Billy Cannon who owned a large plantation near Marion, South Carolina. The number of slaves on the plantation from what they told me was about fifty. Slaves were quartered in small houses built of logs. They had plenty of rough food and clothing. They were looked after very well in regard to their health, because the success of the master depended on the health of his slaves. A man can't work a sick horse or mule. A slave occupied the same place on the plantation as a mule or horse did, that is a male slave. Some of the slave women were looked upon by the slave owners as a stock raiser looks upon his brood sows, that is from the standpoint of production. If a slave woman had children fast she was considered very valuable because slaves were valuable property.

"There was classes of slavery. Some of the half-white and beautiful young women who were used by the marster and his men friends or who was the sweetheart of the marster only, were given special privileges. Some of 'em worked very little. They had private quarters well fixed up and had a great influence over the marster. Some of these slave girls broke up families by getting the marster so enmeshed in their net that his wife, perhaps an older woman, was greatly neglected. Mother and grandmother tole me that they were not allowed to pick their husbands.

"Mother tole me that when she became a woman at the age of sixteen years her marster went to a slave owner near by and got a six-foot nigger man, almost an entire stranger to her, and told her she must marry him. Her marster read a paper to them, told them they were man and wife and told this negro he could take her to a certain cabin and go to bed. This was done without getting her consent or even asking her about it. Grandmother said that several different men were put to her just about the same as if she had been a cow or sow. The slave owners treated them as if they had been common animals in this respect.

"Mother said she loved my father before the surrender and just as soon as they were free they married. Grandmother was named Luna Williams. She belonged to a planter who owned a large plantation and forty slaves adjoining Mr. Cannon's plantation where mother and father stayed. My grandmother on my mother's side lived to be 114 years old, so they have tole me.

"I ran away from home at the age of twelve years and went to Charleston, South Carolina. I worked with a family there as waitin' boy for one year. I then went to Savannah, Ga. I had no particular job and

I hoboed everywhere I went. I would wait all day by the side of the railroad to catch a train at night. I rode freight trains and passenger trains. I rode the blind baggage on passenger trains and the rods on freight trains. The blind baggage is the car between the mail car and the engine. The doors are on the side and none at the end. I hoboed on to Miami over the Florida East Coast Railroad. I next went from Miami to Memphis, Tenn. after staying there a few days and working with a contractor, I again visited Charleston, S.C. I had been there only two days when I met some Yankees from Minnesota. They prevailed on me to go home with them, promising if I would do so they would teach me a trade. I went with them. We all hoboed. We were halted at the Blue Ridge mountains but we got by without going to jail. We then went to N.J. From N.J. to Chicago, Ill., then into Milwaukee, Wis., then on into Minneapolis, Minn. Many towns and cities I visited on this trip, I did not know where I was. My Yankee companions looked out for me. They taught me the trade of making chairs and other rustic furniture. They taught me 164 ways of making different pieces of furniture. I spent 11 years in Minnesota but during that time I visited the South once every three years, spending several days in the county of my birth. Mother and father farmed all their lives and they often begged me to settle down but the wanderlust had me and for 30 years I travelled from place to place. Even while in Minnesota I did not stay in Minneapolis all the time. I visited most every town in the state during the eleven years I stayed there and made hobo trips into most of the adjoining states.

"The main Yankee who taught me the trade was Joe Burton. He and the gang helped me to get food until I learned the trade well enough so I could make a living working at it.

"I have made a lot of money making and selling rustic furniture, but now I am getting old. I am not able to work as I used too. Not long ago I made a trip from Raleigh to Charleston, S.C., but the trip was different from the old days. I hitch-hiked the entire distance. I rode with white folks. On one leg of the trip of over 200 miles I rode with a rich young man and his two pals. They had a fruit jar full of bad whiskey. He got about drunk, ran into a stretch of bad road at a high rate of speed, threw me against the top of his car and injured my head. I am not over it yet.

"I quit the road in 1924. My last trip was from Raleigh, N.C. to Harrisburg, Penn. and return. I have made my home in Raleigh ever since. Done settled down, too ole to ramble anymore."

LE

N.C. District: No. 2
Worker: T. Pat Matthews
No. Words: 1,477
Subject: JAMES TURNER McLEAN
Storyteller: James Turner McLean
Editor: Daisy Bailey Waitt

# JAMES TURNER McLEAN

Lillington, N.C.
Route 1

"My name is James Turner McLean. I was born in Harnett County near Cape Fear River in the Buies Creek Section, Feb. 20, 1858. I belonged to Taylor Hugh McLean, and he never was married. The plantation was between Buies Creek and the Cape Fear river; the edge of it is about 75 yards from where I now live. The place where I live belongs to me. 'Way back it belonged to the Bolden's.

"The Boldens came from Scotland, and so did the McLeans. There were about five hundred acres in this plantation and Marster Hugh McLean had about fifty slaves. The slaves lived in quarters and Marster lived in the big house which was his home. Marster took good care o' his darkies. He did not allow anybody to whip 'em either. We had good food, clothes and places to sleep. My father was Jim McLean and my mother was named Charlotta McLean. My grandmother was named Jane. I called my mother 'Sissie' and called my grandmother 'mammy' in slavery time. They did not have me to do any heavy work just tending to the calves, colts, and goin' to the post office.

"The post office was at Mr. Sexton's and we called it Sexton's post office, on the Raleigh and Fayetteville Road. The stage run on this road and brought mail to this place. This post in my yard is part of a stage coach axle. You see it? Yes sir, that's what it is. I got it at Fayetteville when they were selling the old stage coach. We bought the axle and wheels and made a cart. We got that stuff about 1870; my father bought it. He gave twelve dollars for jes' the wheels and axle. This was after we had taken the iron clad oath and become more civilized.

"We were daresome to be caught with a paper book or anything if we were tryin' to learn to read and write. We had to have a pass to go around on, or the patterollers would work on us. I saw a lot of patterollers. Marster gave his Negroes a pass for twelve months. He sent his timber to Wilmington, and worked timber at other places so he gave his slaves yearly passes. Then when the war was about up me and him went to the post office, and he got the paper. All the niggers were free. We stopped on the way home at a large sassafras tree by the side o' the road where he always stopped to read, and he read, and told me I was free.

"I did not know what it was or what it meant. We came on to the house where my mother was and I said, 'Sissie, we is free.' She said, 'Hush, or I will put the hickory on you.' I then went to grandma, the one I called mammy and threw my arms around her neck and said, 'Mammy we are free, what does it mean?' and mammy, who was grandma, said, 'You hush sich talk, or I will knock you down wid a loom stick.'

"Marster was comin' then, and he had the paper in his hand and was cryin'. He came to the door and called grandma and said, 'You are free, free as I am, but I want you to stay on. If you go off you will perish. If you stay on now the crop is planted and work it, we will divide.' Marster was cryin' and said, 'I do not own you any longer.' He told her to get the horn and blow it. It was a ram's horn. She blew twice for the hands to come to the house.

"They were workin' in the river lowground about a mile or more away. She blew a long blow, then another. Marster told her to keep blowin'! After awhile all the slaves come home; she had called them all in. Marster met them at the gate, and told them to put all the mules up, all the hoes and plows, that they were all free. He invited all to eat dinner. He had five women cooking. He told them all he did not want them to leave, but if they were going they must eat before they left. He said he wanted everybody to eat all he wanted, and I remember the ham, eggs, chicken, and other good things we had at that dinner. Then after the dinner he spoke to all of us and said, 'You have nowhere to go, nothin' to live on, but go out on my other plantation and build you some shacks.'

"He gave them homes and did not charge any rent. He bought nails and lumber for them, but he would not build the houses. Some stayed with him for fifteen years; some left. He gave them cows to milk. He said the children must not perish.

"Marster was a mighty good man, a feelin' man. He cried when some of his slaves finally left him. Mother and father stayed till they got a place of their own. I waited on him as long as he lived. I loved him as well as I did my daddy. I drove for him and he kept me in his house with him. He taught me to be honest, to tell the truth, and not to steal anything.

"When freedom came marster gave us a place for a school building and furnished nails and gave the lumber for the floors. He instructed them in building the windows. He was goin' to put his sister Jenette McAllister in as teacher. She had married Jim McAllister at the Bluff Church, right at the lower part of the Averysboro Battleground where some of the last fightin' between the North and South was done, but a man by the name of George Miller of Harnett County told him he knew a nigger who could teach the school. He employed the nigger, whose name was Isaac Brantley, to teach the school. He came from Anderson's Creek in the lower part of Harnett County. We learned very little, as the nigger read, and let us repeat it after him. He would hold the book, and spell and let us repeat the words after him without lettin' us see in the book. He stayed there two months, then a man by the name of Matthews, Haywood Matthews, son of Henderson Matthews came. They were white folks, but went for negroes. Haywood teached there. He got the children started and most of 'em learned to read and write.

"I saw the Yankees come through. Also Wheeler's Cavalry. The Yankees took chickens and things, and they gave us some things, but Wheeler's Cavalry gave us nothin'. They took what they wanted and went on. Marster hid his horses and things in the Pecosin.

"When the Yankees came Marster was hid. They rode up to my mother and asked her where he was. She said, 'I do not know.' They then asked her where was de silver, his money, an' de brandy, an' wine. They got one demijohn full o' brandy. They went into the house, tore up things got his china pipe, fixed for four people to smoke at one time. You could turn a piece and shett off all de holes but one, when one man wanted to smoke. They threw away his old beaver hat, but before they left they got it and left it in the house. Wheeler's Cavalry stomped things and broke up more den de Yankees.

"Daddy hid marster's money, a lot of it, in the jam o' de fence. He covered it with sand that he threw out of a ditch that ran along near the fence. The Yankees stopped and sat on the sand to eat their dinner and never found the money.

"I have never seen a slave sold, and none never ran away from marster's plantation. When any of his men went to visit their wives he let them ride the stock, and give them rations to carry. There was a jail for slaves at Summerville. I saw it.

"We went to the white folks church at Neill's Creek. Mother used herbs to give us when we were sick. Dr. Turner, Dr. John Turner, looked after us. We were bled every year in the spring and in the fall. He had a little lance. He corded your arm and popped it in, and the blood would fly. He took nearly a quart of blood from grandma. He bled according to size and age.

"We ought to think a lot o' Abraham Lincoln and the other great men such as Booker T. Washington. Lincoln set us free. Slavery was a bad thing and unjust."

AC

N.C. District:        No. 2
Worker:               T. Pat Matthews
No. Words:            857
Subject:              FRANK MAGWOOD
Person Interviewed:   Frank Magwood
Editor:               G.L. Andrews

# FRANK MAGWOOD

"I was born in Fairfield County, South Carolina, near the town of Ridgeway. Ridgeway was on the Southern Railroad from Charlotte, N.C. to Columbia, South Carolina. I was born Oct. 10, 1864. I belonged to Nora Rines whose wife was named Emma. He had four girls Frances, Ann, Cynthia, and Emma and one son named George. There was about one thousand acres of land inside the fences with about two hundred acres cleared. There were about seventy slaves on the place. My mother and father told me these things. Father belonged to a man by the name of John Gosey and mother belonged to ole man Rines. My father was named Lisbon Magwood and my mother was named Margaret Magwood. They were sold and resold on the slave auction block at Charleston, South Carolina, but the families to whom they belonged did not change their names until mother's name was changed when she married father in 1862.

"There were twelve children in the family, three boys and nine girls. Only two boys of this family are living, Walter and myself.

"Mother and father said at the beginning of the war that the white folks said it would not last long and that in the first years of the war they said one southern soldier could whup three Yankee soldiers, but after awhile they quit their braggin. Most everything to eat and wear got scarce. Sometimes you couldn't git salt to go in the vegetables and meat that was cooked. People dug up the salty earth under their smoke houses, put water with it, drained it off and used it to salt rations.

"There came stories that the Yankees had taken this place and that they were marching through Georgia into South Carolina. They burned Columbia, the Capitol of South Carolina, and had both whites and black scared, they were so rough. The Yankees stole, burned, and plundered. Mother said they hated South Carolina cause they started the war there. They burned a lot of the farm houses. The army, so my father and mother said, was stretched out over a distance of sixty-two miles. Jest think of a scope of country sixty two miles wide with most of the buildings burned, the stock killed, and nothing to eat. The southern army and the northern army had marched back and forth through the territory until there was nothing much left. Where Sherman's army stopped and ate and fed their horses the Negroes went and picked up the grains of corn they strowed there and parched and ate them. People also parched and ate acorns in South Carolina.

"Father and mother got together after the war and they moved to a widow lady's place by the name of Ann Hunter, near Ridgeway. She was good to us and we stayed there sixteen years. Ann Hunter had three sons, Abraham, George and Henry. Abraham went to South America on a rambling trip. He decided to stay there. He was a young man then and he married a Spaniard. When he came home to see his mother it was the year of the earthquake in 1886. He was a grown man then and he brought his wife and children with him. He had three children, all of them spoke Spanish and could not understand their grandmother's talk to them. His wife was a beautiful woman, dark with black hair and blue eyes. She just worshipped her husband. They stayed over a month and then returned to South America. I have never seen 'em since or had any straight news of them.

"Mother and father lived on the farm until they died, with first one ex-slave owner and another. They said they had nothing when the war ended and that there was nothing to do.

"I stayed with my mother and father near Ridgeway until I was 21 years of age. I left the farm then and went to work on the railroad. I thought I was the only man then. I was so strong. I worked on the railroad one year then I went to the Stone mountain Rock Quarry in Georgia.

"I got my hand injured with a dynamite cap after I had worked there a year and I came home again. I went back to working on the farm as a day hand. I worked this way for one year then I began share croppin'.

"I farmed ever since I came to Wake County 15 years ago. I farmed on Mr. Simpkins place one year then Mr. Dillon bought the place and I stayed there nine more years then I became so near blind I could not farm. I came to Raleigh to this house four years ago. I have been totally blind since the fifteenth of last December.

"I married Alice Praylor near Ridgeway when I was 23 years of age. We had nine children.

"My last marriage was to Mamie Williams. I married her in South Carolina. We had four children. They are all living, grown and married off. My chief worry over being blind is the fact that it makes me unable to farm anymore."

LE

| | |
|---|---|
| N.C. District: | No. 2 |
| Worker: | T. Pat Matthews |
| No. Words: | 1120 |
| Subject: | JACOB MANSON |
| Person Interviewed: | Jacob Manson |
| Editor: | G.L. Andrews |

# JACOB MANSON

**317 N. Haywood St. Raleigh, N.C. 86 years of age.**

"It has been a long time since I wus born—bout all my people am dead 'cept my wife an one son an two daughters. De son an' one daughter live in N.C. an de other daughter lives in Richmond, Va.

"I belonged to Col. Bun Eden. His plantation wus in Warren County an' he owned 'bout fifty slaves or more. Dere wus so many of 'em dere he did not know all his own slaves. We got mighty bad treatment an' I jest wants to tell you a nigger didn't stan' as much show dere as a dog did. Dey whupped fur mos' any little trifle. Dey whupped me, so dey said, jes to help me git a quicker gait. De patterollers come sneakin' round often an' whupped niggers on marster's place. Dey nearly killed my uncle. Dey broke his collar bone when dey wus beatin him an marster made 'em pay for it 'cause uncle never did git over it.

"Marster would not have any white overseers. He had nigger foremen. Ha! ha! he liked some of de nigger 'omans too good to have any udder white man playin' aroun' 'em.

"We wurked all day an some of de night an' a slave who made a week, even atter doin dat, wus lucky if he got off widout gettin' a beatin. We had poor food an' de young slaves wus fed outen troughs. De food wus put in a trough an de little niggers gathered round an' et. Our cabins wus built of poles an had stick an dirt chimleys one door an one little winder at de back end of de cabin. Some of de houses had dirt floors. Our clothin' was poor an homemade.

"Many of de slaves went bareheaded an barefooted. Some wore rags roun dere heads an some wore bonnets. Marster lived in de great house. He did not do any work but drank a lot of whiskey, went dressed up all de time an had niggers to wash his feet an comb his hair. He made me scratch his head when he lay down so he could go to sleep. When he got to sleep I would slip out. If he waked up when I started to leave I would have to go back an' scratch his head till he went to sleep agin. Sometimes I had to fan de flies way from him while he slept. No prayer-meetings wus allowed, but we sometimes went to de white folks church. Dey tole us to obey our marsters an be obedient at all times. When bad storms come dey let us rest but dey kept us in de fields so long sometimes dat de storm caught us 'fore we could git to de cabins. Niggers watched de wedder in slavery time an de ole ones wus good at prophesyin' de wedder.

"Marster had no chilluns by white women. He had his sweethearts 'mong his slave women. I ain't no man for tellin false stories. I tells de truth an dat is de truth. At dat time it wus a hard job to find a marster dat didn't have women 'mong his slaves. Dat wus a ginerel thing 'mong de slave owners.

"One of de slave girls on a plantation near us went to her missus an tole her 'bout her marster forcing her to let him have sumthin to do wid her an her missus tole her, 'Well go on you belong to him.'

"Another marster named Jimmie Shaw owned a purty slave gal nearly white an he kept her. His wife caught 'im in a cabin in bed wid her. His wife said sumthin to him 'bout it an' he cussed his wife. She tole him she had caught him in de act. She went back to de great house an got a gun. When de marster come in de great house she tole 'im he must let de slave girls alone dat he belonged to her. He cussed her agin an sed she would have to tend to her own dam business an' he would tend to his. Dey had a big fuss an den marster Shaw started towards her. She grabbed de gun an let him have it. She shot 'im dead in de hall. Dey had three chillun, two sons an one married daughter. Missus Shaw took her two sons an' left. De married daughter an her husband took charge of de place. Missus an her sons never come back as I knows of.

"A lot of de slave owners had certain strong healthy slave men to serve de slave women. Ginerally dey give one man four women an' dat man better not have nuthin' to do wid de udder women an' de women better not have nuthin to do wid udder men. De chillun wus looked atter by de ole slave women who were unable to work in de fields while de mothers of de babies worked. De women plowed an done udder work as de men did. No books or larnin' of any kind wus allowed.

"One mornin' de dogs begun to bark an' in a few minutes the plantation wus kivered wid Yankees. Dey tole us we wus free. Dey axed me whur marster's things wus hid. I tole 'em I could not give up marster's things. Dey tole me I had no marster dat[Pg 99] dey had fighted four years to free us an' dat marster would not whup me no more. Marster sent to de fields an' had all de slaves to come home. He told me to tell 'em not to run but to fly to de house at once. All plow hands an' women come running home. De Yankees tole all of 'em dey wus free.

"Marster offered some of de Yankees sumtin to eat in his house but dey would not eat cooked food, dey said dey wanted to cook dere own food.

"I saw slaves sold in slavery time. I saw 'em whupped an many ran away. Some never come back. When we wus sick we took lots of erbs an roots. I married Roberta Edwards fifty-one years ago. We had six sons and three daughters. Atter the war I farmed around from one plantation to another. I have never owned a home of my own. When I got too ole to work I come an' lived wid my married daughter in Raleigh. I been here four years. I think slavery wus a mighty bad thing, though it's been no bed of roses since, but den no one could whup me no mo."

LE

| | |
|---|---|
| N.C. District: | No. 2 |
| Worker: | T. Pat Matthews |
| No. Words: | 1060 |
| Subject: | ROBERTA MANSON |
| Person Interviewed: | Roberta Manson |
| Editor: | G.L. Andrews |

# ROBERTA MANSON

**317 N. Haywood Street, Raleigh, N.C. Age 74.**

"I wus borned de second year of de war an' de mos' I know 'bout slavery wus tole to me by other colored folks. My marster wus Weldon Edwards and my missus wus Missus Lucy. The plantation wus in Warren County near Ridgeway. My father wus named Lanis Edwards and my mother wus named Ellen Edwards. They both 'longed to Weldon Edwards. Father and mother said he wus mighty rough to 'em. I heard my mother say dat marster whupped father so bad dat she had to grease his back to git his shirt off.

"Marster allowed de overseers to whup de slaves. De overseers wus named Caesar Norfeir, Jim Trissel, and David Porter.

"Dere wus a ole man dere by de name of Harris Edwards who fed up the hogs an' things. He wus sick an' he kept him sick. Well after awhile de ole marster tried to make him work. De overseers den took him out way down in the plum orchard. Dey pulled his tongue out an whupped him. He died an' wus found by de buzzards. De overseers wus named Jim Trissel an David Porter dat did dat. Dis ole slave 'longed to missus; and when she found it out dere wus a awful fuss. One of de white overseers tried to put it off on de udder. It finally fell on Jim Trissel and dey soon got rid of him. Missus tole him, 'you have killed my poor ole sick servant.' Mr. Jim Trissel killed several slaves an dey wus shore 'fraid of him. He knocked my father down wid a stick an when he fell my father knocked his hip out of place. Dey whupped father 'cause he looked at a slave dey killed an cried.

"Dey didn't allow no prayermeetings or parties in de houses. No books in de houses. No books or papers, no edication.

"Some of de owners when dey knowed freedom wus commin' dey treated de slaves wusser den ever before. De ole men an women dat wus unable to work wus neglected till dey died or was killed by beatin' or burnin'. Col. Skipper did dat thing. He lived near Clarksville, Va. He put a lot of ole men an women on a island in the Roanoke River. De river rose an stayed up eighteen days an dey parished to death. Dey were sent dere when sick and dey died. Mr. Skipper had over two hundred slaves. He wus one of the richest men in the south and Mr. Nick Long wus another rich man. Nick Long owned de plantation now known as the Caledonia State's Prison Farm. Gen. Ransom's plantation wus a part of de land 'longing to the Caledonia State Prison Farm now. It joined Nick Long's plantation.

"Father and mother had bad fare, poor food, clothes an shoes. Dey didn't sift slave meal. Dey had no sifters. Sometimes de collards and peas was not cleaned 'fore cookin'. Dey said de more slaves a man had de wusser he wus to slaves. Marster had dirt floors in de cabins. Dey slept on straw bunks made outen baggin' and straw. Some slept on wheat, straw an' shucks an' covered wid baggin.

"Ole man Mat Bullock, a negro slave, an' his mother Ella an' grandmother Susan, also slaves, froze to death. Mat Bullock the son of Ole man Mat Bullock tole me this. Dese slaves 'longed to Jim Bullock who's plantation wus near Townsville, N.C.

"Weldon Edwards who owned father and mother had a whuppin post an dey said dey whupped ole man Jack Edwards to death 'cause he went to see his sick wife. He crawled from de whuppin post to de house atter bein whupped and died. Dey tole him 'fore dey whupped him dat dey wus goin to stop him from runnin' away. Families wus broken up by sellin'. Dey couldn't sell a slave dat wus skinned up. Aunt Millie, Agie, Gracy and Lima wus sold from the Edwards family. Aunt Millie cried so much cause she had to leave her young baby dat dey talked of whuppin her, ut den dey say 'we cannot sell her if we whup her an' so dey carried her on. Mother sed Marster Weldon Edwards sole four women away from dere young chilluns at one time.

"We lived in log cabins with dirt floors, one door, and one small winder at de back. De cabins had stick an dirt chimbleys.

"When freedom come mother and father stayed on wid marster cause dey didn't have nuthin. Dey couldn't leave. Dey farmed for shares. Next year the overseer who had beat father so bad come atter him to go an work with him. It wus Mr. David Porter. I axed pa ain't dat de man who beat you so when you wus a slave? An pa say, 'you shet your mouth.' He stayed with Mr. Porter two years den we went to Mr. William Paschal's. We stayed there four years. Endurin' the next fifteen years we moved a good many times. We farmed round and round an' finally went to Mr. Peter Wyms' place near where I wus borned.

"I wus married there to Jack Manson, 52 years ago in January. I had eight chilluns five girls an' three boys. Three are living now. One boy and two girls. Two of the chilluns are in N.C. and one, a girl, is in Virginia.

"I think slavery wus a bad thing but when freedom come there wus nuthin' else we could do but stay on wid some of de white folks 'cause we had nuthin to farm wid an nuthin to eat an wear.

"De men who owned de plantations had to have somebody to farm dere lan' an' de slaves had to have somewhur to stay. Dats de way it wus, so if dere wus a lot of movin' about de exslaves kept doin de wurk cause dat's de only way dey had to keep from perishin'. De marsters needed 'em to farm dere lan' an' de exslaves just had to have somewhur to live so both parties kept stayin' an' wurkin together.

"De nigger made mos' dey has out of workin' fer white folks since de war 'cause dey didn't have nuthin' when set free an dat is all dere is to it."

N.C. District: 2  
Worker: Travis Jordan  
No. Words: 700  
Subject: MILLIE MARKHAM'S STORY  
Interviewed: Millie Markham  
615 St. Joseph St., Durham, N.C.

[TR: Date stamp: JUN 1 1937]

# EX-SLAVE STORY AS TOLD BY MILLIE MARKHAM

## OF 615 ST. JOSEPH ST., DURHAM, N.C.

"I was never a slave. Although I was born somewhere about 1855, I was not born in slavery, but my father was. I'm afraid this story will be more about my father and mother than it will be about myself.

"My mother was a white woman. Her name was Tempie James. She lived on her father's big plantation on the Roanoke River at Rich Square, North Carolina. Her father owned acres of land and many slaves. His stables were the best anywhere around; they were filled with horses, and the head coachman was named Squire James. Squire was a good looking, well behaved Negro who had a white father. He was tall and light colored. Tempie James fell in love with this Negro coachman. Nobody knows how long they had been in love before Tempie's father found it out, but when he did he locked Tempie in her room. For days he and Miss Charlottie, his wife, raved, begged and pleaded, but Tempie just said she loved Squire. 'Why will you act so?' Miss Charlottie was crying. 'Haven't we done everything for you and given you everything you wanted?'

"Tempie shook her head and said: 'You haven't given me Squire. He's all I do want.'

"Then it was that in the dark of the night Mr. James sent Squire away; he sent him to another state and sold him.

"But Tempie found it out. She took what money she could find and ran away. She went to the owner of Squire and bought him, then she set him free and changed his name to Walden Squire Walden. But then it was against the law for a white woman to marry a Negro unless they had a strain of Negro blood, so Tempie cut Squire's finger and drained out some blood. She mixed this with some whiskey and drank it, then she got on the stand and swore she had Negro blood in her, so they were married. She never went back home and her people disowned her.

"Tempie James Walden, my mother, was a beautiful woman. She was tall and fair with long light hair. She had fifteen children, seven boys and eight girls, and all of them lived to be old enough to see their great-grandchildren. I am the youngest and only one living now. Most of us came back to North Carolina. Two of my sisters married and came back to Rich Square to live. They lived not far from the James plantation on Roanoke River. Once when we were children my sister and I were visiting in Rich Square. One day we went out to pick huckleberries. A woman came riding down the road on a horse. She was a tall woman in a long grey riding habit. She had grey hair and grey eyes. She stopped and looked at us. 'My,' she said, 'whose pretty little girls are you?'

"'We're Squire Walden's children,' I said.

"She looked at me so long and hard that I thought she was going to hit me with her whip, but she didn't, she hit the horse. He jumped and ran so fast I thought she was going to fall off, but she went around the curve and I never saw her again. I never knew until later that she was Mis' Charlottie James, my grandmother.

"I don't know anything about slavery times, for I was born free of free parents and raised on my father's own plantation. I've been living in Durham over sixty-five years."

N.C. District: No. 2
Worker: T. Pat Matthews
No. Words: 680
Subject: A SLAVERY STORY
Story teller: MAGGIE MIALS
Editor: George L. Andrews

[TR: Date stamp: SEP 10 1937]

# MAGGIE MIALS

**73 years old, of 202 Maple Street, Raleigh, North Carolina.**

"I'll never forgit de day when de Yankees come through Johnston County.

"I belonged to Tom Demaye an' ole missus in slavery time wus named Liza.

"De Demayes lived in Raleigh when I wus born, so mother tole me, but dey moved to a place near Smithfield. He had 'bout a dozen slaves. We had little cabins to live in, but marster had a big house to live in that set in a grove. De food I got wus good because I was a pet in de family. My mother was a cook an' a pet. My marster wus good to all of us an' I fared better den dan I do now. Ole marster thought de world of me and I loved him. Marster allowed his slaves to visit, have prayer meetings, hunt, fish, an' sing and have a good time when de work wus done. Some of de slave owners did not like marster cause he wus so good to his slaves. They called us 'Ole Man Demayes damn free niggers.' I don't know my age zackly but I was a big gal, big enough to drag a youngin roun' when de Yankees come through. I wus six years old if no older.

"When de Yankees come dey called us to de wagons an' tole us we wus free. Dey give each of us a cap full of hard-tack. Dey took clothes an' provisions an' give us nothin'. One crowd of Yankees would come on an' give us something an' another would come along an' take it away from us. Dey tole us to call marster an' missus Johnny Rebs, that we wus free an' had no marsters. Dat wus a day for me. Some of de Yankees wus ridin', some walkin', an' some runnin'. Dey took de feather beds in marsters house to de windows, cut dem open an' let de feathers blow away. It wus a sad time to me 'cause dey destroyed so much of marster's stuff.

"After de Yankees left we stayed right on with marster a long time, den we moved away to other members of de family. Mother would not give up de family an' she an' daddy stayed wid dem as long as dey lived. I love de family now an' I rather be livin' wid 'em den like I is. Dere is only a few of de younger set of de Demayes livin'. Ole marster an' missus' had three boys, Sye, Lee, Zoa; girls, Vick, Correna and Phidelia, six chilluns in all. Dey is all dead but I can't never forgit 'em if I live to be a hundred years ole.

"I tries to live right before God an' man cause I knows I haint got much longer on dis earth. I knows I got to lay down sometime to rise no more till Judgment Day, den I wants to meet ole marster, missus an' de family in dat country where dere'll be no more goodbyes.

"I was married at twenty years ole to Theodore Miles at de ole Mack Powell place near de Neuse River, in Wake County. I wus hired as a house girl at dis place wid Mr. Alango Miles family. Dey wus some of de Demaye family. I had ten chillun, four boys an' six girls. Six of my chillun are livin' now. Two boys an' four girls. My husband been dead 'bout 16 years. He died in Oct. 1921. Buried on de third Sunday in October.

"I have farmed most of my life an' have raised a big family. Sometimes we wus hongry an' sometimes we had plenty. None of my chilluns wus never arrested an' none ever went to prison. I thinks dats something to knock on wood about.

"Slavery was a good thing by all niggers who happened to have good marsters. De owners wus to blame for slavery gettin' such a bad reputation. Some of 'em jus' done a little too much an' sich caused de war an' give de niggers freedom. Slavery wus good for some an' bad for others."

EH

N.C. District: No. 2
Worker: Mary Hicks
No. Words: 344
Subject: Ex-Slave Story
Teller: Anna Mitchel
Editor: Daisy Bailey Waitt

# ANNA MITCHEL
## Ex-slave story.

**An interview with Anna Mitchel, 76 of 712 S. Person Street, Raleigh, North Carolina.**

"I wus borned in Vance County an' I 'longed ter Mr. Joseph Hargrove, de same man what owned Emily an' Rufus Hargrove, my mammy an' pappy. He also owned Joseph an' Cora, my bruder an' sister. My mammy uster 'long ter 'nother man what lived in Virginia, but Mr. Hargrove buyed her when she wus sold on de choppin' block at Richmon'. He already had my pappy so dey got married dar on his plantation.

"Marster ain't neber whup nobody, case he am too much de gentleman, but de oberseer done nuff fer 'em all.

"Dar wasn't no Sadday evenin's off 'cept fer de wimen what had eight or ten chilluns an' dey got off ter wash 'em up. In de rush time, dat is, when de fodder wus burnin' up in de fiel's or de grass wus eatin' up de cotton dey had ter wuck on Sunday same as on Monday.

"My mammy wus a seamstress, an' I'se knowed her ter wuck all night an' half de day ter make clothes fer de slaves.

"We ain't had but two meals a day an' dey wus scant. We had a few frolicks, dances an' sich lak onct in a while[Pg 115] an' onct a year we all went ter a show, sorter lak a circus.

"I 'members dat we sung 'Swing Low Sweet Chariot,' 'De Promised Lan',' 'Ole Time Religion,' an' one dat goes:

"'Dark wus de night an' col' de groun'On which my Saviour lay,An' sweat lak drops of blood run downWhile ter de God he pray.'

"Dar wus a few mo' but I done fergit.

"Does you know dat I can't 'member much 'bout de slave days? I doan recoleck when de Yankees comed, mebbe dey ain't come ter our part o' de country. I 'members when Marse Joseph comed out ter de slave cabins an' tells us dat we can leave case we am free. I think dat dat wus de las' of August, case de fodder wus in.

"I still knows a lady an' gentleman do'. A lady or gentleman speaks nice ter you, case dey wus borned wid a silver spoon in dey mouth, but de other kin' what talks biggety shows plain dat de spoons which dey am borned wid am brass."

N.C. District: No. 2
Worker: T. Pat Matthews
No. Words: 1,474
Subject: A SLAVE STORY
Reference: Patsy Mitchner
Editor: George L. Andrews

[TR: Date stamp: JUL 24 1937]

# PATSY MITCHNER

**84 years old, of 432 McKee Street, Raleigh, N.C.**

"Come right in, honey, I been expectin' some of you white folks a long time from what I dreampt an' I wants to tell you my story. You see I is umble an' perlite 'cause my white folks teached me dat way.

"Come right in, I'm not feelin' well. My husban' has been dead a long time. I cannot stan' up to talk to you so have a seat.

"I belonged to Alex Gorman, a paper man. He printed the 'Spirit of the Age,' a newspaper. I reckon you can find it in the Museum. I reckons dey keeps all way back yonder things in dere jest to remember by. He had a lot of printers both black an' white. De slaves turned de wheels de most of de time, an' de white mens done de printin'. Dere wus a big place dug out at each side of de machine. One man pulled it to him an' de other pulled it to him. Dey wurked it wid de han's. It wus a big wheel. Dey didn't have no printers den like dey got now.

"De ole printin' place is standin' now. It stands in front of de laundry on Dawson Street, where a lot of red wagons stan's goin' up towards the bus station. De ole buildin' wid stairsteps to go up. Dey sot de type upstairs an' de machine wus on de groun' floor.

"Marster married Gormans twice an' dey wus both named Mary. Don't know whether dey wus sisters or not, but dey wus both Virginia women. So my missus name wus Mary Gorman.

"I do not know my age, but I wus 'bout 12 years old when Wheeler's cavalry come through. Dey skeered me so much I squatted like a rat. Dey pulled clothes off de line an' stole clothes from stores an' went down to de depot an' changed clothes. Dey stole de womens drawers an' filled 'em wid things. Dey stole meat, corn an' other things an' put 'em in womens drawers, throwed 'em across dere horses backs an' went on. You know women den wore long drawers open in front, ha! ha!

"Wheeler's cavalry tied up de legs an' front of 'em an' filled de legs an' seat full of things dey stole. Dey jest grabbed everything an' went on. Dey had a reason for leavin'; de Yankees wus at dere heels.

"Jest as soon as dey lef' de Yankees come. You know, dere wus a man here by de name of Governor Holden an' de flag wus a red an' white flag, an' when de Yankees come dere wus another flag run up.

"I want to try to tell de truth 'cause I wus teached dat way by marster an' missus.

"De flag brought peace 'cause de Yankees did not tear up de town. Dey had guards out around de houses an' dey marched back an' forth day an' night to keep everybody from robbin' de houses.

"De Yankees wid dere blue uniforms on jest kivered de town. Dey wus jest like ants. Dey played purty music on de ban' an' I liked dat. I wus fraid of 'em dough 'cause marster an' missus said dey were goin' to give us to 'em when dey come. I stayed hid mos' of de time right after de surrender 'cause I didn't want de Yankees to ketch me. When de others lef' after de surrender I run away an' went to Rev. Louis Edwards, a nigger preacher. He sent me to my aunt at Rolesville. My Aunt wus named Patsy Lewis. I stayed dere bout three weeks when my uncle rented whur Cameron Park is now an' tended it dat year. We all come to Raleigh an' I have lived here all my life, but the three weeks I stayed at Rolesville.

"I have wurked for white folks, washin', cookin', an' wurkin' at a laundry ever since freedom come.

"I never seed my father in my life. My mother wus named Tempe Gorman. Dey would not talk to me 'bout who my father wus nor where he wus at. Mother would laf sometime when I axed her 'bout him.

"Marster treated his niggers mean sometimes. He beat my mother till de scars wus on her back, so I could see 'em.

"Dey sold my mother, sister an' brother to ole man Askew, a slave speculator, an' dey were shipped to de Mississippi bottoms in a box-car. I never heard from mother anymore. I neber seed my brother agin, but my sister come back to Charlotte. She come to see me. She married an' lived dere till she died.

"In slavery time de food wus bad at marsters. It wus cooked one day for de nex', dat is de corn bread wus baked an' de meat wus biled an' you et it col' fer breakfas'. De meat wus as fat as butter an' you got one rashen an' a hunk of corn bread fer a meal. No biscuit wus seen in de slave houses. No sir, dat dey wus not. No biscuit for niggers at marsters.

"Our clothes wus bad an' our sleepin' places wus jest bunks. Our shoes had wooden bottoms on 'em.

"I heard 'em talk about patterollers so much I wus skeered so I could hardly sleep at night sometimes. I wus 'fraid dey would come an' catch me but I neber seed one in my life.

"I neber seed any slaves sold, in chains, or a jail for slaves. I neber seed a slave whupped. Marster took 'em in de back shed room to whup 'em.

"We was not teached to read an' write. You better not be caught wid no paper in yore han' if you was, you got de cowhide. I darsent to talk back to 'em no matter what happen'd dey would git you if you talked back to 'em.

"I married Tom Mitchner after de war. I went by de name of Patsy Gorman till I wus married. Now I goes by de name of Patsy Mitchner. My husban', Tom Mitchner, was born a slave. My marster lived whar de bus station now is on de corner of Martin an' McDowell Streets in dat ole house dat stan's near dere now. I wus born an' bred in Raleigh an' have neber libed out of Wake County.

"Ole Dr. Jim McKee, who is dead an' gone, looked atter us when we wus sick. He give us medicine an' kep us clean out better en people is clean out now. Dr. John McKee at de City Hall is his son. Dey pays no 'tention to me now; guess dey has forgotten me.

"Did you say ghosts, Lawsy, no I neber seed one but our spirits is always wonderin' aroun' eben before we dies. Spirits is wonderin' eberywhere an' you has to look out for 'em.

"Witches is folks. I neber had a spell put on me by one, but I knowed a woman once who had a spell put on 'er, an' it hurt her feet, but a ole white man witch doctor helped take de spell off, but I think it wus de Lord who took it off. I is a Christain an' I believes eberythin' is in His han's.

"De people is worser now den dey was in slavery time. We need patterollers right now. 'Twould stop some uv dis stealin' an' keep a lot of folks out of de penetentiary. We need 'em right now.

"Slavery wus better for us den things is now in some cases. Niggers den didn't have no responsibility, jest wurk, obey an' eat. Now dey got to shuffle around an' live on jest what de white folks min' to give 'em.

"Slaves prayed for freedom. Den dey got it dey didn't know what to do wid it. Dey wus turned out wid nowhere to go an' nothin' to live on. Dey had no 'sperence in lookin' out for demselves an' nothin' to wurk wid an' no lan'.

"Dey made me think of de crowd onetime who prayed for rain when it wus dry in crap time. De rain fell in torrents an' kept fallin' till it was 'bout a flood. De rain frogs 'gin to holler an' callin' mo' rain an' it rained an' rained. Den de raincrow got up in a high tree an' he holler an' axed de Lord for rain. It rained till ebery little rack of cloud dat come ober brought a big shower of large drops. De fiel's wus so wet an' miry you could not go in 'em an' water wus standin' in de fiel's middle of ebery row, while de ditches in de fiel's looked like little rivers, dey wus so full of water. It begun to thunder agin in de southwest, right whar we call de 'Chub hole' of de sky, whar so much rain comes from an' de clouds growed blacker an' blacker back dere.

"Den one of de mens who had been prayin' for rain up an' said, 'I tell you brothers if it don't quit rainin' eberything goin' to be washed away.' Dey all looked at de black rain cloud in west wid sor'ful faces as if dey felt dey didn't know what use dey had for rain after dey got it. Den one of de brothers said to de other brothers kinder easy an' shameful like, 'Brothers don't you think we overdone dis thing?' Dats what many a slave thought 'bout prayin' for freedom.

"Before two years had passed after de surrender dere wus two out of every three slaves who wushed dey wus back wid dere marsters.

"De marsters kindness to de niggers after de war is de cause of de nigger havin' things today. Dere wus a lot of love between marster an' slave en dar is few of us dat don't love de white folks today.

"Slavery wus a bad thing an' freedom, of de kin' we got wid nothin' to live on wus bad. Two snakes full of pisen. One lyin' wid his head pintin' north, de other wid his head pintin' south. Dere names wus slavery an' freedom. De snake called slavery lay wid his head pinted south an' de snake called freedom lay wid his head pinted north. Both bit de nigger, an' dey wus both bad."

EH.

N.C. District: II
Worker: Mrs. W.N. Harriss
No. Words: 396
Subject: Emeline Moore, Ex-slave.
Interviewed: Emeline Moore,
707 Hanover Street, Wilmington, N.C.
Edited: Mrs. W.N. Harriss

# EMELINE MOORE, EX-SLAVE

**707 Hanover Street, Wilmington, N.C.**

"I don' exac'ly know how ole I is, but dey say I mus' be eighty. No mam, I ain' got nothin' in no fam'ly Bible. Where'd I git a fam'ly Bible? My mammy (with a chuckle) had too many chillun to look after to be puttin' 'em down in no Bible, she did'n have time, an' she did'n have no learnin' nohow. But I reckon I is eighty because I 'members so much I's jes' about forgotten it all.

"My folks belonged to Colonel Taylor. He an' Mis' Kitty lived in that big place on Market Street where the soldiers lives now, (The W.L.I. Armory) but we was on the plantation across the river mos' of the time.

"Of co'se I was born in slavery, but I don' remember nothin' much excep' feedin' chickens. An' up on Market Street Mis' Kitty had chickens an' things, an' a cow. The house had more lan' around it than it got now. I do remember when they thought eve'ybody 'roun' here was goin' to die an' I got skeered. No'm t'want no war it was the yaller fever. We was kept on the plantation but we knowed folks jes died an' died an' died. We thought t'would'nt be nobody left. I don't remember nothin' about Lincoln travelin' aroun'. I always heard he was President of the Lunited States, an' lived in Washington, an' gave us freedom, an' got shot. Of co'se I knows all about Booker Washington, a lot of our folks went to his school, an' he been here in Wilmington. I'd know a lot about slave times only I was so little. I have heard my mammy say she had a heap easier time in slavery than after she was turn' loose with a pa'cel of chilluns to feed. I married as soon as I could an' that's how I got this house. But I can't work, an' I disremembers so much. The Welfare gives me regerlar pay, an' now an' then my friends give me a nickel or a dime.

"I lives alone now, until I can git a decent 'ooman to live with me. I tells you Missus these womens an' young girls today are sumpin else. After you had 'em aroun' awhile you wish you never knowed 'em.

"Sometimes when I jes sets alone an rocks I wonder if my mammy didn't have it lots easier than I does."

| | |
|---|---|
| **N.C. District:** | Asheville |
| **Worker:** | Marjorie Jones |
| **No. Words:** | 2,300 |
| **Subject:** | **Interview with Fannie Moore, Ex-slave.** |
| **Story teller:** | Fannie Moore |
| **Editor:** | Marjorie Jones |
| **Date:** | September 27, 1937 |

[TR: Cover page is in a format labeled "STATE EDITORIAL IDENTIFICATION FORM".]

Fannie Moore

| | |
|---|---|
| Interviewer: | Marjorie Jones, |
| Date: | Sept. 21, 1937. |
| Interview With: | Fannie Moore, Ex-slave,<br>151 Valley Street,<br>Asheville, N.C. |

"Nowadays when I heah folks a'growlin an' a'grumblin bout not habbin this an' that I jes think what would they done effen they be brought up on de Moore plantation. De Moore plantation b'long to Marse Jim Moore, in Moore, South Carolina. De Moores had own de same plantation and de same niggers and dey children for yeahs back. When Marse Jim's pappy die he leave de whole thing to Marse Jim, effen he take care of his mammy. She shore was a rip-jack. She say niggers didn't need nothin' to eat. Dey jes like animals, not like other folks. She whip me, many time wif a cow hide, til I was black and blue.

"Marse Jim's wife war Mary Anderson. She war the sweetest woman I ebber saw. She was allus good to evah nigger on de plantation. Her mother was Harriet Anderson and she visit de Missus for long time on de farm. All de little niggers like to work fo' her. She nebber talk mean. Jes smile dat sweet smile and talk in de soffes' tone. An when she laugh, she soun' jes like de little stream back ob de spring house gurglin' past de rocks. An' her hair all white and curly, I can 'member her always.

"Marse Jim own de bigges' plantation in de whole country. Jes thousands acres ob lan'. An de ole Tiger Ribber a runnin' right through de middle ob de plantation. On one side ob de ribber stood de big house, whar de white folks lib and on the other side stood de quarters. De big house was a purty thing all painted white, a standin' in a patch o' oak trees. I can't remember how many rooms in dat house but powerful many. O'corse it was built when de Moores had sech large families. Marse Jim he only hab five children, not twelve like his mammy had. Dey was Andrew and Tom, den Harriet, Nan, and Nettie Sue. Harriett was jes like her granny Anderson. She was good to ebberbody. She git de little niggers down an' teach em dey Sunday School lesson. Effen ole Marse Jim's mammy ketch her she sho' raise torment. She make life jes as hard for de niggers as she can.

"De quarters jes long row o' cabins daubed wif dirt. Ever one in de family lib in one big room. In one end was a big fireplace. Dis had to heat de cabin and do de cookin too. We cooked in a big pot hung on a rod over de fire and bake de co'n pone in de ashes or else put it in de skillet and cover de lid wif coals. We allus hab plenty wood to keep us warm. Dat is ef we hab time to get it outen de woods.

"My granny she cook for us chillens while our mammy away in de fiel. Dey wasn't much cookin to do. Jes make co'n pone and bring in de milk. She hab big wooden bowl wif enough wooden spoons to go 'roun'. She put de milk in de bowl and break it up. Den she put de bowl in de middle of de flo' an' all de chillun grab a spoon.

"My mammy she work in de fiel' all day and piece and quilt all night. Den she hab to spin enough thread to make four cuts for de white fo'ks ebber night. Why sometime I nebber go to bed. Hab to hold de light for her to see by. She hab to piece quilts for de white folks too. Why dey is a scar on my arm yet where my brother let de pine drip on me. Rich pine war all de light we ebber hab. My brother was a holdin' de pine so's I can help mammy tack de quilt and he go to sleep and let it drop.

"I never see how my mammy stan' sech ha'd work. She stan' up fo' her chillun tho'. De ol' overseeah he hate my mammy, case she fight him for beatin' her chillun. Why she git more whuppins for dat den anythin' else. She hab twelve chillun. I member I see de three oldes' stan' in de snow up to dey knees to split rails, while de overseeah stan off an' grin.

"My mammy she trouble in her heart bout de way they treated. Ever night she pray for de Lawd to git her an' her chillun out ob de place. One day she plowin' in de cotton fiel. All sudden like she let out big yell. Den she sta't singin' an' a shoutin', an' a whoopin' an' a hollowin'. Den it seem she plow all de harder. When she come home, Marse Jim's mammy say: 'What all dat goin' on in de fiel? Yo' think we sen' you out there jes to whoop and yell? No siree, we put you out there to work and you sho' bettah work, else we git de overseeah to cowhide you ole black back.' My mammy jes grin all over her black wrinkled face and say: 'I's saved. De Lawd done tell me I's saved. Now I know de Lawd will show me de way, I ain't gwine a grieve no more. No matter how much yo' all done beat me an' my chillun de Lawd will show me de way. An' some day we nevah be slaves.' Ole granny Moore grab de cowhide and slash mammy cross de back but mammy nebber yell. She jes go back to de fiel a singin'.

"My mammy grieve lots over brothah George, who die wif de fever. Granny she doctah him as bes' she could, evah time she[Pg 131] git way from de white folks kitchen. My mammy nevah git chance to see him, 'cept when she git home in de evenin'. George he jes lie. One day I look at him an' he had sech a peaceful look on his face, I think he sleep and jes let him lone. Long in de evenin I think I try to wake him. I touch him on de face, but he was dead. Mammy nebber know til she come at night. Pore mammy she kneel by de bed an' cry her heart out. Ol' uncle Allen, he make pine box for him an' carry him to de graveyard over on de hill. My mammy jes plow and cry as she watch em' put George in de groun'.

"My pappy he was a blacksmith. He shoe all de horses on de plantation. He wo'k so hard he hab no time to go to de fiel'. His name war Stephen Moore. Mars Jim call him Stephen Andrew. He was sold to de Moores, and his mammy too. She war brought over from Africa. She never could speak plain. All her life she been a slave. White folks never recognize 'em any more than effen dey was a dog.

"It was a tubble sight to see de speculators come to de plantation. Dey would go through de fields and buy de slaves dey wanted. Marse Jim nebber sell pappy or mammy or any ob dey chillun. He allus like pappy. When de speculator come all de slaves start a shakin'. No one know who is a goin'. Den sometime dey take 'em an' sell 'em on de block. De 'breed woman' always bring mo' money den de res', ebben de men. When dey put her on de block dey put all her chillun aroun her to show folks how fas she can hab chillun. When she sold her family nebber see her agin. She nebber know [HW: how] many chillun she hab. Some time she hab colored children an' sometime white. Taint no use to say anything case effen she do she jes git whipped. Why on de Moore plantation Aunt Cheney, everbody call her Aunt Cheney, have two chillun by de overseeah. De overseeah name war Hill. He war as mean as de devil. When Aunt Cheney not do what he ask he tell granny Moore. Ole Granny call Aunt Cheney to de kitchen and make her take her clothes off den she beat her til she jest black an' blue. Many boys and girls marry dey own brothers and sisters an' nebber know de difference lest they get to talkin' bout dey parents and where dey uster lib.

"De niggers allus hab to get pass to go anywhere offen de plantation. Dey git de pass from de massa or de missus. Den when de paddyrollers come dey had to show de pass to dem, if you had no pass dey strip you an' beat you.

"I remember one time dey was a dance at one ob de houses in de quarters. All de niggers was a laughin an' a pattin' dey feet an' a singin', but dey was a few dat didn't. De paddyrollers shove de do' open and sta't grabbin' us. Uncle Joe's son he decide dey was one time to die and he sta't to fight. He say he tired standin' so many beatin's, he jes can't stan' no mo. De paddyrollers start beatin' him an' he sta't fightin'. Oh, Lawdy it war tubble. Dey whip him wif a cowhide for a long time den one of dem take a stick an' hit him over de head, an' jes bus his head wide open. De pore boy fell on de flo' jes a moanin' an' a groanin. De paddyrollers jes whip bout half dozen other niggers an' sen' em home and leve us wif de dead boy.

"None o' the niggers have any learnin', warn't never 'lowed to as much as pick up a piece o' paper. My daddy slip an' get a Webster book and den he take it outen de fiel and he larn to read. De white folks 'fraid to let de children learn anythin'. They fraid dey get too sma't and be harder to manage. Dey nebber let em know anything about anythin'. Never have any church. Effen you go you set in de back of de white folks chu'ch. But de niggers slip off an' pray an' hold prayer-meetin' in de woods den dey tu'n down a big wash pot and prop it up wif a stick to drown out de soun' ob de singin'. I 'member some of de songs we uster sing. One of dem went somethin' like dis:

"'Hark from de tomb a doleful soun'My ears hear a tender cry.A livin' man come through the groun'Whar we may shortly lie.Heah in dis clay may be you bedIn spite ob all you toilLet all de wise bow revrant headMus' lie as low as ours.'

"Then dey sing one I can hardly remember but dis is some of de words:

"'Jesus can make you die in bedHe sof' as downs in pillow thereOn my bres' I'll lean my headGrieve my life sweetly there.In dis life of heaby loadLet us share de weary travelerAlong de heabenly road.'

[Pg 134]

"Back in dose time dey wasn't no way to put away fruit and things fo' winter like dey is today. In de fall of de yeah it certainly was a busy time. We peel bushels of apples and peaches to dry. Dey put up lots o' brandied peaches too. De way dey done dey peel de peaches and cut em up. Then dey put a layer ob peaches in a crock den a layer ob sugar den another layer ob peaches until de crock was full. Den dey seel de jar by puttin' a cloth over de top then a layer o' paste then another cloth then another layer ob paste. Dey keep dey meat bout de same way foks do today 'cept dey had to smoke it more since salt was so sca'ce back in dat day. Dey can mos' ob de other fruit and put it in de same kin' o' jars dat dey put de peaches in. Dey string up long strings o' beans an' let 'em dry and cook em wif fat back in de winter.

"Folks back den never heah tell of all de ailments de folks hab now. Dey war no doctahs. Jes use roots and bark for teas of all kinds. My ole granny uster make tea out o' dogwood bark an' give it to us chillun when we have a cold, else she make a tea outen wild cherry bark, pennyroil, or hoarhound. My goodness but dey was bitter. We do mos' enythin' to git out a takin' de tea, but twarnt no use granny jes git you by de collar hol' yo' nose and you jes swallow it or get strangled. When de baby hab de colic she git rats vein and make a syrup an' put a little sugar in it an' boil it. Den soon [HW: as] it cold she give it to de baby. For stomach ache she give us snake root. Sometime she make tea, other time she jes cut it up in little pieces an' make you eat one or two ob dem. When you hab fever she wrap you up in cabbage leaves or ginsang leaves, dis made de fever go. When de fever got too bad she take the hoofs offen de hog dat had been killed and parch em' in de ashes and den she beat em' up and make a tea. Dis was de most tubble of all.

"De yeah fore de war started Marse Jim died. He war out in de pasture pickin' up cow loads a throwin' em in de garden an' he jes drop over. I hate to see Marse Jim go, he not sech a bad man. Ater he die his boys, Tom an' Andrew take cha'ge of de plantation. Dey think dey run things diffe'nt from dey daddy, but dey jes git sta'ted when de war come. Marse Tom and Marse Andrew both hab to go. My pappy he go long wif dem to do der cookin. My pappy he say dat some day he run four or five miles wif de Yankees ahind him afore he can stop to do any cookin. Den when he stop he cook wif de bullets a fallin all roun de kettles. He say he walk on ded men jes like he walkin on de groun'. Some of de men be dead, some moanin' an' some a groanin', but nobody pay no tention, case de Yankees keep a comin. One day de Yankees come awful close Marse Andrew hab de Confed'rate flag in his han'. He raise it high in de air. Pappy say he yell for him to put de flag down case de Yankees was a comin' closer an' was agoin' to capture him anyway. But Marse Andrew jes hol' de flag up an run 'hind a tree. De Yankee sojers jes take one shot at him an' dat was de las' of him. My pappy bring him home. De fambly put him in alcohol. One day I went to see him and there he was a swimmin' round in de water. Mos' ob his hair done come off tho. He buried at Nazereth. I could go right back to de graveyard effen I was there. Den my pappy go back to [HW: stay] with Marse Tom. Marse Tom was jes wounded. Effen he hadn't had a Bible in his pocket de bullet go clear through his heart. But yo' all kno' no bullet ain't goin' through de Bible. No, you can't shoot through God's word. Pappy he bring Marse Tom home an' take care of him til he well. Marse Tom give pappy a horse an' wagon case he say he save his life.

"Many time de sojers come through de plantation an' dey load up dey wagons wif ebberthing dey fin', lasses, hams, chickens. Sometime dey gib part of it to de niggers but de white folks take it way when dey git gone. De white folks hide all de silverware from de soldiers. Dey fraid dey take it when dey come. Some time dey make us tell effen dey think we know.

"After de war pappy go back to work on de plantation. He make his own crop, on de plantation. But de money was no good den. I played wif many a Confed'rate dollar. He sho was happy dat he was free. Mammy she shout fo' joy an' say her prayers war answered. Pappy git pretty feeble, but he work til jest fore he die. He made patch of cotton wif a hoe. Dey was enough cotton in de patch to make a bale. Pappy die when he 104 years old. Mammy she live to be 105.

"After de war de Ku Klux broke out. Oh, miss dey was mean. In dey long white robes dey scare de niggers to death. Dey keep close watch on dem afeared dey try to do somethin'. Dey have long horns an' big eyes an' mouth. Dey never go roun' much in de day. Jes night. Dey take de pore niggers away in de woods and beat 'em and hang 'em. De niggers was afraid to move, much les try to do anything. Dey never kno' what to do, dey hab no larnin. Hab no money. All dey can do was stay on de same plantation til dey can do better. We lib on de same plantation till de chillun all grown an' mammy an' pappy both die then we leave. I don' know where any of my people are now. I knows I was bo'n in 1849. I was 88 years old de fust of September."

N.C. District: No. 2
Worker: Mary A. Hicks
No. Words: 944
Subject: RICHARD C. MORING
Story teller: Richard C. Moring
Editor: Daisy Bailey Waitt

# RICHARD C. MORING
## Ex-Slave Story

**An interview with Richard C. Moring 86 of 245 E. South Street, Raleigh, N.C.**

"My mammy wus Cherry, an' my pappy wus Jacob. Mr. Anderson Clemmons owned mammy, an' Mr. Fielding Moring owned pappy.

"I doan know much 'bout Mr. Moring, case we stayed wid Mr. Clemmons near Apex, in dis same county.

"Mr. Clemmons owned less'n a dozen slaves, but he wus good ter 'em. De oberseer, Mr. Upchurch, whupped de slaves some, but not very much.

"We had nuff ter eat an' w'ar an' we wuck hard, but no harder dan we has since dat time. Marster 'lowed us our own gyarden an' tater patch, we also had our own hawgs.

"Dey 'lowed us some fun lak dancin', wrestlin' matches, swimmin', fishin', huntin' an' games. We also had prayer meetin's at our cabins.

"When dere wus a weddin' dar wus fun fer all, case hit wus a big affair. Dey wus all dressed up in new clothes, an' marster's dinin' room wus decorated wid flowers fer de 'casion. De ban' which wus banjoes, an' fiddles 'ud play an' de neighborin' folks 'ud come.

"De preacher married 'em up good an' tight jist lak he done de white folks, an' atter hit wus ober an' de songs wus sung marster's dinin' table wus set an' dar was a weddin' supper fer all.

"I doan 'member so much 'fore de war but I 'members dat de Rebs go by an' dat de Yankees chase 'em. (I is on Mr. Morings' place den clost ter Morrisville.)

"De Yankees am so busy chasin' de Rebs dat dey doan stop ter bodder us much, 'cept ter kill de chickens an' so on.

"Dar's a place out from Morrisville whar de Yankees an' de Rebels had er little skirmish on dat trip. We could hyar de guns go boomin', an' atter hit wus ober we chilluns went dar an' pick up de balls an' boxes of dese hardtacks whar de soldiers had fit.

"I fergit ter tell you 'bout de fust gang o' Yankees what come by. Dey wus lookin' fer food an' when dey got ter our place dey comes in an' he'ps dereselbes ter marster's stuff. Dey kilt all de live things, took all de hams an' sich, an' dey foun' 'bout a bushel o' aigs. Dey put 'em in de big wash pot an' biled 'em an' dey goes ter de spring house an' gits seben er eight poun's o' butter. When de aigs am biled dey splits 'em open an' puts de butter on 'em an' eats 'em dat way. Dat's de fust aigs dat eber I tasted, an' dey shore give me all I wants.

"We went back ter Mr. Clemmons' 'fore de surrender, case when dat happen Mis' Jane Clemmons tells us'n herself dat we am free. All o' we chilluns, Duncan, Candice, Mariah, Len, Willis, William, Sidney, Lindy, Mary, Rilda, an' me, all of mammy's chilluns was dar at de en' of de war.

"We stayed on at Mr. Clemmons fer seberal years, in fac' till de ole folks died. My young Missus Mis' Katy Ellis lives on Hillsboro Street, an' I often goes ter see her an' she sometimes gives me money, so you sees de feelin' dat 'zists twixt me an' my white folkses.

"I'll tell you de story 'bout de witch at de mill iffen you wants ter hyar hit, I hyard my grandmammy tell hit when I wus a little feller."

## THE WITCH AT THE MILL

"Onct dar wus a free nigger what ownes a mill an' he am makin' a heap o' money. He married a han'some nigger wench an' hit 'peared lak his luck all went bad. De folkses quit bringin' dere co'n ter be groun' an' he 'gan ter git pore.

"'Long in dem times de slaves sometimes runned away from deir cruel marsters an' dey'd go ter dis nigger at de mill. He'ud put 'em ter sleep in de mill, but dey can't sleep on de 'count of fusses an' scratchin'.

"'Last one night a nigger what has runned away comed ter spen' de night, an' he sez dat he am not skeerd o' nothin' De owner can put him ter sleep in de house if he wants ter, case his wife am spendin' de night wid a friend of hern, but he 'sides ter put him in de mill.

"He tells de runaway nigger 'bout de witch, but atter de nigger gits hisself a butcher knife he ain't skeered no mo' an' he goes on ter de mill.

"'Way in de night de nigger sees somethin', an' de whites o' his eyes shines lak lamps. De things comes nearer an' nearer an' he sees dat hit am a big black cat wid de savage notion o' eatin' him.

"De nigger swings his knife an' off comes one of de ole cat's feets. She gives a awful screech an' goes outen de winder.

"De nex' mornin' de owner's wife am sick in de bed an' she' fuses ter git up. De man tells her ter git up an' cook his breakfas', but she 'fuses ter stir.

"'You better git up, you lazy trollop', de man shouts an' wid dat he drags de 'oman outen de bed. He am 'mazed when he sees dat her han' am cut off, an' he yells fer de neighbors.

"When de neighbors gits dar dey makes a big bresh pile an' dey ties her on hit an' burns her up. Atter dat de man had good luck, eben atter he married ag'in."

Note: This witch story is a variant of <u>The Old Brownrigg Mill</u> by Doctor Richard Dillard.

N.C. District: No. 2
Worker: Mary A. Hicks
No. Words: 689
Subject: JULIUS NELSON
Story teller: Julius Nelson
Editor: Daisy Bailey Waitt

Julius Nelson

# JULIUS NELSON
## Ex-Slave Story

**An interview with Julius Nelson, 77 of State Prison, Raleigh, N.C.**

"I doan 'member no slavery, of course, so 'taint no use ter ax me no questions. I does know dat my mammy wus named Ann an' my pappy wus named Alex. Dey 'longed ter a Mr. Nelson in Anson County. Dere wus 'leben o' us youngins but dey am all daid now 'cept me.

"I doan reckon dat I is but roun' sebenty, case I wus jist five years old at de close o' de war. What's dat, I'se sebenty seben? Lan' how de time do fly!

"Anyhow I jist barely does 'member how de ho'n blowed 'fore de light o' de day an' how we got up an' had our breakfast an' when de ho'n blowed at sunrise we went ter de fiel's in a gallop. At dinner time de plantation bell rung an' we'd fly fer home.

"One big fat nigger 'oman cooked de dinner fer us fifty er sixty slaves an' in er hour or so we'd go back ter de fiel's fer mo' wuck. I sez us, but I means dem what could wuck. I did pull weeds an' pick up apples, an' dem things.

"Dese dinners hyar 'min's me o' de plantation dinners somehow. Maybe case it am 'bout de same quantity. Great big pots o' turnip salet, collards, peas, beans, cabbages, potatoes or other vege'ables, an' a oben full o' sweet' taters in de winter. Dar wus a heap o' pies in de summertime, an' honey, an' 'lasses, an' lasses cake in de winter time. Dar wus big pones o' co'n bread all de year roun' an' whole sides o' meat, an' on New Years' Day hogshead an' peas.

"Fur supper we gine'ly had pot licker, lef' from dinner, 'taters maybe an' some sweetnin'. Dar wus ash cakes fur supper an' breakfas' most o' de time an' hominy, which de marster had grown hisself. De smart nigger et a heap o' possums an' coons, dar bein' plenty o' dem an' rabbits an' squirrels in abundance.

"Did yo' eber eat any kush? Well dat wus made outin meal, onions, salt, pepper, grease an' water. Hit made a good supper dish. Sometimes in de heat o' de day marster let us pick blackberries on de hedgerow fer our supper. We little' uns often picks de berries, an' den we have a big pan pie fer supper.

"On holidays we sometimes had chicken pie an' ham an' a lot o' other food. Dem wus de happy times, 'specially on Christmas mornin' when we all goes ter de big house ter celebrate an' ter git our gif's. Dey give us clothes, food, an' fruit. One Christmas we had a big tub of candy, I reckolicts. 'Bout twict a year we had a sociable when de niggers from de neighborin' plantations 'ud be invited an' dey'd come wid deir banjoes an' fiddles an' we'd dance, all o' us, an' have a swell time.

"We little'uns 'ud play fox-on-de-wall, tag, mulberry bush, drap handerchief, stealin' sticks an' a whole heap of others dat I disremembers right now.

"We shucked our co'n on rainy days mostly, but de marster lets us have one big co'n shuckin' eber' year an' de person what fin's a red year can kiss who dey pleases. Hit wus gran' times dat we had den.

"We also had regular weddin's wid a preacher an' all de fixin's an' de marster usually give us a big supper case he knowed dat he wuz gwine ter soon habe more slaves from de union.

"Iffen de Yankees comed ter our part o' de country I don't 'member seein' dem but I does know dat de Ku Kluxes done give us a heap of trouble.

"I'se libed a long time, 'specially de fifteen years dat I'se spent hyar, but I knows how ter treat white folkses, an' I knows dat de wuck an' de healthy rations dat de niggers got 'fore de war am why dey am stronger dan de young niggers o' dis day."

N.C. District: No. 2
Worker: Mary A. Hicks
No. Words: 679
Subject: PLANTATION LIFE
Teller: Lila Nichols
Editor: Daisy Bailey Waitt

[TR: Date stamp: JUN 1 1937]

Lila Nichols

# PLANTATION LIFE

**An Interview with Lila Nichols 89 of Cary, Wake County, N.C. May 18, 1937.**

"We belonged ter Mr. Nat Whitaker atter his marriage. His daddy, Mr. Willis, give us to him. We lived near Rhamkatte wid Mr. Willis, an' we wuz happy. My pappy wuz named Yancey an' my mammy wuz named Sabra. Dar wuz two brothers named Yancey an' Add, an' five sisters: Alice, Sally, Martha, Betty an' Helia.

"Ole massa wuz good ter his slaves, but young massa Nat wuzn't. We ain't had half nuff ter eat most o' de time, an' we ain't had no shoes till we wuz twenty-one. We had jist a few pieces of clothes an' dey wuz of de wust kind. Our cabins wuz shacks, an' we got seberal whuppin's near 'bout ever' day. Fer example I had de job of gittin' up de aigs in de ebenin', an' if de ain't de right number of dem Missus Mae whupped me. I also looked atter de bitties, an' iffen one of' em died I got a whuppin' too.

"Once missus wuz sick, an' a slave gal named Alice brung her some water an' somethin' ter eat. Missus got sick on her stomick, an' she sez dat Alice done try ter pizen her. Ter show yo' how sick she wuz, she gits out of de bed, strips dat gal ter de waist an' whups her wid a cowhide till de blood runs down her back. Dat gal's back wuz cut in gashes an' de blood run down ter 'er heels. Atter dat she wuz chained down by de arms an' laigs till she got well; den she wuz carried off ter Richmond in chains an' sold.

"We wucked all de week, my mammy plowin' wid a two-horse plow, all de year when she warn't cleanin' new ground or diggin' ditches; an' she got two days off when her chilluns wuz borned. We ain't had no passes ter go nowhar, an' we ain't allowed offe'n de groun's.

"I know one time do' missus 'cides ter whup a 'oman fer somethin' an' de 'oman sez ter her, 'No sir, Missus, 'ain't 'lowin' nobody what wa'r de same kind of shirt I does ter whup me.'

"We wuz glad when de Yankees comed, aldo' dey acted lak a pack o' robbers. Dey burned de cotton, dey stold eber' thing dey could lay han's on, an' dey tored up ever' thing scand'lous. Dey'd go ter de house an' knock at de do', den missus would lock it an' yell at 'em dat she warn't gwinter open it. Dey doan keer, dey jist kicks it down an' walks right in.

"Dey snatch pictures frum de side o' de house an' throw 'em down an' break 'em. Dey drunk up all of massa's brandy, an' dey insults de white wimmen an' de blacks alike.

"De Yankees comed on a Thursday an' we lef' on Sunday. When we left de yard wuz full of dem Yankees, cussin', an' laughin', an' drinkin'. We went to Raleigh, an' de fust winter wuzen't so bad atter all. We doan keer nothin' 'bout Mr. Lincoln, case he ain't keerin' 'bout us. He wuz lak de rest of de Yankees, he jist doan want de south ter git rich. Dey tol' us dat de warn't no slaves in de no'th but we done found out dat de only reason wuz 'cause dey can't stan' de cold weather dar, an' dat de No'th am greedy of us.

"I 'members de Ku Klux Klan, an' I ain't got nothin' 'ginst 'em, case dey had ter do somethin' wid dem mean niggers an' de robber Yankees, who had done ruint us all. I knowed some niggers what ain't got 'long so well an' dey done mean, case dey blame de white folks; but atter awhile dey sees dat it am Massa Lincoln's fault, so dey gits quiet. I said dat we wuz glad dat de Yankees comed. We wuz, jist cause our massa warn't good lak some massas, an' at dat, we ain't want ter be free."

N.C. District:       No. 2
Worker:              Mary A. Hicks
No Words:            273
Subject:             A SLAVERY STORY
Person Interviewed:  Martha Organ
Date of Interview:   May 18, 1937
Editor:              Daisy Bailey Waitt

# A STORY OF SLAVERY

**As told by Martha Organ of Cary as she heard her mother tell it many years ago.**

"I doan know nothin' 'bout slavery 'cept what I hyard my mother tell, an' dat ain't so much.

"I know dat my pappa's name wuz Handy Jones an' my mammy's name wuz Melisa. She belonged to a Mr. Whitaker but atter she married my pappa she belonged ter Mr. Rufus Jones, Mr. Rufus wuz Mr. Wesley Jones' brother at de ole Fanning Jones place; an' he owned a sizable plantation. Mr. Jones wuz good ter 'em. Dey ain't nebber give him no trouble an' he ain't nebber whip none of 'em.

"I've hyarn her tell a whole heap 'bout de patterollers an' de Ku Klux Klan but of course I wuz borned atter de surrender, I now bein' jist sixty one.

"I 'members 'specially what mammy said 'bout when de Yankees come. She said dat it wuz on a Thursday an' dat de ole master wuz sick in de bed an' had sent some slaves ter de mill wid grain. When dese men started back frum de mill de Yankees overtook 'em an' dey killed de oxes in de harness, cut off de quarters an' rid [HW: ter] de house wid dat beef hangin' all over de horses. Dey throwed what dey ain't wanted away, but of course dey took de meal an' de grain.

"De ole master had hyard dat dem Yankees wuz comin' an' he had buried de silverware in a san' bar, but Lawd dem Yankees foun' hit jist lak it were on top o' de groun'. Dey stold eber'thing dat day git dere han's on, 'specially de meat frum de smoke house. Dey went down inter de cellar an' dey drunk up master's brandy an' dey got so drunk dat dey ain't got no sense atall. When dey left dey carried my bruther off wid 'em, an' nobody ever hyard frum him ag'in. Dey said dat de president was'nt thought much of dem days.

"Mr. Jones died a few days atter de surrender an' hit 'pears lak he made a will what give all of his niggers a little piece o' land. Somehow dis Mr. Whitaker, what my mammy uster belong to had somepin' ter do wid it, so he went ter de co't house in Raleigh ter have de will broke up; an' he draps daid. Mr. Jones an' Mr. Whitaker wuz buried de same day.

"Speakin' 'bout ghosts, my mammy tol' me 'bout a ghost what she'd seed an' when I wuz a chile, I seed it too.

"It wuz closter Ephues Church on de Durham highway, an' de ghosts wuz three wimmen, dressed, in white an' widout heads. De rize an' flewed ober de wagin an' went ter de churchyard, an' dat wuz de las' time I seed 'em. I doan believe in ghosts much, but fo' de Lawd I seed dat one an' my mammy an' pappy seed it 'fore I wuz borned.

"My mammy said dat she'd seed some slave sales but dat dey warn't so bad. She nor my pappy ain't neber had no whippin's an' she said dat de wust thing she eber seed wuz a gal burnt. Hit wuz dis way: Missus Jones had sold a gal dat she raised named Alice ter a neighborhood 'oman. Alice had been ust ter goin' to de Missus house an' warmin', so when she went inter dis 'omans house ter warm de 'oman made her stand fore de fire till her legs burned so bad dat de skin cracked up an' some of it drapped off. Missus Jones found it out an' she give de 'oman back her money an' took Alice home wid her."

MH/EH

N.C. District: No. 2
Worker: Mary A. Hicks
No Words: 435
Subject: ANN PARKER
Person Interviewed: Ann Parker
Editor: Daisy Bailey Waitt

# ANN PARKER
## Ex-Slave Story

**An interview with Ann Parker in the Wake County Home, Raleigh, North Carolina.**

"I reckon dat I is a hundert an' three or a hundert an' four years old. I wuz a 'oman grown at de end o' de war.

"I ain't had no daddy case queens doan marry an' my mammy, Junny, wuz a queen in Africa. Dey kidnaps her an' steals her 'way from her throne an' fetches her hyar ter Wake County in slavery.

"We 'longed ter Mr. Abner Parker who lived near Raleigh an' he had maybe a hundert slaves an' a whole heap of lan'. I ain't neber laked him much, case we had ter wuck hard an' we ain't got much ter eat. He ain't 'lowed us no fun, but we did have some, spite o' him.

"We uster git by de patterollers an' go ter de neighborin' plantations whar we'd sing an' talk an' maybe dance. I know onct do' dat we wuz in a barn on Mr. Liles' place when de patterollers comed, all dat could git out scated, but de ones dat got ketched got a whuppin'.

"I got seberal whuppin's fer dis, dat an' tother; but I specks dat I needed 'em. Anyhow we wuz raised right, we warn't 'lowed ter sass nobody an' we ole'uns still knows dat we is got ter be perlite ter yo' white ladies.

"Daughter, did I tell yo' 'bout my mamny bein' a queen. Yes, she wuz a queen, an' when she tol' dem niggers dat she wuz dey bowed down ter her. She tol' dem not ter tell hit an' dey doan tell, but when dey is out of sight of de white folkses dey bows down ter her an' does what she says.

"A few days 'fore de surrender mammy, who am also a witch, says ter dem dat she sees hit in de coffee grounds dat dey am gwine ter be free so all o' us packs up an' gits out.

"We got along pretty good atter de war, an' on till lately. Atter I gits too ole ter wuck I sets on de post-office steps an' begs. I got a good pile o' money too, but somebody done stole hit an' now I'se hyer in de County Home.

"I fell an' broke my arm sometime ago, case my right side am daid an' I tries ter crawl offen de bed. When I gits back from de hospital dey ties me in dis cheer ter keep me from fallin' out, but I want ter git a loose. De nigger boy what helps me up an' down ain't raised lak I wuz, he fusses an' he he ain't got de manners what he ort ter habe."

L.E.

N.C. District: 2
Worker: T. Pat Matthews
No. Words: 448
Subject: A SLAVE STORY
Reference: AMY PENNY
Editor: George L. Andrews

[TR: Date stamp: AUG 17 1937]

# AMY PENNY

**811 Cannister Street, Raleigh, North Carolina.**

"I do not know my age. I wus borned in Mecklenburg [HW: County], Virginia. My marster give my age in a Bible but I lost it by lendin' it out. My mother died 'fore I 'membered her. She wus named Dinah Epps. My grandmother wus named Eliza Epps. She lived to be 107 years old. My father wus named Jerry Epps. Marster's name wus Victor Epps, an' my missus wus named Martha. I married Bob Penny.

"De plantation wus at Mecklenburg, Virginia, near Boylan, [HW: Boydton, in Mecklenburg Co., Va.] Virginia. I don't 'member how many slaves but dere wus a good number. I never heard 'em numbered out as I knows of. I never saw a slave sold. I never saw one whupped. I heard 'em talk about paterollers but I never saw one.

"I don't 'member when I come to Raleigh. I have been here so long. My grandmother an' grandfather come here an' I come too.

"I plowed in Virginia, an' I cooked too. Dey did not pick any work fur me. We lived in log houses. Yes, indeed, we had plenty to eat. I never suffered for sumptin' to eat till I come to Raleigh. On de plantation we got plenty allowance. We had good clothes on de plantation.

"I am more naked now den I ever been before in my life.

"We went to both de white an' colored churches in Virginia. I never could learn to read an' write. I never could learn to make a number correct. I just can't learn. I tried my bes' to write. I went to four sessions of school but couldn't learn. I wus raised by some mighty good white people. I wanted to learn so bad I slept wid my books under my head but I couldn't learn.

"I am well thought of at my home in Virginia. Dey have sent me rations since I been here. I had de worse time of my life since de surrender. I don't know nothin' 'bout de Yankees comin' through only what I heard others say. I heard 'em talkin' 'bout freedom an' de war but I didn't know or care nothin' 'bout it. My father went to Manassas Gap to de war. I heard him talk 'bout de breastworks but I don't know nothin' 'bout 'em.

"I wus my father's only chile. He didn't have any chillun by his las' wife. I fergot de name of his las' wife.

"I heard 'em say Abraham Lincoln come through de south an' just learned ever'thing 'bout de folks. He wus 'guised so nobody knowed who he wus. Yes, I heard 'bout dat an' when dey foun' out he been here he done come through an' gone back.

"Slavery wus better den it is now. Shore it wus. I don't know much 'bout de war but my first life in Virginia[Pg 161] wus better den it is now. I never did have any mean white folks. De Lord made me lucky in dat way. De Yankees took, stole, an' carried off a lot of things an' dere wus a lot of talk 'bout 'em, but I never saw 'em 'cept when dey wus paradin'. I never seed any of 'em down dere at my marster's plantation.

"My grandfather died in Raleigh. Grandmother wus de mother of thirteen chilluns but none of 'em 'cept two ever seed Raleigh. Dey wus so scattered 'bout 'cept de two younges', a boy an' a girl. Dey come to Raleigh atter de surrender when grandmother an' me come. We lived worser in Raleigh den we did in Virginia, an' if I wus back home wid my white folks I would git plenty to eat but I don't git it here. Dey sends me a little money now an' den. Here is some of dere letters where dey sent me money. You can see by dese letters dat my Virginia white folks loves me an' I love dem.

"I wus 'bout ten years ole when de war wus goin' on. I think slavery wus not such a bad thing 'pared wid de hard times now."

EH

N.C. District: No. 2
Worker: Mary A. Hicks
No. Words: 794
Subject: SLAVERY DAYS IN FRANKLIN COUNTY
Story teller: Lily Perry
Editor: Geo. L. Andrews

[TR: Date stamp: JUL 24 1937]

# SLAVERY DAYS IN FRANKLIN COUNTY

**An interview with Lily Perry, 84 years old, of 9 McKee Street, Raleigh, N.C.**

"I wus borned on de plantation of Mister Jerry Perry near Louisburg, about eighty-four years ago. My daddy, Riddick, 'longed ter him an' so did my mammy, do she 'longed ter a Mis' Litchford 'fore she married daddy.

"De fust things dat I can remember wus bein' a house gal, pickin' up chips, mindin' de table an' feedin' de hogs. De slop buckets wus heavy an' I had a heap of wuck dat wus hard ter do. I done de very best dat I could but often I got whupped jist de same.

"When dey'd start ter whup me I'd bite lak a run-mad dog so dey'd chain my han's. See hyar, hyars de scars made by de chains. Dey'd also pick me up by de years an' fling me foun',[TR: roun'] see hyar, I can wiggle my years up an' down jist lak a mule can, an' I can wiggle 'em roun' an' roun' lak dat, see!

"One day I ain't feelin' so good an' de slops am so heavy dat I stops an' pours out some of it. De oberseer, Zack Terrell, sees me an' when I gits back ter de house he grabs me ter whup me.

"De minute he grabs me I seize on ter his thumb an' I bites hit ter de bone, den he gits mad an' he picks me up an' lifts me higher dan my haid an' flings me down on de steel mat dere in front of de do'.

"Dey has ter revise me wid cold water from de spring an' I wus sick fer a week. We ain't had good food which makes me weak an' I still has ter do heavy wuck.

"Dar wus a slave block in Louisburg an' I'se seed many a slave sold dar. Very few wus put in chains, most of 'em wus put in a kivered wagon wid a guard an' wus chained at night. I'se seed many a 'oman cryin' fer her chile when one er de tother wus put on de slave block in Louisburg.

"I wus 'bout twelve years old when de Yankees come. I wus pickin' up chips in de yard when dey comes by wid dere hosses steppin' high an' dere music playin' a happy chune. I wus skeered, but I don't dasent run case marster will sho have me whupped, so I keeps on wid my wuck.

"Dey pass fast on down de road an' dey doan bother nothin' in our community but de white folkses hates 'em jist de same.

"Marster Jerry tells us 'bout a week later dat we am free an' all of de two hundret 'cept 'bout five er six goes right off. He tells all of us dat he will pay us effen we will stay an' wuck, so me an' my family we stays on.

"We lives dar fer seberal years den I marries Robert Perry who lives on de same plantation wid us. We ain't had but one daughter an' dat's Kate, who still libes wid me.

"Me an' Robert wus raised up tergether, he bein' five years older'n me an' I loved him frum de time I wus borned. I know how he uster hate ter see me git dem beatin's an' he'd beg me not ter let my mouth be so sassy, but I can't help hit. He uster take my beatin's when he could an' a heap of times he sneak out ter de fiel's in de ebenin' an' toted dat slops ter de pigs.

"Onct when marster wus whuppin' me Robert run up an' begged marse ter put de whuppin' on him 'stead of me. De result wus marse whupped us both an' we 'cided ter run away.

"We did run away, but night brung us back ter another whuppin' an' we ain't neber run away no mo'.

"We wus at a frolic at Louisburg when he proposes ter me an' he do hit dis way, 'Honey gal, I knows dat you doan love me so powerful much, but will you try ter do hit fer me?'

"Course I sez, 'Go long, nigger, iffen I doan love yo' den dar ain't no water in Tar Riber.' Den I sez, 'We can git Marse Henry outen de bed an' he'll marry us ternight.'

"Rob wus tickled pink an' sho nuff we wus married right away dat very night.

"We lived pore, dat I knows, but we wus too happy in ourselves ter worry 'bout sich things an' de lack.

"I laughs now ter think how ignorant we niggers wus. We'd do our washin' an' 'bout de time we hung hit on de line, we'd see a string of folks comin' home frum de Prospect Church an' we'd know dat we'd done our washin' on a Sunday."

AC

N.C. District:        No. 2
Worker:              Mary Hicks
No. Words:           615
Subject:             A SLAVE STORY, THE WOMAN OVERSEER
Person Interviewed:  Valley Perry
Editor:              George L. Andrews

[TR: Date stamp: AUG 17 1937]

# THE WOMAN OVERSEER

**An interview with Valley Perry, 50 years of age, of Cary, North Carolina, Route #1.**

"Course bein' no older dan I is I can't recollect 'bout de war, but I'se heard my manny [TR: mammy] tell a little an' my gran'mammy tell a right smart 'bout dem slavery times yo's talkin' 'bout.

"Gran'mammy Josephine, an' mammy Clarice 'longed ter a Mr. Nat Whitaker in Wake County.

"Mr. Nat's wife wus named Mis' Lucy, an' she wus so good dat ever'body what ever seed her 'membered her. Dar is eben de belief among de niggers dat she riz up ter heaben alive, like Elijah.

"Dey said dat Mr. Nat's oberseer wus kinder mean ter de slaves, an' when he whupped dem dey 'membered hit ter de longest day dey lived. Mr. Nat wusen't near so bad an' Mis' Lucy wus a angel. She'd beg Mr. Nat ter make de oberseer stop, but Mr. Nat 'fused, 'case he said dat de niggers won't obey him iffen he teaches dem he won't let de oberseer punish dem good an' plenty. Den Mis' Lucy 'ud cry an' she'd run an' grab de oberseer's arm an' beg him ter stop. She'd cry so hard dat he'd hafter stop.

"Finally de oberseer goes ter Mr. Nat an' complains, an' he sez dat he am gwine ter quit de job iffen Mr. Nat doan make Mis' Lucy keep outen his business.

"Mr. Nat axes him ter tell him 'fore he starts ter beat 'em, an' ter set a time fer de beatin' an' dat he will git Mis' Lucy offen de place. Well, de oberseer does what Mr. Nat sez an' waits ter whup eber'body on Chuesday an' on Chuesday Mr. Nat takes Mis' Lucy ter town.

"Mis' Lucy am tickled pink dat she am a-goin' shoppin' an' she ain't suspicion nothin' at all. When she gits ter shoppin' do' she ain't satisfied, an' terreckly she tells Mr. Nat dat she wants ter go home. Mr. Nat tries to git her ter go ter a concert but Mis' Lucy sez no, dat she feels lak somethin' am happenin' at home.

"Mr. Nat begs her ter stay on an' enjoy herself, but when she won't listen ter no reason at all he starts home. De mules creep an' poke, but Mis' Lucy herself whups 'em up, an' dey gits home sooner dan dey am expected.

"When dey drives up in de yard de oberseer am so busy whuppin' de niggers what has done bad dat he ain't seed Mis' Lucy till she am right on him, den she snatch de heavy bullwhup an' she strikes him two or three times right in de face.

"Mis' Lucy look delicate, but she cuts de blood outen[Pg 170] his cheek an' she shets up one of his eyes an' brings de blood a-pourin' from his nose. Den de meek little 'oman draws back de whup ag'in an' she 'lows, 'Git offen dis plantation, an' iffen ever I ketches you here ag'n I'll shoot you, you beast.'

"Dat settled de oberseer's hash an' atter he left Mis' Lucy went ter doctorin' cut up backs. Gran'mammy said dat dar wusn't no more trouble wid de niggers an' Mis' Lucy done all of de punishin' herself.

"She made de meanest ones l'arn a whole passel of scripture, she punish de chillun by makin' dem memorize poems an' sich. Sometimes she sont 'em ter bed widout supper, sometimes she make 'em work at night, sometimes she prayed fer 'em, an' once in a coon's age she whupped. Dey said dat she could really hurt when she meant to, but she whupped as de las' thing ter do an' she whupped wid a keen little switch 'stead of de leather.

"Once atter she had whupped a little nigger she said, 'Clarice, dis hurt me wusser dan hit did yo'.'

"Clarice look at Mis' Lucy den she sez, 'Iffen hit hurt yo' wusser dan hit did me I'se powerful sorry fer you.' Dat little gal wus my mammy.

"My gran'father wus named Jake, an' he 'longed ter a family by de name of Middleton some whar in de neighborhood. Marse Nat ain't had no use fer Mr. Middleton 'case he tried ter act up, an' he wus a New York Yankee ter boot, what thought that he owned de heabens an' de yearth. When gran'father Jake fell in love wid gran'mammy nobody ain't knowed hit, 'case dere marsters am mad at each other an' dey knows dat dere won't be no marryin' twixt de families.

"Time goes on an' gran'father runs away an' comes ter see gran'mammy, but one night Mr. Middleton follers gran'father an' fin's him in gran'mammy cabin.

"Mr. Middleton doan wait ter say nothin' ter nobody, when he peeps in at de winder an' sees dem a-settin' at de table eatin' musk melons what gran'pappy had stole outen his patch. He jist comes in a-rarin' an' a-tarin' an' starts a-whuppin' wid his ridin' quirt. He whups gran'father fer a while, den he pitches in on gran'mammy.

"While all dis am a-goin' on somebody runs fer Marster Nat an' when he gits dar dere am trouble in de shack. Marse Nat ain't so heaby as Mr. Middleton, but man, he puts de beatin' on Mr. Middleton, den he makes him sell Jake ter him an' he pays him spot cash right den an' dar.

"De nex' day he thinks ter ax gran'mammy what Jake am a-doin' in her cabin, an' gran'mammy tells him dat she loves Jake an' dat she wants ter marry him. Marse Nat laugh fit ter kill an' he sez dat dey'll have a big weddin' at de house fer dem.

"Dey did habe a big weddin' an' gran'mammy wore a red dress dat Mis' Lucy give her. She said dat she wish dat gran'father could of wore red too.

"She said dat when mammy wus borned dat ole Doctor Freeman 'tended her an' dat she stayed in de bed two weeks. Mis' Lucy wus good ter de niggers lak dat.

"I 'members gran'mammy tellin' 'bout de Yankees comin' an' how she stood front of Mis' Lucy's door wid de ax an' tol' 'em dat she'd chop out anybody's brains what tried ter go in. De door wus open an' dey could see Mis' Lucy a-settin' dere white as a sheet, so dey went on sarchin' fer valuables, an' all de time dem valuables wus in Mis' Lucy's room."

N.C. District:      No. 2
Worker:             Mary A. Hicks
No. Words:          389
Subject:            TEMPE PITTS
Person Interviewed: Tempe Pitts
Editor:             Daisy Bailey Waitt

Tempe Pitts

# TEMPE PITTS
## Ex-Slave Story

**An interview with Tempe Pitts, 91 of 307 Tarboro St., Raleigh, N.C.**

"I wuz borned in Halifax County ninety-one years ago. See dis paper, hit wuz writ our fer me by ole marster's granddaughter dis year. Hit says not only dat I is ninety-one but dat I wuz her mammy, an' dat I wuz a good an' trus'worthy servant.

"My mammy wuz Phillis Pitts, an' my daddy wuz Isaac Williams. We 'longed fust ter Mr. Mason L. Wiggins dar in Halifax, den through de marriages we 'longed ter Captain Hardy Pitts. Both o' dem fambles wuz good ter me an' dey ain't neber done me dirty yit.

"De Pitts' owned ober two hundert slaves, case dey also had a plantation in Firginia. We had all we could eat an' good, do' tough clothes. Hit's de Lawd's truff dat I ain't lakin' fer nothin' den. When we wuz sick we had de bes' doctor an' all de medicine dat he said dat we ought ter habe; an' we ain't wuck when we wuz sick nother.

"I 'members jist one whuppin' dat I got, an' I needed hit too. Missus Pitts sont me out in de yard ter scrub de wilverware [TR: silverware] wid some san'. I knowed dat I wuz supposed to scrub hit good an' den wash it all off, but 'stid of dat I leaves hit layin' dar in de yard wid de dirt on it. She whups me fur it, but she jist stings my laigs wid a little switch.

"I seed de oberseer whup a slave man but de best I 'members hit de nigger warn't whupped much.

"I ain't neber seed no slave sales, do' I did see a whole slew o' slaves a-marchin' ter be sold at Richmond. Dey neber wuz chained do', an' sometimes I 'specks dat dese niggers what claims dat dey seed sich things am a-tellin' a lie.

"De maddest dat I eber git, an' de only time dat eber I cuss bad wuz when de Yankees come. Dey stold de meat an' things from de smoke house, an' eber thing else dat dey can git. Dey ain't done nothin' ter me, but de way dey done my white folkses made me mad, an' I jumps straight up an' down an' I yells, 'Damn dem Yankees an' damm ole Abraham Lincoln too!'

"At de surrender did I leave? Naw sir, I stay right on dar. Missus die fust, den Marster, an' atter dat I leaves, an' I gits married.

"My mammy an' pappy, dey tells me, wuz married in de marster's dinin' room by jumpin' de broom. I ain't sayin' nothin' 'bout de ceremony case I ain't sayin' nothin' 'bout my white folkses, but sometimes I does wonder why I'se red-headed when my pappy an' mammy wuz black as tar. Maybe I is part white, but I ain't sayin' nothin' 'bout my white folkses as I done tol' yo'."

L.E.

| | |
|---|---|
| N.C. District: | No. 2 |
| Worker: | T. Pat Matthews |
| No. Words: | 1213 |
| Subject: | HANNAH PLUMMER |
| Person Interviewed: | Hannah Plummer |
| Editor: | Daisy Bailey Waitt |

# HANNAH PLUMMER

**412 Smith Street**

"My name is Hannah Plummer. I was born near Auburn, in Wake County, January 7, 1856. My father was Allen Lane and my mother was named Bertcha Lane. We belonged to Gov. Charles Manly, that is mother and myself, father belonged to some maiden ladies, Susan and Emma White. The governor had large plantations, but mother and myself lived with them on their lot right where the Rex Hospital now stands on South and Fayetteville Streets. Governor Manly owned the block down to the railroad, and we chillun went into [HW: ?] grove, it was a grove then, to pick up walnuts and hickory nuts.

"My father was a stonecutter and he hired his time and gave it to his missus and lived with us. Mother was at Governor Manly's. He said father was a high-headed fellow and said he was livin' on his lot and in his house and that he didn't do anything for him, and that he ought to keep up his family. Mother was the washerwoman for the governor and his family. Missus Manly, the Governor's wife, I forget her first name, did not take any particular interest in her servants. She had slave servants for everything: a wash and ironer, a drawing room and parlor cleaner, a cook, waiting men, waitresses and a maid who did nothing but wait on her.

"Governor Manly was a mighty rich man, and he had several plantations and a lot o' slaves. I don't remember how many slaves he owned. Mother was given meal and meat and had to cook it just the same as she would now. They didn't allow her food from the great house. Mother had ten children, and at times we did not have enough to eat. We went hungry a lot. The boys were named Fred, David, Matthew, Allen, and Thomas. Girls, Cinderilla, Corinna, Hannah, Victoria, and Mary. All were born slaves but two. Thomas and Mary. David and myself are all that are left alive.

"I remember that we lived in a plank house, with three rooms and a shed porch. Mother washed clothes under the porch. The house had two rooms downstairs and one upstairs. (Oh! I have thought of the Governor's wife's name, missus name, it was Charity.) We used trundle beds of wood. Mother made our bed clothes at night. She also made bonnets and dresses. Sometimes she made bonnets and sold them. The child that set up with her she gave some kind o' sweets. I set up with her a lot because I liked to eat. Mother was allowed the little money she made makin' bonnets and dresses at night.

"They whupped slaves on the place. I could hear the blows and hear 'em screamin' cryin' an' beggin', but I never saw it. I never saw a slave sold an' I never saw any in chains.

"I do not remember how many children old marster had, I only remember one; he was Marster Basil Manly. He was an officer in the Confederate Army. He used to come home with his pretty clothes an' his hat with plumes on it. Mother tole me that before she was married Marster gave her to his son Basil as a maid for his wife Caroline.

"Missus Caroline whupped her most every day, and about anything. Mother said she could not please her in anything, no matter what she done or how hard she tried. Missus would go up town and come back and whup her. Mother was a young girl then. One day Miss Caroline went up town, an' come back mad. She made mother strip down to her waist, and then took a carriage whup an' beat her until the blood was runnin' down her back. Mother said she was afraid she would kill her, so she ran for the woods and hid there, and stayed three weeks. She made up her mind she wasn't comin' back.

"The old Governor Charles Manly, went to mother's father, Jimmie Manly an' tole him if he did not get Bertcha back he would whup him. Her father tole him he did not know where she was, an' that he belonged to him an' he could do with him as he liked, but he was not goin' one step to hunt Bertcha, my mother. Then the governor went to grandmother an' tole her she had to find her. He tole her to leave the lot an' stay away until her daughter came back. Grandmother did not know where she was.

"The niggers on different plantations fed mother by carrying things to certain hidin' places and leavin' it. Grandmother got word to her, an' she said she would come back, but not to Mis' Caroline. She told marster, so marster let her stay with grandmother until Christmas, then they allowed her to hire herself out. She hired herself to Mrs. Simpson. She was good to her and allowed her to work for herself at night, sit up as long as she wanted to, and she stayed with her until she was married. Then she went back to old marster's.

"When the war ended mother went to old marster and told him she was goin' to leave. He told her she could not feed all her children, pay house rent, and buy wood, to stay on with him. Marster told father and mother they could have the house free and wood free, an' he would help them feed the children, but mother said, 'No, I am goin' to leave. I have never been free and I am goin' to try it. I am goin' away and by my work and the help of the Lord I will live somehow'. Marster then said, 'Well stay as long as you wish, and leave when you get ready, but wait until you find a place to go, and leave like folks.' Marster allowed her to take all her things with her when she left. The white folks told her good bye.

"We went to a colored Methodist Church in slavery time but we had a white pastor. His name was Dr. Pell. He was a mighty nice man and all the colored people loved him. After the surrender it was a long time that the colored people had white preachers in their churches. It was a long time after the war before any of the colored churches had Negro preachers. William Warrick was the first colored preacher in Raleigh. He preached in the basement of the Baptist Church now standing on the corner of Hillsboro and Salisbury Streets. I went to church and Sunday school there after the surrender.

"I went to school in Raleigh and taught school in Ft. Payne, Alabama. My husband was a carpenter and went there where he could get good wages. Slavery was a very bad thing. Abraham Lincoln was one of the best men that ever lived.

"Roosevelt is just grand. He is no doubt one of the greatest men of any age. I love to look at his picture. I love him because he has done so much for humanity. I pray to the Lord to let him live to serve his country, and help his people."

LE

| N.C. District: | No. 2 |
|---|---|
| Worker: | T. Pat Matthews |
| No. Words: | 2036 |
| Subject: | PARKER POOL |
| Person Interviewed: | Parker Pool |
| Editor: | Daisy Bailey Waitt |

# PARKER POOL

"Good Morning, how is yer? Dat front door am locked Mister, but I'll come 'round and undo it."

"I'm not feeling ve'y well an' it looks lak dey'll rob me out'n all I got. Dey had a mortgage on my home fer $850. I paid it, an' den dey got to gamblin' on it, an' tuk it. I didn't git de right receipts, when I paid: dat's de truf. I got a farm loan on de house part, yes sir, an' I still has it.

"I wuz born near Garner, Wake County, North Carolina. I belonged to Aufy Pool. He wuz a slave owner. His plantation wuz near Garner. I am 91 years old. I wuz born August 10, that's what my grandmammie tole me, an' I ain't never fergot it.

"My missus name wuz Betsy. My fust master, I had two, wuz Master Aufy Pool. Den he give us to his son, er his son bought us in at de sale when Master Aufy died. After Master Aufy died, his son, Louis Pool wuz my master den, an' his plantation wuz in Johnston County. My mother wuz named Violet Pool. She died in child-birth two years atter I wuz born. My father wuz named Peter Turner. He belonged to John Turner in Johnston County, right near Clayton.

"My grandfather, I had two grandfathers, one on my mother's side and one on my father's side. On my mother's side Tom Pool, on my father's side Jerry Beddingfield. I never seed my great-grandparents, but my great-grandfather wuz name Buck. He wuz right out o' Africa. His wife wuz name Hagar. I never have seen dem, but my grandmother wuz deir daughter. Dey had three chillun here in America. My grandmammie and grandfather told me this. My brothers were name, oldest one, Haywood, den Lem, an' Peter, an' me, Parker Pool. De girls, oldest girl wuz Minerva Rilla.

"I had good owners. My missus and master dey took jes as good keer o' me as they could. Dey wuz good to all de han's. Dey giv' us plenty to eat, an' we had plenty o' clothes, sich as they wuz, but de wuz no sich clothes as we have now. Dey treated us good, I will have to say dat. Dey are dead in their graves, but I will have to say dis fer 'em. Our houses were in de grove. We called master's house 'de great house'. We called our homes 'de houses'. We had good places ter sleep.

"We got up at light. I had to do most o' the nursin' o' de chillun, case when choppin' time come de women had to go to work. We had plenty ter eat, an' we et it. Our some'in to eat wuz well fixed an' cooked. We caught a lot o' 'possums, coons an' other game, but I tell yer a coon is a lot harder to ketch den a possum. We had one garden, an' de colored people tended the garden, an' we all et out'n it.

"Dere wuz about 2000 acres in de plantation. All de farm lan' wuz fenced in wid wood rails. De hogs, cows an' stock wuz turned out in de woods, an' let go. The cows wuz drived home at night, dat is if dey didn't come up. Dat is so we could milk de ones we wanted ter milk.

"We dug ditches to drain de lan', blin' ditches; we dug 'em an' den put poles on top, an' covered 'em wid brush an' dirt. We put de brush on de poles to keep de dirt from runnin' through. Den we ploughed over de ditches.

"We tanned our leather in a tan trough. We used white oak bark an' red oak bark. Dey put copperas in it too, I think.

"I knows how to raise flax. You grow it an' when it is grown you pull it clean up out of de groun' till it kinder rots. Dey have what dey called a brake, den it wuz broke up in dat. De bark wuz de flax. Dey had a stick called a swingle stick, made kinder like a sword. Dey used dis to knock de sticks out o' de flax. Dey would den put de flax on a hackle, a board wid a lot of pegs in it. Den dey clean an' string it out till it looks lak your hair. Dey flax when it came from de hackles wuz ready for de wheel whur it wuz spun into thread. I tell you, you couldn't break it either.

"When it wuz spun into thread dey put it on a reel. It turned 100 times and struck, when it struck it wuz called a cut. When it come from de wheel it wuz called a broach. De cuts stood fer so much flax. So many cuts made a yard, but dere wuz more ter do, size it, and hank it before it wuz weaved. Most of the white people had flax clothes.

"We had no church on de plantation. We had prayer meetin' an' candy pullin's, an' we would ask slaves from udder plantations. My master had no public corn shuckin's. His slaves shucked his corn. He had about 50 head. De slaves dey went to de white folks church. Dey had a place separate from de white folks by a railin'. We could look at de preacher an' hear him preach too.

"No, sirree, dey wouldn't let us have no books. Dey would not let none o' de chilluns tell us anything about a book. I cain't read an' write, not a bit. Dey preached ter us to obey our master. Preacher John Ellington wuz my favorite preacher. No nigger wuz allowed ter preach. Dey wuz allowed ter pray and shout sometimes, but dey better not be ketched wid a book. De songs dat dey sung den, dey hardly ever sing 'em now. Dey were de good ole songs. 'Hark from de tomb de doleful sound'. 'My years are tender,' 'Cry, You livin' man,' 'Come view dis groun' where we must shortly lie'.

"No one ran away from our plantation, but dey did from some other plantations. When some o' de niggers were carried by their masters to wait on 'em as servants up no'th, some o' de other people would see how dey were treated an' git 'em to run away. When dere master started home dey couldn't find 'em. Dey took and educated 'em and made women an' men out'en 'em.

"We visited at night during slavery time. De men went courtin'. When a man, a slave, loved a 'oman on another plantation dey axed der master, sometimes de master would ax de other master. If dey agreed all de slave man an' 'oman had ter de [HW: do] Sa'dy night wuz fer him to come over an' dey would go to bed together. Dere wuz no marriage—until atter de surrender. All who wanted to keep de same 'oman atter de surrender had to pay 25¢ fer er marriage license, den $1.50, den $3.00. If de magistrate married you, you didn't have to pay anything, less he charged you.

"We got de holidays, Christmas, and atter lay-by-time o' de crops. Dey had big dinners den. Dey had big tables set in de yard, de rations wuz spread on 'em, an' everybody et. We had brandy at Christmas.

"I have been whupped twice, an' I have seen slaves whupped. Ha! Ha! missus whupped me. She wouldn't let nobody else whup me neither. I 'members what it wuz about as if it wuz yesterday. She wuz fretted 'bout de cook. We wuz skinnin' i'sh taters. She tole us to make haste, if we didn't make haste an' peel de taters she would whack us down. I laughed, she sent me to git a switch. She hit me on de legs. When we were whupped we would say, 'oh! pray,' and dey would quit. If you acted stubborn dey would whup you more. She axed me, 'ain't you gwine ter say 'oh! pray?' I wuz mad. She wuz not hurtin' me much, an' I wouldn't say nuthin'. Atter awhile I said, 'oh! pray', an' she quit. I had good owners all o' dem. My masters never did hit me. Missus would not whup me much. She jes wanted ter show off sometimes.

"We had good doctors when we got sick. I 'members Dr. James o' Clayton comin' to our house. Dey carried dere pills an' medicine den, an' lef' it at de house fer you.

"My master had a son in de war, Walter Pool. He wuz a footso'dier at first. He got sick an' he come home sick on er furlough. He hired er man to go in his place at first, den de man went. Atter awhile de men got so skurce, he had to go agin; den he got de chance to go in de cavalry. Ole master bought him a horse, an' he could ride nex' time. He belonged to the 1st. Ga. Reg. 2nd Cavalry Gen. Dange's Brigade, C. Co. N.C. Volunteers.

"I saw de Confederates' General Johnson come through[Pg 190] Clayton, an' de Yankees come de 2nd [HW: second] day atter dey come through. I think I seed enough Yankees come through dere to whup anything on God's earth. De Yankees camped three miles from our plantation at Mrs. Widow Sarah Saunders across White Oak Creek on de Averysboro road. Her son, Capt. Ed. Saunders wuz in de Confederate Army. She wuz a big slave owner. She had about 100 slaves. She wuz called a rich 'oman.

"De Yankees played songs o' walkin' de streets of Baltimore an' walkin' in Maryland. Dey really played it. Dey slaughtered cows and sometimes only et de liver. I went to de camp atter dey lef' an' it wuz de awfulest stink I ever smelt in my life. Dey lef' dem cows part o' 'em lying whur dey were in de camp. Dey killed geese an' chickens, an' skinned 'em. Sometimes dey skinned de hind quarters uv a cow, cut 'em off an' lef' de res'.

"When dey tole me I wuz free I didn't notice it, I stayed on and worked jest lak I had been doin', right on wid missus and master. I stayed dere a year atter de surrender.

"I dunno what ter think o' Abraham Lincoln. Dey said he wuz all right. I guess he wuz a man God loved, er all right man. I think some o' de slaves wuz better off when dey had owners and wuz in slavery den dey is now. De colored people are slaves now more den dey wuz den. I can show you wherein de nigger's got all his expenses ter bear now. He gits his pay out'en de white man and de white man don't pay him much. De nigger in de South is jest as much a slave as ever. De nigger now is a better slave den when dey owned him, 'cause he has his own expenses to bear. If you works a horse an' doan have him ter feed, you is better off, dan if you had ter feed and care fer him. Dat is de way dat thing is now.

"I seed many patterollers durin' slavery. If dey caught you out at night without a pass dey would whup you.

"I think Mr. Roosevelt is a mighty nice man. He has done me a lot o' good. No man can make times real good till everybody is put to work. Wid de lan' lyin' out dere can't be real good times. Dis is my 'lustration. My horse died las' year. I ain't got no money ter buy nother and can't git one. You see dat lan' lyin' out dere I have farmed it every year fer a long time. Through part o' de year I always had vegetables and sich ter sell, but now my horse is dead an' I can't farm no more. I ain't got nothin' ter sell. I is bad out o' heart. I shore hope sumpin' will be done fer me."

N.C. District: No. 2
Worker: T. Pat Matthews
No. Words: 779
Subject: RENA RAINES
Person Interviewed: Rena Raines
Editor: G.L. Andrews

[TR: Date stamp: AUG 17 1937]

# RENA RAINES

"I wus three years ole when de Yankees come through. I do not 'member much 'bout slavery, but I knows a lot my mother tole me.

"My mother wus named Vicey Rogers an' my father wus named Bob Hunter. He 'longed ter de Hunters of Wake County an' mother longed ter Marster John Rogers. Her missus' name wus Ann Rogers. I 'members my grandfather on my mother's side but do not 'member any more of my grandparents.

"Marse John Rogers wus a ole batchelor before he wus married an' he had 'bout twelve slaves when he married Mis' Ann Hunter. She owned one slave, a colored boy, when she wus married. Her father gave her the slave. The plantation wus between Apex an' Holly Springs in Wake County. All my people lived in Wake County an' I wus born on de plantation. Marster wus good ter his niggers before he wus married, but when she came in it got mighty rough. It got wusser an' wusser till 'bout de time of de surrender. De place wus a Hell on earth, mother said, if dere could ever be one. Missus had slaves whupped fur most any little thing an' den she wud not allow 'em to have much ter eat. My mother tole me all about it, atter de surrender. Mother said Missus runned the plantation an' made it hard fur all de slaves. She jist liked ter see slaves beat almost ter death. Dere wus a lot of niggers whupped in dat neighborhood by the overseers, owners an' patterollers.

"Slaves wus sold 'round from one to a nother 'mongst de white folks. Mother said you jist couldn't tell when you would git whupped. De wurk wus hard from sun to sun. Poor food ter eat, poor clothes, barefooted most of de time, an' a general hard time, till freedom put an end to it. My mother tole me ole man Pasqual Bert who lived near 'em in Wake County had his niggers whupped all day sometimes. He beat 'em unmercifully an sometimes made away wid 'em an' dey wus not seed no more. She said de way he whupped his slaves wus ter lay 'em up an' down on a log wid de bark off. He made 'em lie flat down on dere stomachs an' den buckled 'em on den de overseers beat 'em unmercifully. One time a overseer's wife heard a pat, pat, pat, down at de whuppin' log an' she ax him what it wus an' why he beat niggers from sun to sun an he tole her ole man Bert made 'im do it or else leave. So his wife says 'We will leave, you must not beat any more niggers if we perish to death,' an de overseer left. Mother said ole man Bert fed his little niggers out of a trough like hogs. Ole man Bert also had niggers tied to barrels an whupped.

"De grown slaves got one pair shoes a year. Dey wus give ter dem at Xmas. an de chillun didn't have no shoes at all. De clothes wus homemade. De houses wus made out of logs an had stick an dirt chimleys to 'em. De sleepin' places wus bunks fer de grown niggers an de chillun slept on de floor on pallets. A pallet wus made by spreadin' a quilt made of towbaggin' or rags on de floor, dat's where de chillun slept in our neighborhood before de surrender.

"Mother and father married by jumpin' de broom. Dey put de broom down on de floor den day helt one another's hands an den dey jumped de broom, den day went ter de slave house an' went ter bed. Mother an' father come ter Raleigh atter de surrender an wus married right. Mother an' father lef' ole man Rogers as soon as dey wus free. Dey lived on hardtack an' pickled meat de Yankees give for sometimes den dey went an' stayed wid Mr. Gray Jones an' when I wus a great big girl we lef' an moved ter Chatham County. Pa bought a place, paid for it, built a little house on it an' lived dere until he died.

"I married in Chatham County an' lived dere till my husband died den I kept stayin' till all my chillun married off an' I come ter Raleigh ter live wid my son. I had four chilluns. Dey are all dead but de one I live wid.

"I have been unable to git out of de house widout help fur a long time. I have heart trouble an' high blood pressure. Slavery wus a right bad thing. I thank God it is over."

LE

N.C. District: No. 2
Worker: Mary A. Hicks
No. Words: 203
Subject: ANTHONY RANSOME
Person Interviewed: Anthony Ransome
Editor: Daisy Bailey Waitt

[TR: Date stamp: JUN 2 (unclear)]

# ANTHONY RANSOME
# Ex-Slave Story (Free)

**An interview with Anthony Ransome of 321 S. Tarboro St. Raleigh, N.C.**

"I reckon dat I is eighty years old, an' I wus borned in Murfreesboro in Hertford County. My mammy wus named Annice an' my father wus named Calvin Jones. My brothers wus named Thomas, Wesley, Charlie, Henry an' William.

"We wus borned free, my mammy bein' de daughter of a white 'oman, an' my paw's paw onct saved do life o' his master's chile, an' wus freed.

"My paw wus a shoemaker an' he made a putty good livin' fer us. Course we ain't knowed so much 'bout slavery, but Doctor Manning who lived near us owned some slaves an' he treated 'em bad. We could hyar 'em screamin' at de top of dere voices onct in a while, an' when dey got through beatin' 'em dey wus tied down in de cellar. Dey ain't had much ter eat nother.

"Dar wus a preacher what tol' us 'bout a member of his congregation durin' de war. De wife wus sold from de husban' an' he married ag'in. Atter de war his fust wife comed back an' atter his secon' wife died he married de fust one ober ag'in."

N.C. District: No. 2
Worker: Mary A. Hicks
No. Words: 1083
Subject: **CAROLINE RICHARDSON**
Person Interviewed: Caroline Richardson
Editor: G.L. Andrews

# CAROLINE RICHARDSON

**An interview with Caroline Richardson who does not know her age. She resides near the northern city limits of Selma.**

"I reckin dat I is somers 'bout sixty year old. Anyhow I wus ten or twelve when de Yankees come ter Marse Ransome Bridgers' place near Clayton. Dat's whar I wus borned an' my pappy, my mammy an' we 'leben chilluns 'longed ter Marse Ransome an' Mis' Adeline. Dar wus also young Marse George an' young Miss Betsy who I 'longed to.

"Mis' Adeline wus little an' puny an' Marse Ransome wus big an' stout, dat's why it am funny dat mammy won't let Mis' Adeline whup her but she don't say nothin' when de marster gits de whup. Dere ain't nobody got many whuppin's nohow an' a slave on marster's place had ter be mean ter git a whuppin'. You see mammy would sass dem all.

"We ain't heard much 'bout de war, nothin' lak we heard 'bout de world war. I knows dat nobody from our plantation ain't gone ter dat war case Marse Ransome was too old an' Marse George wus a patteroller, or maybe he wus just too young. Dar was a little bit of talk but most of it we ain't heard. I tended to de slave babies, but my mammy what cooked in de big house heard some of de war talk an' I heard her a-talkin' to pappy about it. When she seed me a-listenin' she said dat she'd cut my year off iffen I told it. I had seen some of de slaves wid clipped years an' I wanted to keep mine, so I ain't said nothin'.

"One day Mis' Betsy come out ter de yard an' she sez ter we chilluns, 'You has got de habit of runnin' ter de gate to see who can say howdy first to our company, well de Yankees will be here today or tomorrow an' dey ain't our company. In fact iffen yo' runs ter de gate ter meet dem dey will shoot you dead.'

"Ober late dat evenin' I heard music an' I runs ter de gate ter see whar it am. Comin' down de road as fast as dey can I sees a bunch of men wid gray suits on a-ridin' like de debil. Dey don't stop at our house at all but later I heard dat dey wus Wheeler's cavalry, de very meanest of de Rebs, though 'tis said dat dey wus brave in battle.

"About a hour atter Wheeler's men come by de Yankees hove into sight. De drums wus beatin', de flags wavin' an' de hosses prancin' high. We niggers has been teached dat de Yankees will kill us, men women an' chilluns. De whole hundert or so of us runs an' hides.

"Yes mam, I 'members de blue uniforms an' de brass buttons, an' I 'members how dey said as dey come in de gate dat dey has as good as won de war, an' dat dey ort ter hang de southern men what won't go ter war.

"I reckin dat dey talk purty rough ter Marse Ransome. Anyhow, mammy tells de Yankee Captain dat he ort ter be 'shamed of talkin' ter a old man like dat. Furder more, she tells dem[Pg 201] dat iffen dat's de way dey're gwine ter git her freedom, she don't want it at all. Wid dat mammy takes Mis' Betsy upstairs whar de Yankees won't be a-starin' at her.

"One of de Yankees fin's me an' axes me how many pairs of shoes I gits a year. I tells him dat I gits one pair. Den he axes me what I wears in de summertime. When I tells him dat I ain't wear nothin' but a shirt, an' dat I goes barefooted in de summer, he cusses awful an' he damns my marster.

"Mammy said dat dey tol' her an' pappy dat dey'd git some land an' a mule iffen dey wus freed. You see dey tried ter turn de slaves agin dere marsters.

"At de surrender most of de niggers left, but me an' my family stayed fer wages. We ain't really had as good as we done before de war, an' 'cides dat we has ter worry about how we're goin' ter live.

"We stayed dar at de same place, de ole Zola May place, on de Wake an' Johnston line, fer four or five years an' I went to school a little bit. Atter we left dar we went to Mr. John H. Wilson's place near Wilson's Mill. It wus at de end of dese ten years dat mammy wus gwine ter whup Bill, my brother, so he went off ter Louisanna an' we ain't seed him since.

"At de end of dis time I married Barney Richardson an' we had three chilluns, who am all dead now. We worked an' slaved till we bought dis house an' paid fer it, den in 1918 he died. I married John Haskins de second time but he's been[Pg 202] dead now fer about ten years.

"I told you dat I owned dis shack but you see how de top has come ter pieces an' de steps has fell down. I'm behind in my taxes too so I'm 'spectin' dem ter take it away from me at any time. I has been dependent on de white folks now fer four or five years. De county gives me two dollars a month an' de white folks gives me a little now an' den. You see dat I can't straighten up so I can't work in five years.

"Drawin' water out of dat well wid no curb shore bothers me too, come an' look at it."

I looked at the well and in the well and was horrified. There was no curbing at all, only a few rotting planks laid over the hole, and on these she stood right over the water while she drew up the heavy bucket with a small rope and without the aid of a wheel. "I reckin dat some of dese days somebody will draw me outen dis well," she continued briskly. "Anyhow hit don't matter much.

"You see dat little patch, wid de roastin' ears comin' an' de peas a-bloomin'. I grubbed it up wid my hoe an' planted it myself. Iffen you can spare it I wish you'd give me a quarter an' iffen you're round here 'bout three weeks stop an' git you a mess of peas."

N.C. District: No. 2
Worker: T. Pat Matthews
No. Words: 638
Subject: CHARITY RIDDICK
Story teller: Charity Riddick
Editor: Daisy Bailey Waitt

[TR: Date stamp: JUN 2 (unclear)]

# CHARITY RIDDICK

**813 E. D. Street.**

"I am 80 years old, you know after 79 comes 80, dats how old I am. A year ago, a little over a year ago, I wus 79 by de age in de Bible. My son Ernest Riddick tole me dat. He is gone to Greensboro to work. He carried de Bible wid him. If I had de Bible I could tell de story better den I can. My full name is Charity Riddick and my husband wus Weldon Riddick. He is dead. My father wus named Lewis Jones. Mother wus named Haley Jones. I had three brothers, Washington, William and Turner, two sisters Mary and Celia. All my people are dead except my sons. I have three sons livin'.

"I got sick an' I got way down in my taxes. I am payin' a dollar on' em every time I can get it. I ain't able to work much. I chops in de garden to make a little to eat. My sons help me some. Dey have children you know, but dey send me a little. Dey is all married. One has eight chillun, the other five chillun and de third has four chillun. Dey can't help me much.

"I belonged to Madison Pace in slavery time. He dead an' gone long ago do'. My missus wus name Mis' Annie Pace. Sometimes I got plenty to eat and sometimes I didn't. All I got came through my mother from marster and missus. I was in my mother's care. I wus so young dey didn't have much to do with me. The plantation wus about three miles east o' Raleigh.

"Dis house did belong to me, but I am a long way behind on it. Dey lets me stay here and pay what I kin. I rents a room to an old lady fer 75 cents a week. I buys oil and wood wid it. De lights has been cut off. I uses a oil lamp fur light. Lights done cut off. I can't pay light rent, no sir, I haint been able to pay dat in a long time.

"In slavery time when de people you call de Yankees come, I wus small, but father took us and left the plantation. We lived in Raleigh after that. Father did not stay on de plantation anymore but he farmed around Raleigh as long as he lived. He made corn, peas, potatoes and other things to feed us with. I used to hear 'em talk about de Ku Klux. We wus mighty afraid of dem.

"I used to hear my father say he had a very good master. My min' is not good but I remember we used water from a spring and lived in a little log house out from my master's 'great house'. I remember sein' de slaves but I do not remember how many dere wus. I never saw a slave whupped. My mother's son wus sold, that wus my brother Washington wus sold away from her before de surrender. Mother cried a lot about it. I remember sein' her cry about my brother bein' sold.

"I remember sein' de Yankees. Dey told us dey were the Blue Jackets dat set us free. I wus afraid o' dem. I am old enough to have been dead long ago. Guess it is the mercy of the Lord dats lets me live.

"All I know about Abraham Lincoln is what I been told. Dey say, I think dey said he set de slaves free. I don't know much good or bad about Mr. Roosevelt. I can't read and write. Dey would not let a nigger have any books. Dey were perticular 'bout dat. When dey tole us 'bout de Bible dey say it say obey your marster. Dis is 'bout all I 'members. Yes, 'bout all I 'members."

AC

N.C. District: No. 2
Worker: T. Pat Matthews
No. Words: 736
Subject: SIMUEL RIDDICK
Story teller: Simuel Riddick
Editor: Daisy Bailey Waitt

# SIMUEL RIDDICK

**2205 Everette Ave.**

"My name is Simuel Riddick. I was born the fourth day February, 1841. My owners, my white people, my old mistress wrote me a letter telling me my age. My mother was Nancy Riddick; she belonged to the Riddicks in the Eastern part of the State. My father was named Elisha Riddick. My master was named Elisha and my mistress Sarah Riddick. They had three daughters, Sarah, Christine, and Mary, one boy named Asbury Riddick.

"I was born in Perquimans County, North Carolina and I have lived in North Carolina all my life. We had good food, for marster was a heavy farmer. There were about 200 acres cleared on the plantation, and about 25 slaves. The great house was where marster lived and the quarters was where we lived. They were near the great house. I saw only one slave whupped. I had mighty fine white people, yes, mighty fine white people. They did not whup their slaves, but their son whupped my mother pretty bad because she did not bale enough corn and turnips to feed the fattening hogs.

"He was a rang tang. He loved his liquor, and he loved colored women. The ole man never whupped anybody. Young marster married in the Marmaduke family in Gates County. He sold one man who belonged to his wife, Mary. I never saw a slave sold.

"I have seen lots o' paterollers. They were my friends. I had friends among 'em because I had a young missus they run with. Dats why they let me alone. I went with her to cotton pickin's at night. They came, but they didn't touch me. My young missus married Dr. Perry from the same neighborhood in Perquimans County. Bill Simpson married her sister. He was from the same place. Watson White married the other one. He was from Perquimans.

"There were no half-white children on Marster's plantation, and no mixups that ever came out to be a disgrace in any way. My white folks were fine people. I remember marster's brother's son Tommy going off to war. Marster's brother was named Willis Riddick. He never came back. I got a letter from my missus since I been in Raleigh. She was a fine lady. She put fine clothes on me. I was a foreman on the plantation and looked after things in general. I had charge of everything at the lots and in the fields. They trusted me.

"When the war broke out I left my marster and went to Portsmouth, Virginia. General Miles captured me and put me in uniform. I waited on him as a body servant, a private in the U.S. Army. I stayed with him until General Lee surrendered. When Lee surrendered I stayed in Washington with General Miles at the Willard Hotel and waited on him. I stayed there a long time. I was with General Miles at Fortress Monroe and stayed with him till he was in charge of North Carolina. He was a general, and had the 69th Irish brigade. He also had the Bluecats and Greentorches.

"I waited on him at the Abbeck House, Alexandria, Virginia after the war. I stayed with the general a long time after the war. I didn't go with General Miles when he was ordered to the plains of the west.

"I stayed on the Bureau here in Raleigh. Dr. H.C. Wagel was in charge. After I left the Bureau I worked at the N.C. State College several years then I worked with the city at the city parks. I never left the state after coming here With General Miles.

"I had mighty good white people, was treated all right, was made foreman and treated with every kindness. I haven't anything to say against slavery. My old folks put my clothes on me when I was a boy. They gave me shoes and stockings and put them on me when I was a little boy. I loved them and I can't go against them in anything. There were things I did not like about slavery on some plantations, whuppin' and sellin' parents and children from each other but I haven't much to say. I was treated good.

"Don't know much about Abraham Lincoln, haven't much to express about Mr. Roosevelt. He is a mighty pleasant man tho'. I learned to read and write after the war. I could not read and write when I was a soldier."

AC

N.C. District:     No. 2
Worker:            Mary A. Hicks
No. Words:         453
Subject:           Ex-Slave Stories
Person Interviewed: Adora Rienshaw
Editor:            Daisy Bailey Waitt

[TR: Date stamp: JUN 1 (unclear) 1937]

Adora Rienshaw

# EX-SLAVE STORIES

**An interview with Adora Rienshaw, 92, of 431 South Bloodworth Street, Raleigh.**

"I wuz borned at Beulah, down hyar whar Garner am now, an' my parents wuz Cameron an' Sally Perry. When I wuz a month old we moved ter Raleigh.

"We wuz called 'Ole Issues', case we wuz mixed wid de whites. My pappy wuz borned free, case his mammy wuz a white 'oman an' his pappy wuz a coal-black nigger man. Hit happened in Mississippi, do' I doan know her name 'cept dat she wuz a Perry.

"She wuz de wife of grandfather's marster an' dey said dat he wuz mean ter her. Grandfather wuz her coachman an' he often seed her cry, an' he'd talk ter her an' try ter comfort her in her troubles, an' dat's de way dat she come ter fall in love wid him.

"One day, he said, she axed him ter stop de carriage an' come back dar an' talk ter her. When he wuz back dar wid her she starts ter cry an' she puts her purtty gold haid on his shoulder, an' she tells him dat he am her only friend, an' dat her husban' won't eben let her have a chile.

"Hit goes on lak dis till her husban' fin's out dat she am gwine ter have de baby. Dey says dat he beats her awful an' when pappy wuz borned he jist about went crazy. Anyhow pappy wuz bound out till he wuz twenty-one an' den he wuz free, case no person wid ary a drap of white blood can be a slave.

"When he wuz free he comed ter Raleigh an' from de fust I can remember he wuz a blacksmith an' his shop wuz on Wolcot's Corner. Dar wuz jist three of us chilluns, Charlie, Narcissus, an' me an' dat wuz a onusual small family.

"Before de war Judge Bantin's wife teached us niggers on de sly, an' atter de war wuz over de Yankees started Hayes's school. I ain't had so much schoolin' but I teached de little ones fer seberal years.

"De Southern soldiers burned de depot, which wuz between Cabarrus an' Davie Streets den, an' dat wuz ter keep de Yankees from gittin' de supplies. Wheeler's Cavalry wuz de meanest troops what wuz.

"De Yankees ain't got much in Raleigh, case de Confederates has done got it all an' gone. Why fer a long time dar de way we got our salt wuz by boilin' de dirt from de smoke house floor where de meat has hung an' dripped.

"I'm glad slavery is ober, eben do' I ain't neber been no slave. But I tell yo' it's bad ter be a 'Ole Issue.'"

N.C. District: No. 2
Worker: T. Pat Matthews
No. Words: 712
Subject: CELIA ROBINSON
Story teller: Celia Robinson
Editor: Daisy Bailey Waitt

# CELIA ROBINSON

**611 E. Cabarrus St.**

"My name, full name, is Celia Robinson. I can't rest, I has nuritus so bad; de doctor says it's nuritus. I do not know my age, I wus eight or ten years old at de close o' de war. De ole family book got burned up, house an' all. I wuz borned a slave. Dat's what my father and mother tole me. My father, he 'longed to Dr. Wiley Perry of Louisburg, N.C., Franklin Co., an' my mother 'longed to McKnight on an adjoining plantation. I do not know McKnight's given name. My father wus named Henderson Perry. He wuz my marster's shop man (blacksmith). My mother wus named Peggy Perry. McKnight's wife wus named Penny. I member her name.

"I member when de Yankees came ter my mother's house on de McKnight plantation near Louisburg an' dey went inter her things. When de Yankees came down my brother Buck Perry drug me under de bed and tole me to lie still or de Yankees would ketch me. I member de sweet music dey played an' de way dey beat de drum. Dey came right inter de house. Dey went inter her chist; they broke it open. Dey broke de safe open also. Dey took mother's jewelry. But she got it back. Missus went ter de captain an' dey give back de jewelry. My missus wus de cause of her gittin' it back.

"I wuz old enough to go up ter where my brother kept de cows when de war ended. I member where he kept de calves. My brother would carry me up dere ter hold de calves off when dey wus milking de cows. My marster would take me by de hand and say 'Now, Celia, you must be smart or I will let de bull hook you.' He often carried me up to de great house an' fed me. He give me good things ter eat. Yes, I am partly white. It won't on my mother's side tho', but let's not say anything about dat, jist let dat go. Don't say anything about dat. Marster thought a lot o' me. Marster and missus thought there wus nothin' like me. Missus let me tote her basket, and marster let me play wid his keys.

"I cannot read an' write. I have never been ter school but one month in my life. When I wus a little girl I had plenty ter eat, wear, an' a good time.

"I 'member when my father would come ter see mother. De patterollers tole him if he didn't stop coming home so much dey wus goin' ter whip him. He had a certain knock on de door, den mother would let him in.

"I 'member how mother tole me de overseer would come ter her when she had a young child an' tell her ter go home and suckle dat thing, and she better be back in de field at work in 15 minutes. Mother said she knowed she could not go home and suckle dat child and git back in 15 minutes so she would go somewhere an' sit down an' pray de child would die.

"We lived at Dr. Wiley Perry's one year atter de war, then we moved ter de plantation of Seth Ward, a white man who was not married, but he had a lot of mulatto children by a slave woman o' his. We stayed dere four years, den we moved ter de Charles Perry plantation. Father stayed dere and raised 15 children an' bought him a place near de town o' Franklinton. I got along during my early childhood better dan I do now. Yes, dat I did. I plowed, grubbed an' rolled logs right atter de war, I worked right wid de men.

"I married Henry Robinson. We married on de Perry plantation. We had two children born ter us, Ada an' Ella. Dey are both dead. I wish I had had two dozen children. I have no children now. If I had had two dozen, maybe some would be wid me now. I am lonesome and unable to work. I have been trying to wash and iron fer a livin', but now I am sick, unable to work. I live with my grandson an' I have nothing."

| | |
|---|---|
| N.C. District: | No. 2 |
| Worker: | T. Pat Matthews |
| No. Words: | 1239 |
| Subject: | GEORGE ROGERS |
| Person Interviewed: | George Rogers |
| Editor: | Daisy Bailey Waitt |

# GEORGE ROGERS
## Ex-Slave Story

"George Rogers is the name. I has carried fur 94 years an' over. I will be 95 the first day o' this comin' August. Louis Rogers wuz my father. My mother wuz Penny Rogers. All my brothers an' sisters are dead except one sister. She is livin' in Buffalo, New York. She is somewhere in seventy years old. She wuz the baby in our home. My mother an' father an' all o' us belonged to Felix Rogers. He lived in the edge o' Wake County next to Greenville County. My mother came from Canada. My master came here from Canada an' married here. He married old man Billy Shipp's daughter. Her name wuz Matilda Shipp.

"I cannot read an' write. Dey did not 'low no niggers to handle no papers in dem days. Master had three plantations an' about one hundred slaves. We had good houses an' plenty to eat. My master wuz a good man. We had no church on the plantation, but we had prayermeeting in our houses. He 'lowed dat an' when dey had big meeting, he made us all go. We had dances or anything else we wanted to at night. We had corn shuckings, candy pullings, an' all the whiskey an' brandy we wanted. My daddy didn't do nuthin' but 'still for him. Whiskey wuz only ten cents a quart den.

"I have never seen him really whup a slave any more dan he whupped his own chilluns. He whupped us all together when we stole watermelons and apples. He made us chillun, white and black, eat together at a big table to ourselves. We had ordinary clothes, but we all went alike. In the summer and winter we all went barefooted and in our shirt tails mos' er de time. His chilluns wuz just as bad fer goin' barefooted as we niggers wuz.

"We had our patches, and he allowed us to have the money we made on 'em. Our houses were called slave quarters. Our marster's house wuz a big fine two story-house. We slaves called it 'de great house'. None er de slaves from Marster Roger's plantation never run away.

"We chillun played de games uv marbles, cat ball, an' we played base, prison base. At night we all played peep squirrel in the house. We played blindfold and tag.

"We fished a lot in Briar Creek. We caught a lot o' fish. Sometimes we used pin hooks we made ourselves. We would trade our fish to missus for molasses to make candy out uv.

"When we got sick we had a doctor. His name wuz Dr. Hicks. I never wuz sick, but some uv de res' wuz. We had an old colored man who doctored on all us chillun. He give us roots an' herbs.

"Yes sir, I have seen slaves sold. My marster died the year the war started; den dey had a big sale at our house. Dey had a sale, an' old man Askew bought a whole lot o' our niggers. I don't know his name only dey called him 'old man Askew'. He lived on Salisbury Street Raleigh, down near de Rex

Hospital, Corner Salisbury and Lenoir Streets. Old man Askew wuz a slave speculator. He didn't do nothin' but buy up slaves and sell 'em. He carried de ones he bought at our house to Texas. He bought my half-sister and carried her to Texas. Atter de surrender I saw her in Texas once, never no more.

"When de war begin dey carried young marster off. His name wuz William Rogers, an' dey sent me to wait on 'im. I wuz in camp wid 'im up here by de old Fair Grounds. Atter we got there I seed old Colonel Farrabow, he wuz Colonel o' dat regiment. We all lef' Raleigh on wagons, an' I don't know whur we went atter we lef' Raleigh; I wuz las'. We got on de train at Fayetteville, whur dey kept de rations. We went to a place whur dere wuz a lot o' water. I don't know its name. We were dere about three days when dey had a battle, an' den Colonel Farrabow come round an' tole me marster wuz gone. He told us to go to the breas'works and work. I stayed dere three years and eight months. Den dey had anudder battle dar jus' befo' I lef', and de Yankees tuc' de place.

"I went to de Yankees den. Dey give me clothes, shoes, sumtin to eat, and some money too. I worked for 'em while dey were camped in Raleigh. I come wid' em back to Raleigh. Dey were camped on Newbern Avenue and Tarboro Street and all out in Gatlin' Field in de place now called Lincoln Park. De Yankees, when dey tuc' us, tole us ter come on wid' em. Dey tole us to git all de folks's chickens and hogs. We wuz behind 'em, an' we had plenty. Dey made us steal an' take things fur 'em. Wheeler's Calvary went before us, dat's why dey wuz so rich. Dey got all de silver, an' we got de chickens and hogs.

"De Yankees skinned chickens and geese. Dey cut hogs an' cows up an' den skinned 'em. Dey took jis' part of a cow sometime, jis' de hind quarters an' lef' de res'. We went to one place, an' de white 'oman only had one piece o' meat an' a big gang o' little chillun. I begged de Yankees to let dat piece of meat alone, she wuz so po', but de officer tole 'em to take it, an' dey took her las' piece o' meat.

"I stayed wid de Yankees two years arter de surrender. Dey carried me to Florida when I lef' Raleigh. When I lef' 'em in Florida I went ter Texas to min' cattle. I stayed in Texas seven years. Den Mr. Hardie Pool from down here at Battle Bridge, Wake County come out dere. When he started home I couldn't stan' it no longer, an' I jis tole him I wuz goin' back home to North Carolina. No Sir, when I got home, I would not go back. No mo mindin' cattle in Texas fur me. I married arter I come back here. I married Polly Bancomb first, den a 'oman named Betsy Maynard, and las', Emily Walton.

"When de surrender come marster wuz dead, but he lef' it so dat all his slaves who had families got a piece o' lan'. Dere were four of 'em who got lan'. He wuz dead do', but missus done like he had it fixed.

"We had white overseers. Old man John Robinson stayed there till de surrender; den he lef'. We used to kill squirrels, turkeys, an' game wid guns. When marster went off some o' us boys stole de guns, an' away we went to de woods huntin'. Marster would come back drunk. He would not know, an' he did not care nuther, about we huntin' game. We caught possums an' coons at night wid dogs. Marsa an' missus wuz good to us.

"I heerd a heap uv talk about Abraham Lincoln, but I don't know nuthin' bout him. I like Mr. Roosevelt all right. He is all right as fur as I know of 'im. I digs fish worms fer a livin'; I can't work much. I jist works awhile in the mornin'. I don't git anything from charity, de county, ner de State. I don' have much. Dese are de bes' shoes I has. Dey flinged dem away, an' I picked 'em up. Dey is jist rags uv shoes. I shore need shoes."

L.E.

N.C. District: No. 2
Worker: T. Pat Matthews
No. Words: 1172
Subject: HATTIE ROGERS
Person Interviewed: Hattie Rogers
Editor: G.L. Andrews

[TR: Date stamp: AUG 4 1937]

# HATTIE ROGERS

"I was born a slave in New Bern, N.C., Craven County, the 2nd day of March 1859. My full name is Hattie Rogers. My mother's name was Roxanna Jeffreys. Her husband was named Gaston Jeffreys, but he was not my father. My father was Levin Eubanks, a white man. I was born before my mother was married. I called my father Marse Levin. We belonged to Allen Eubanks of New Bern, N.C. and his sister's son was my father. His sister was named Harriot and I was named after her. Marster didn't care who our fathers was jest so the women had children. My father died in 1910. My mother was 15 years old when I was born. When I was a little girl they moved us out to the plantation on the White Oak River in Onslow County where we had plenty to eat and wear. We made the stuff and we ate it. Our marster was good to us. Marster carried me around in his arms a whole lot. He would say to me, 'Come on Harriot, and let's go get a dram. If you're like your daddy I know you like it.'

"Our marster did not whip us or allow anyone else to whip us.

"When the Yankees took New Bern, two years before the war ended, we all were refuged to Franklin County to keep them from setting us free. All who could swim the river and get to the Yankees were free. Some of the men swum the river and got to Jones County, then to New Bern and freedom. One of these was Alec Parker. The White Oak River was in Onslow County bordering Jones County. There was a lot of slaves who did this, but he is the only one I personally remember.

"When we got to Franklin County, we saw plenty of patterollers, and many of the men were whipped. Mother's husband was beat unmercifully by them.

"There was no churches on the plantation, but we went to the white folks church and sat on the back seats. The white people was friendly to us in the eastern part of the state. Indeed it was more stiff up in Franklin County. Some of the slave-owners was very mean to their slaves. I remember seeing some of the slaves almost beat to death. Lawsy mercy, that was a time. I saw a slave-owner whip a colored woman named Lucy, his servant. He was named John Ellis, Judge Ellis's son in Franklinton.

"My mother cooked for Judge Ellis then. John Ellis whipped Lucy because he found a piece of pickle outside the pantry door. He accused her of stealing it. There was a string attached to a bell, near where Lucy stayed. She was a house girl. He accused her of stealing the pickle and leaving it there when the bell rung, and she had to go in the house. He made her strip to her waist and then he made her hug a tree. He whipped her with a cowhide whip until she could only say in a weak voice, 'Oh pray! Marster John'. Major Thomason was there, and he went to Marse John and said 'John, don't kill the dam nigger.'

"A lot of the white folks hid in the woods and in caves and swamps. They hired slaves out when they didn't need 'em themselves. They hid jewelry in hoss stables by digging holes, putting the jewelry in, and then replacing the straw.

"When the slaves was sent from White Oak to Franklinton before Lee surrendered they had to walk all the way. We children was carried in dump carts drawn by mules. My marster nor none of his boys was ever in the Confederate Army. When they got us to Franklinton they put us in jail for safe keeping.

"If a woman was a good breeder she brought a good price on the auction block. The slave buyers would come around and jab them in the stomach and look them over and if they thought they would have children fast they brought a good price.

"Just before the war started when the birds would sing around the well, Missus would say, 'War is coming, them birds singing is a sign of war; the Yankees will come and kill us all.' I can see the old well now jest as plain. It had a sweep and pole. You pulled the sweep over by pulling the pole and bucket down into the well. When it sunk into the water, the heavy sweep pulled it up again.

"I wouldn't tell anything wrong on my ole marster for anything. He was good to all of us. He offered my mother a piece of land after the war closed, but mother's husband would not let her accept it. My grandmother took a place he offered her. He gave her fifty acres of land and put a nice frame building on it.

"The man we belonged to never was married. He bought a woman who had two little girls, on [TR: one] named Lucy and the other Abbie. He took Lucy for a house girl to wait on his mother. She had eleven children by him. They're all dead except one. All the missus I ever had was a slave, and she was this same Lucy. Yes, sir he loved that woman, and when he died he left all his property to her.

"When the slaves on the plantation got sick they relied mostly on herbs. They used sage tea for fever, poplar bark water for chills.

"When the husbands and brothers and sweethearts were gone to the war the white ladies would sing. Annie Ellis and Mag Thomas would sing these pitiful songs. 'Adieu my friends, I bid you adieu, I'll hang my heart on the willow tree and may the world go well with you.'

"When I was three years old I remember hearing this song. 'Old Beauregard and Jackson came running down to Manassas, I couldn't tell to save my life which one could run the fastest, Hurray boys, hurray!'

"When the surrender came the Yankees rocked the place where we were in. We were in a box car. They wanted to get a light-colored slave out.

"The Yankee officers came and gave mother's husband a gun and told him to shoot anyone who bothered us. They put a guard around the car, and they walked around the car all night.

"My mother was dipping snuff when the Yankees came. One rode up to her and said, 'Take that stick out of your mouth.' Mother was scared when the Yankees tried to break in on us. She cried and hollered murder! and I cried too. I din't know about freedom. I was too young to realize much about it. When the war ended I had just been hired out. I was never sent off. I think slavery was an awful thing, and that Abraham Lincoln was a good man because he set us free."

LE

| | |
|---|---|
| N.C. District: | No. 2 |
| Worker: | Mary A. Hicks |
| No. Words: | 669 |
| Subject: | HENRY ROUNTREE |
| Person Interviewed: | Henry Rountree |
| Editor: | G.L. Andrews |

# HENRY ROUNTREE

**Henry Rountree, 103 years old, of near Newsom's Store in Wilson County.**

"I wus borned an' bred in Wilson County on de plantation of Mr. Dock Rountree. I wus named fer his oldest son, young Marse Henry. My mammy, Adell, my pappy, Shark, an' my ten brothers an' sisters lived dar, an' aldo' we works middlin' hard we has de grandes' times ever.

"We has two er three corn shuckings ever' fall, we has wood splittin' days an' invite de neighbors in de winter time. De wimmen has quiltin's an' dat night we has a dance. In de col' winter time when we'd have hog killin's we'd invite de neighbors case dar wus a hundret er two hogs ter kill 'fore we quit. Yes, mam, dem wus de days when folkses, white an' black, worked tergether.

"Dar wus Candy pullin's when we makes de 'lasses an' at Christmas time an' on New Year's Eve we has a all night dance. On Christmas mornin' we serenaded de marster's family an' dey gived us fruits, candy an' clothes.

"My marster had game cocks what he put up to fight an' dey wus valuable. When I wus a little feller he had one rooster that 'ud whup me ever' time I got close ter him, he'd whup young Marse Henry too, so both of us hated him.

"One day we set down wid bruised backs ter decide how ter git rid of dat ole rooster, not thinkin' 'bout how much he cost. We made our plans, an' atter gittin' a stick apiece ready we starts drappin' a line of corn to de ole well out in de barnyard. De pesky varmint follers de corn an' when he gits on de brink of de well we lets him have it wid de sticks an' pretty shortly he am drownded. Marse ain't never knowed it nother.

"De missus had a ole parrot what had once 'longed ter her brother who wus a sea captain. Dat wus de cussingest thing I ever seed an' he'd cuss ever'body an' ever'thing. One day two neighborhood men wus passin' when dey heard somebody holler 'Wait a minute.' When dey turns 'roun' de ole parrot sez, 'Go on now, I jist wanted ter see how you looks, Great God what ugly men!' An' de ole thing laughs fit ter bust.

"Dat ole parrot got de slaves in a heap of trouble so de day when de hawk caught him we wus tickled pink. De hawk sailed off wid de parrot screamin' over an' over, 'Pore polly's ridin'. We laughed too quick case de hawk am skeerd an' turns de ole fool parrot loose.

"Hit's things lak dat dat I 'members mostly, but I does 'member when de news of de war come. Ole missus says dat de will of de Lord be done. Den ole Marse sez dat his slaves won't be no happier in heaben dan dey will wid him an' dat de Yankees better keep outen his business.

"De war comes on an' as de niggers l'arns dat dey am free dar am much shoutin' an rejoicin' on other plantations, but dar ain't nothin' but sorrow on ours, case de marster sez dat he always give us ever'thing dat we needs ter make us happy but he be drat iffen he is gwine ter give us money ter fling away. So we all has ter go.

"Ole marster doan live long atter de war am over, but till de day dat he wus buried we all done anything he ax us.

"I has done mostly farm work all of my life, an' work aroun' de house. Fer years an' years I lives on a part of Marse's land an' atter dat I lives here. I ain't got no kick comin' 'bout nothin' 'cept dat I wants my ole age pension, I does, an' I'd like to say too, Miss, dat de niggers 'ud be better off in slavery. I ain't seed no happy niggers since dem fool Yankees come along."

LE

By Miss Nancy Watkins
Madison, Rockingham County

# Biography Sketch of Ex-Slave, Anderson Scales, 82

Three fourths of a mile from his master's mansion in Madison on Hunter Street, with his large plug tobacco factory across the street on the corner (where [HW: in] 1937 stands the residence of Dr. Wesley McAnally,) in some "quarters" which Nat Pitcher Scales had near Beaver Island Creek, Anderson was born to slave mother, Martha Scales of a father, "man name uh Edwards." Baby Anderson was the slave of William Scales, at one time the world's largest manufacturer of plug or chewing tobacco and he was named for Henry Anderson, the husband of Mrs. William Scales' sister. Cabins here "quarters" consisting of three or four log ones. Cabins were near the old "free white schoolhouse" or rather the "schoolhouse" for whites.

Rolling around the yards with the other pickaninnies, Anderson passed his babyhood, and when he was a boy he went to be house boy at Marse Jim Dick Cardwell's on Academy Street facing Nat Pitcher Scales' home, later that of Col. John Marion Gallaway. Here he learned good manners and to be of good service. Later he was houseboy in the big house just beyond the Methodist church at James Cardwell's who had a mill five miles west of Madison and whose wife was Sallie Martin; granddaughter of Governor Alexander Martin. Here Anderson learned more good manners and rendered more good house boy service such as sweeping floors, bringing in "turns" (armfuls) of fireplace wood, drawing water from the yard well and toting it into the house, keeping flies off the dining table, carrying out slops and garbage, for every town house had its back lot pigs.

Larger [HW correction: Later] Anderson was hired to Nat Wall, (colored) farmer and blacksmith, then to Joshua Wall, white planter of Dan Valley northeast of town a few miles.

White men would get contracts to have the mail carried to various towns and Anderson Scales was hired by one of these contractors to carry the mail from Madison to Mt. Airy, fifty miles distant in northwest Surry County. He would go by horse and sulky (sulky) on Monday, return on Wednesday; go on Thursday, return on Saturday. This was in the late 1870's and 1880's.

During the tobacco season, he worked in factories in Winston (no Salem then) and Greensboro. Then he worked in Nat Scales' factory in Madison and in that of his former Marster, William Scales. He married Cora Dalton and started his home a mile up the Ayresville road from town.

The railroads having come with the consequent transporting of freight to and fro, Anderson started a public draying business of one horse and a wagon, which lasted thirty eight years and was given up by him to his son-in-law, Arthur Cable who now, in 1937, has an auto-truck and hauls large paper boxes from the Gem Dandy Suspender and Garter Company located across Franklin Street from Anderson's house boy home, that of James Cardwell, to the post office. From the freight train depot, Arthur hauls merchandise also in paper cartons to the feed stores which do not own an auto truck of their own, and he hauls to the garter factory a few two by three foot wooden boxes loaded with metal fillings for the suspenders. This is a complete contrast to the loads "drayed" by Anderson through the 1880's, 1890's and the 1900's to about 1915 when the automobile began to change the world of transportation, and Anderson's one horse wagon dray business along with it.

For thirty-eight years Anderson met every train to capture the trunks of visitors or "drummers" in town. Two immense hogheads packed with leaf tobacco was sold on the floors of Webster's ware house and

Planters' warehouse. Two stacks of tobacco baskets loaded with the bundles of leaf, Anderson, five feet high, and his lean horse could dray from the sales floors to the packing houses where the tobacco was packed and pressed into the hogsheads or else stored for removal at a greater profit. One such packing house was converted into the Gem Dandy Garter Factory about 1915, and today three of the original five remain. One or two are still used for tobacco packing, though the season of 1936-1937 marked the hauling of immense loads of tobacco direct from the sales floors to the Winston-Salem buyers. One pack house is used as a fertilizer sales house. One loaded to the roof comb with heavily insured tobacco was mysteriously burned during the World War where such insurance collections were the fashion! Thus Anderson's dray business dwindled. Any kind of hauling he could get done, and his horses, as they died from strenuous work, would be replaced by others who in no time learned the meaning of Anderson's constant pulls on their reins and his constant and meaningful clucks. With no swivel features to his wagon, Anderson could nevertheless work the horse and wagon into any kind of close position for loading and unloading. He always said the baggage of the writer was the heaviest he carried. This was so because of books packed in the trunk or in boxes and twenty-five cents a piece was the fare!

Anderson's wife and children at home were making the acre homestead pay with cow, pigs, chickens and vegetables quickly grown on soil enriched from his dray horse stable as well as the cow stable: "snaps", tomatoes, Irish potatoes, roasting ears, butterbeans, squash in the summer, in the spring mustard and onions; in the winter "sallet" from the "seven top" and turnips, too. Fruit trees planted in time gave fruit for eating, canning and "pursurving" while all the little darkies knew where wild strawberries, crab apples and black berries grew for the picking. With Mommuh taking in white folks' washing and the dray horse money coming in, Anderson Scales prospered in Madison where he started from zero scratch. He had money in the bank.

Anderson said after "Srenduh", [HW addition: the surrender] he learned to read and write at a negro free school taught by Matilda Phillips. With his wife, Cora Dalton, sister of Sam Dalton, Anderson joined the African Methodist Church fifty years ago. This was located just across the street from the home of his former employer, Nat Wall until 1925 when it was abandoned with its parsonage and a new brick church built on the Mayodan road with stained glass memorial windows, electric lights, piano, well finished interior, and christened St. Stephen's Methodist Episcopal Church. The omission of the word "South" emphasized the fact that the members considered it a northern Methodist church as well as African. In this church, Anderson was exhorter, trustee and class leader. In then religious capacities, his education by the colored teacher, Matilda Phillips was a great help to him.

Anderson's second wife was Dinah Strong who had no children. She died December, 1933 from a goiter on her throat.

For ten years or more Anderson has operated a grocery store in the corner of the Mayodan and the Ayresville roads. Customers come more at night, so Anderson has time in the day to work his garden patches of onions, snaps and the like and to stop and rest on the porch of the small store house. Clad in good dark clothes, a low crowned derby hat, he often snoozes as he rests his eighty-two year old frame.

Anderson and many of his children were distinguished by their very large round eyes with much white showing. One of his sons inherited the blackness of his skin. This was "Little Anderson" who once sought a warrant from a local justice to punish by trial some boy at the tobacco warehouse, who had remarked thus: "Boy, charcoal would leave a light mark on your skin!"

Anderson's son, Will Scales, was the first husband of Bertha who had to nurse him through the terrible spells he would have from liquor debauchery. Will was the servant of the Nat Picket family and once Mrs. Pickett herself went down to their home and nursed Will through one of his terrible "cramping spells." After Will Scales' death, Bertha married Cleve Booker, plumber, ex-World War veteran and of surpassing good nature from Washington, Georgia. Their oldest son they named Chilicothe, Ohio, because at that city, Cleve was in war camp and met Bertha who had gone there to go out in service.

Some of Anderson Scales other children still live in Madison in homes marked by good construction, clean well furnished interior, artistic surroundings. Martha married Arthur Cable who also holds an honored place in the church. One daughter married Odell Dyson. Fannie Sue married Thompson. Walter married Morris Carter's daughter. He died in early 1937 of pneumonia in West Virginia. So his widow went to help take care of "Pap Anderson". Nancy Scales married Eler William Wells.

When told that the pioneer graveyard of the Scaleses which is a mile or so west of his store was a thick tangle of growth and no stones to the once wealthy tobacco manufacturer, William Scales, Unka Anderson exclaimed May 19, 1937: "You don't mean to tell me my ole Marse ain't got no tombstone to his grave".

A merchant's wife stated that about 1930, Anderson had more ready cash in the bank of Madison than any white man in town, but Uncle Anderson disclaimed this.

But the Depression of 1930-1934 did not injure this energetic black man who started in a "quarters" cabin a mile or so west of his present home and store, lived all his life in Madison and faces the "one clear call" with comfortable snoozes on his own front porch. Respected by white and colored, Anderson Scales, 82, has guided his life by the gospel preached by his pastor, also an ex-slave, William Scales of Madison.

By Miss Nancy Watkins
Madison, North Carolina
Rockingham County

# BIOGRAPHY OF EX-SLAVE CATHERINE SCALES

About ten years old at the "Srenduh", now quite feeble, but aristocratic in her black dress, white apron and small sailor hat made of black taffeta silk with a milliner's fold around the edge, Aunt Catherine is small, intensely black with finely cut features and thin lip. Her hand is finely molded, fingers long and slender. Her voice is soft and poise marks her personality. Sallie Martin, a ginger cake colored woman, sixty-five, has lived as a kind of caretaker with Aunt Catherine since 1934 and thereby gets her own roof and refreshment. For Aunt Catherine has gotten "relief" from the county welfare chief, Mrs. John Lee Wilson, and Jeff Scales, seventy, brings Sallie to the "relief" dispensary in his two horse wagon for the apples or onions or grape fruits or prunes with dried bena, milk, canned beef or potatoes as the stores yield. A white horse and a brown mule comprise the team, and several dogs trot along side. Sally also small and frail looking sits in a chair planted in the flat wagon bed behind the drivers' seat, a plank resting on the sides. Jeff drives close to the door, alights and helps Sallie step on to the back of the bed, thence to a chair he has placed, then to the ground, just as polite whites did to their women folks after the war when they would ride to town or to church or to picnics in wagons in order to carry the family, the servants, the dinner, horse feed, water bucket, chairs, cushions. Sallie gets in line, presents Aunt Katherine's card which she has gotten by mail, hears the dispensing lady call to the helping men what Aunt Catherine is to have, and struggles to the door with it where Jeff meets her, transfers the load to his wagon bed. Then with his hands he steadies Sallie as she mounts the chair, then the back of the wagon bed, over the side with voluminous long skirts, and old fashioned ruffled sun bonnet. Off to the hilly north part of Madison called Freetown, Jeff's [TR: Jeff] expertly guides his team through automobile traffi. [TR: traffic] During the worst of the depression Aunt Sallie said she kept her coal reserve in a tub upstairs so nobody could steal it.

Aunt Katherine strengthened by her relief food can talk comfortably.

"I shure did love my white fokes—Ole Marse, Timberlikk (Timberlake) an' Ole Miss Mary Timberlikk. My mother, Lucy Ann Timberlikk bough their portraits at the sale of the old Timberlake things, and kepp them an' brought them with her to Madison, when we moved up here, an kepp them until mummy was in her last sickness, an' two of Ole Misses daughters came over from Greensboro, an' begged,—an mammy sold the pictures to them for a quarter a piece. I still have Ole Misses mother's dish, though. I've got in [TR: it] packed away in a safe place. I'll get it and show it to you." It is a large flat platter of the ware called iron ware and was generally used to serve fried ham and eggs while the gravy came in a small deep dish. In summer, a heap of snaps greasy with middling meat slashed and boiled down dry with Irish potatoes around the edge came to table in the platter.

The keeper of the Timberlake oil portraits was Lucy, slave of Nat Scales, and Lucy's husband was Nathan Scales. Slave Nat Scales (named for Marse Nat) had married a black woman who came "across the water", Sallis [TR: Sallie?] Green who become by purchase Sallie Scales. Thus Aunt Katherine recalls her grandmother as one who "cum over the water with a white lady". The purchaser Mrs. Scales was from the LeSeur family. Her father was clerk of the Rockingham county court as early as [TR: missing date?] and kept the session records of his Presbyterian church in a fine neat script.

"The LeSeurs had as big a house as the Scales house at Deep Springs. I've stayed many a nite in it. It was next to Ole Marse Jimmie Scaleses. John Durham Scales, Marse Jimmy's grandson lived and died in it—his grandmother's house, the old Le Seur place, ten miles down the Dan river towards Leaksville. Miss Mary Le Seur married Marse Gus Timberlikk, an was the grandmother of William Timberlake Lipscomb who used to come up to Madison and go to Dr. Schuck's Beulah Academy just after the Srenduh. When Marse Billy'd get lonesome, he'd go down to Spring Garden and dance with the Scales girls. Ole Marse Le Seur's wife was Miss Lizzie Scales Marse Jimmie's.

"Nome, us slaves didn't have no chuch. Marse Nat Scales ud let his slaves go to the babtizings.

"I could hoe but I didn't do much clean up work. I spun on a great big wheel that went m-m-m-m-m. I wish I had a big wheel to spin on right now. My mammy, Lucy Ann, could weave. She sho loved her white fokes. Cullud fokes didn't have much sence den. She would take cow hair and kyard and spin it with a little cottin in to rolls, and then she'd weave cloth out of it.

"An how they made their shoes den: My father would cut shoes out of the raw cowhide and put them on bottoms (soles) he cut out uv wood. An he couldn't run in them a-tall, just had to stomp along! An day didn't put on shoe till nearly Christmas."

## Schooling

Aunt Katherine said she "learned her letters" in a school fuh cullud fokes only taught by Mr. Sam Allen just after the Srenduh close to the old Timberlake place. Mr. Sam was the son of Mr. Val(entine)[Pg 248] Allen an Miss Betsy Martin (she was the granddaughter of Governor Martin).

"Sometimes Miss Betsy'd git worried with little nigguh rolling roun on de floor thub hader under her feet, an' she'd say: 'Gway! Gway!! Gway fum hyuh! Gway tuh Pamlico!' An the little nigguhs'd say: 'Miss Betsy, whah's Pamplico?'

"'Nine miles tother sede o' hell!'

"Yesin Mr. Sam Allen learn't me my letters. He was crippled. He married a Grogan, an' two Allen girls married Grogans—one, Mary! Mr. Val's father was William Allen. I went to Mr. Vaul Allen's funeral an he was buried on his father's ole place, an Miss Betsy too.

"How de cullud fokes did hate to be sold down south in de cotton country! One time ole Marse Jimmy Scales wuz go sell uh hunduhd down south, and he died, an' all de cullud fokes wuz glad he died cause he wuz go sell um, an oftuh he died, day didn't halftuh be sold way fum home.

"One slave woman wuz sold way fum home—had three chillun, and daze six an eight an ten yuhs ole. She sang a song juss fo day tuh hub off. She put her three children between her knees. She sung, 'Lord, Be With Us.'"

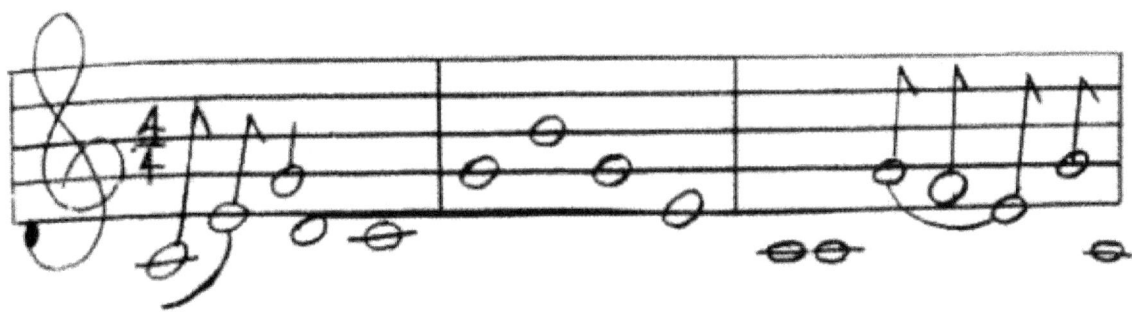

```
do—me—sol—re—do—sol—te—sol—me—do—do—sol—fa—me—sol—do
"Remembuh me      Remembuh me      Oh Lord      remembuh me"
```

This was sung full of quavers and pathos, and entreaty.

"Den she cried! An dey took huh off, and de chillun never saw her no more.

"Aftuh I learned my lettuhs at Marse Sam Allens school, I learned a Bible verse ebry day an if I want bixxy I'd learn ah half uh chaptuh. I read some newspapers, and some story books de Miss Mary Timberlikk give us chillun to read an look ovuh. I learned to write in a copy book, an I'd write stories about Christ, and several different stories. I filled a great big copy book with practice. I learned the most, tho', from Webstuh's Weekly in Reidsville. We took that papuh goin on five yuhs. I read evrything in it.

"Nome, I didn't know Miss Irene McGehiet. Uncle John R. Webster made that paper. It sure wuz a good paper!

"My daddy wuz Marse Nat's slave, an Porter Scales wuz his slave too. Ole Marse Jimmie Scale's sons was Nat Pitcher and John Durham, and John Durham[Pg 250] went to wah. He took Richmond Scales long wiff him to wait on him! Cook fuh him! Make his pallet! Clean his clothes! Rub down his horse! Marse John Durum'd sleep with Richmond in de wintuh to keep him warm. Richmond'd carry him watuh in his canteen during a battle. Marse John Durum had on a ring that wuz carved and he tole Richmond take a good look at this ring sose he'd know him by it, if he didn't kum up aftuh a battle. Richmond ud hole onto his hawse's tail, an go wif him fuhs he could fo a battle.

"Yes'm I ma'd, Richmond Scales when he wuz a widower an had a boy named Jeff. I never had no chillun. Jeff's (70) seventy now, an lives right ovuh cross de street dere in the other hous the Vadens built sixty years ago. I live in one, too."

Aunt Katherine's house has a front room with stairway in the corner leading to one above. A back door leads to a side porch flanked by a two roomed ell, and ended by a pantry. Chimneys with fireplaces once gave heat, but economy had put in Aunt Katherine's tiny stove which she a lump at a time in the winters of depression and relief 1932-1937.

A big fat clean double bed, bureau, wash stand, "centuh" table, chairs and the stairway consumed the living room floor space.

"Nome! I joined de chuch after a big meetin' held by preacher Richard Walker about 1907. I joined the Methodist Chuch an I have always loved to go tuh chuch. This street goes on and goes into the Mayodan road at our new brick (1925) Methodist Chuch. Richmond Scales, my husband died long ago; my mother, about four years ago. She was very old! I wanted to move to Reidsville when we leff de ole plantation whab we could get more wok (waiting) waten on wimmen (obstetries) but the men fokes had kin fokes up hyuh, an we keem hyuh.

"I know whah de ole Sharp graveyard 'bout two miles fum (east) Madison close to Mist Tunnuh (Turner) Peay's; cause lots uh cullud fokes buried there an I went to the funerals. I could go straight tuh it."

By Miss Nancy Watkins, volunteer
Madison, North Carolina

## Story of Ex-Slave, Porter Scales

[TR: Date stamp: JUN 1 1937]

Monday, December 19, 1933, the faithful colored friends of Uncle Porter Scales transported his body from St. Stephen's African Methodist Episcopal Church located on the Madison-Mayodan highway to a plantation grave yard several miles east of town, along roads slippery with sleet. He was buried by the side of his first wife on the 130 acre farm which Uncle Porter said he bought from Mr. Ellick Llewellyn to raise his family on and which he later swapped to Mr. Bob Cardwell for a town house in Pocomo (Kemoca, a suburb from first syllables of promoters' names, Kemp—Moore—Cardwell—Kemoca). In this town house, Uncle Porter passed away aged he thought ninety-seven. For a number of years, he had drawn a pension of $100.00 per year for his services to the Confederate government in hauling foodstuff from Charlotte, North Carolina to Danville, Virginia.

As a slave of Nat Pitcher Scales residing in the brick mansion on Academy Street across from the Methodist church, Porter came to Madison when ten years of age, and his memory held the development of Madison from the erection of the churches around 1845 to details like seeing little Bettie Carter (Mrs. B. Watkin's Mebane) cry from stage fright and pass up her "piece" at school "exhibition" (commencement). He saw Madison grow from a tiny trading village with aristocratic slave holding citizens with "quarters" on their town lots to a town of 1500 with automobiles clipping by to Mayodan, a mill town of 2000, and a thickly populated though unincorporated country side.

In 1930, Uncle Porter was struck by an automobile, and since he [HW addition: has] poked his way about town cautiously with his cane, no longer working as handy man to Thomas R. Pratt's family on the corner of Academy and Market streets. His slavery home was in a two roomed (with loft) cabin next door to the house Mr. Pratt built in 1890 when he moved to Madison from Leaksville. This cabin Col. Gallaway in the 1890's had enlarged to house the Episcopal rector, Mr. Stickney. Uncle Porter's slave home stands in 1937, occupied by Mr. Pratt's daughter, Mrs. Pearl Van Noppen and sons.

Uncle Porter was ever very polite and humble, for all his contacts he thought had always been with the highest of Dan river aristocracy. His medium, lean body, with a head like Julius Caesar's was covered with skin of "ginger cake color".

On the Deep Springs Dan River plantation lived Mrs. Timberlake whose daughter married Mr. Le Seur from an adjoining plantation just across the Dan river from Gov. Alexander Martin's Danbury plantation. She in time married Mr. Scales, and as property of this lady, Porter was born of legally married parents. Porter's brother, Nathan Scales, was given by his mistress to her daughter, when she married another Le Seur, and thus he became Nathan Le Seur. Both brothers have descendants in Madison of a high type of citizenship. Porter, himself was given the choice by his ole Miss of belonging to either of her two sons, John Durham Scales or Nathaniel Pitcher Scales. Porter chose Nat Scales as his young marse and come to Madison to live with him about 1845.

By obeying orders from his marse Nat Pitcher Scales, Porter operated a train of fifteen wagons loaded with corn for the Confederate cavalry from Charlotte, North Carolina to Danville, Virginia. Thus a Confederate soldier, he in his old age received a pension.

Porter said he got lots of practice in managing feed wagons by "Waggoning in Georgia" for his marster between the two cities, Augusta and Wadesboro. His master, he said, traded his services to "Dan River Jim Scales" who "bossed" the teams between Augusta and Wadesboro which were owned by John Durham Scales and Dan River Jim Scales. These wagons also carried corn. Nat Pitcher, Porter's master by choice, operated a store at Wadesboro, Georgia. Uncle Porter's "waggoning in Georgia" shows Madison's connection with the far south not only through the Scales family but through other families.

But the great honor of a tobacco country slave was that of being sold "down south to the cotton country."

So after the war, Porter Scales came back to the Dan river in Rockingham county, and bought his 130 acres farm from Mr. Alex Llewellyn. He liked to recount his matrimonial matters except those of his second wife who married him for a rich nigger widower, and spent his hard won dollars freely for lace curtains and such to adorn the town house in "Pocomo" and finally forced him out of the "town" house into the woodhouse in the yard where he lived some years, dying there. His church friends took charge of his body and kept it until put away by the side of his first wife.

She, Martha Foy, he said in 1932 to me, was bought by Dr. Ben Foy of Madison from Wheeler Hancock of Wentroth. Six of their children are living near Madison and in West Virginia, Stephen and Lindsay Scales at the old place down at Deep Springs. He told of "going tuh see" the attractive Betsy Ann, house girl slave of Mrs. Nancy Watkins Webster but was "cut out" by Noah Black. Aunt Betsy Ann Black is remembered as being the superlative obstetrical nurse in homes of the rich about Madison, and was designated by them as being a "lady" if ever there was a negro lady. She was never dressed except in "cotton checks". "Being cut out" thus, Porter cited as evidence of his aristocratic association: for one of Aunt Betsy's son became a Methodist preacher, and two of her grandaughters teachers in the public schools of North Carolina.

Porter told of the white school teacher, Professor Seeker who taught in the Doll academy, Madison's old "female academy" which still stands (remodeled since 1900 into a dwelling) on Murphy Street at the 60 foot deep well in the street, by the old Dr. Robert Gallway house (standing still in 1937) just south of John H. Moore's five acre homeplace. Professor Seeker, he said left Madison and went up on Baughn's Mountain to teach among the Baughns, Lewises and Higgies and Bibsons, pioneer families of that area. On that May 2, 1932 in his Kemoca yard, Uncle Porter recited the poem which little Bettie Carter forgot in stage fright at Professor Seeker's "exhibition" before Professor Jacob Doll ever started his "female school". All these pupils were pay "scholars".

The free school for Madison, the "old field schoolhouse" was way down the hill from the old Dr. Smith house near Beaver Island Creek. Only white folks intimate with itch, head lice and long standing poverty then sent their children to the "free ole feel schoolhouse".

Porter said as a laborer he helped build a big tobacco factory at Dr. Smith's old place. By 1880, this factory had been purchased by Madison negroes as community and fraternal "Hall" for assemblies. It served thus to 1925 when it was abandoned, and in 1936, it was torn down, the last of the several large plug tobacco factories operated in Madison 1845-1875 by the Scales, Daltons and Hays.

Porter could name and designate vocationally Madison's early white residents, and others, too, whom his Marse Nat Scales visited. His story of some Civil War refugees led to how their slave girl, Rose, acquired a small farm two miles east of town held to this day (1937) by her descendants, the Ned Collins family of Madison. Rose acquired the farm by Kindness to its owners, who willed it to her.

Forced to live in cellars in Petersburg, Virginia, (Mrs. A.R. Holderby, William Holderby, Miss Fannie Holderby, Mrs. Aiken) because of bombording Federal shells 1864 came to Madison afflicted with tuberculosis. Their slave girl was Rose. The whites died except a son, who became a Presbyterian minister. The whites were buried on a hill just north of the pioneer Joel Cardwell home (1937 Siegfired Smiths'). Rose was married to Uncle Henry Collins, and they lived on the place of Mrs. Louise Whitworth and Scylla Bailey. These white women willed their tiny farm to Rose Collins because of her kindness to them in their old age.

N.C. District: No. 2
Worker: T. Pat Matthews
No. Words: 1197
Subject: WILLIAM SCOTT
Story Teller: William Scott
Editor: Daisy Bailey Waitt

[TR: Date stamp: JUN 11 1937]

William Scott

# WILLIAM SCOTT
Ex-Slave Story

**401 Church St., 77 years old.**

"My name is William Scott. I live at 401 Church Street, Raleigh, North Carolina. I wuz born 1860, March 31st. I wuz free born. My father wuz William Scott. I wuz named after my father. My mother wuz Cynthia Scott. She wuz a Scott before she wuz married to my father. She wuz born free. As far back as I can learn on my mother's side they were always free.

"My mother and father always told me my grandfather wuz born of a white woman. My grandfather wuz named Elisha Scott. I have forgot her name. If I heard her name called I have forgot it. My grandfather on my mother's side wuz a Waverly. I can't tell you all about dese white folks, but some of 'em, when they died, left their property to mulattoes, or half-breed children, and several of them are living in this community now. I can tell you exactly where they are, and where they got their property. Some of them are over half white. They were by a Negro woman who wuz a mulatto and a white man. Dey air so near white you can't tell them from white folks. This condition has existed as long ago as I have any recollection, and it still exists, but there are not as many children according to the relations as used to be.

"Free Negroes were not allowed to go on the plantations much. Now you see my father wuz a free man. We lived right here in town. My father wuz a ditcher and slave gitter. One night the man he worked for got up a crowd and come to whup him and take his money away from him. He had paid father off that day. Dat night dey come an' got him an' blindfolded him. He moved the blindfold from over his eyes and run an' got away from 'em. He never did go back o [TR: no] more to the man he had been workin' for. I wuz a little boy, but I heard pappy tell it. Dat wuz tereckly after de surrender. Pappy saw the man he had been workin' for when he slipped the blindfold off his face, and he knowed him.

"I wuz a boy when the Yankees came to Raleigh. They came in on the Fayetteville Road. They stopped and quartered at the edge of the town. I remember they had a guardhouse to put the Yankees in who disobeyed. Later on they came in from the east and quartered at the old Soldiers Home right in there, but not in the buildings. There were no houses there when the Yankees came. They had some houses there. They built 'em. They stayed there a good while until all the Yankees left. When the Yankees first came in they camped over near Dix Hill, when they come into town you hardly knew where they come from. They were jist like blue birds. They jist covered the face of the earth. They came to our house and took our sumpin' to eat. Yes sir, they took our sumpin' to eat from us Negroes. My daddy didn't like deir takin' our rations so he went to de officer and tole him what his men had done, and the officers had sumpin' to eat sent over there.

"My mammy cooked some fur de officers too. Dey had a lot of crackers. Dey called 'em hard tack. The officers brought a lot of 'em over dere. We lived near the Confederate trenches jist below the Fayetteville Crossin' on Fayetteville Street. The breastworks were right near our house.

"I know when the colored men farmed on share craps, dey were given jist enough to live on, and when a white man worked a mule until he wuz worn out he would sell him to de colored man. De colored man would sometime buy 'im a old buggy; den he wuz called rich. People went to church den on steer carts, that is colored folks, most uv 'em. De only man I wurked for along den who wud gib me biscuit through de week wuz a man named June Goodwin. The others would give us biscuit on Sundays, and I made up my mind den when I got to be a man to eat jist as many biscuits as I wanted; and I have done jist dat.

"My mammy used to hire me out to de white folks. I worked and made jist enough to eat and hardly enough clothes to wear to church until I wuz a man. I worked many a day and had only one herrin' and a piece of bread for dinner. You know what a herrin' fish is? 'Twon't becase I throwed my money away, twas cause we didn't git it, nuther to save up. When we farmed share crap dey took all we made. In de fall we would have to split cord wood to live through de winter.

"I will tell you now how I got my start off now, I am going to use dis man's name. I went to work for a man name George Whitaker. I drive a wagon for him. He 'lowed me all de waste wood for my own use. This wuz wood dat would not sell good on de market. I hauled it over home. I worked for him till he died, en his wife lowed me a little side crap. I made this crap, took de money I got for it, and built a little storehouse. I disremember how long I worked fer Mis' Hannah Whitaker. Den I quit work for her and went to work for myself. I owns dat little storehouse yit, de one I worked wid Mis' Hannah Whitaker, en from dat I bought me a nudder home.

"When de Yankees come to Raleigh dere wuz a building dey called de Governor's Palace, it stood whur de Auditorium now stands. Right back o' where de courthouse now stands wuz a jail and a gallows an' a whuppin' pos' all dere together. I know when dey built de Penitentiary dey hauled poles from Johnston County. Dey called dem Johnston County poles. Dey hauled em in on trains. Dis post office wuz not built den. De post office den wuz built of plank set up an' down.

"I remember seeing a man hung down at de jail. His name wuz Mills. He wuz a white man. When he got on de scaffold he said, 'What you gwine to do to me do it quick and be done wid it'.

"I think Abraham Lincoln done the colored man a heap of good. If it hadn't been for Mr. Roosevelt there are many livin' today who would have parished to death. There are plenty of people walkin' about now who would have been dead if Mr. Roosevelt had not helped them. The only chance I had to hold my home wuz a chance given me through him. At my age, I cannot make much at work, but through things he helped me, and I is holding my own."

B.N.

N.C. District: No. 2
Worker: Mary A. Hicks
No. Words: 607
Subject: **TINEY SHAW, EX-SLAVE OF WAKE COUNTY, 76.**
Story Teller: Tiney Shaw
Editor: Daisy Bailey Waitt

Tiney Shaw

# TINEY SHAW

**Ex-Slave of Wake County, 76.**

"My papa wuz a free nigger, case he wuz de son of de master who wuz named Medlin. When a chile wuz borned ter a slave woman an' its pappy wuz de boss dat nigger wuz free from birth. I know dat de family wuz livin' on Mis' Susy Page's place durin' de war an' we wus jist lak slaves alldo' we wuz said to be free den.

"My pappy wuz named Madison Medlin, maybe for de president, an' my mammy wuz a pretty, slim brown-skinned gal when I could remember. Dey said dat she wuz named fer Betsy Ross. I had four brothers, Allison, William, Jeems and John an' five sisters named Cynthy Ann, Nancy, Sally, Caroline an' Molly.

"We hyard a heap 'bout de war, but de white folkses didn't want us to know 'bout it. Most of de white wimmens had ter live by dere selves durin' de time dat de men folkses wuz away at de war, but de niggers in our neighborhood stuck ter de missus an' dar ain't no niggers from other plantations come dar ter insult 'em nother.

"I 'members dat it wuz in April when de Yankees come an' I hyard Mis' Susy cryin', case she wuz a widder 'oman; an' her crops wuz jist started ter be planted. She knowed dat she wuz ruint, I reckon.

"Me an' my mammy wuz sittin' by de fireplace when de Yankees come. I crawled under de wash bench but de Yankee officer drug me out an' he sez, 'Go fetch me a dozen aigs, an' I wants a dozen now, mind yo'.'

"I looked till I found twelve aigs an' I started ter de house wid 'em, but bein' so excited I drapped one uv dem an' cracked it. I wuz sceered stiff now sho' nuff, an' I runned inter de back do' an' crawled under de bed. De officer seed me do' an' he cracks his whup an' makes me come out den he sez, 'Nigger what's dat out dar in dat barrel in de hallway?'

"I sez, 'Lasses sir', an' he sez 'draw me some in dis cup.'

"I draws 'bout a half a cupful an' he sez, 'Nigger dat ain't no 'lasses,' an' he cracks his whup ag'in.

"I den draws de cup full as it could be an' he tells me ter drunk it.

"I drinks dat whole cupful uf 'lasses 'fore he'll lemmie 'lone. Den I runs back ter my mammy.

"Atter awhile de Yankee comes back an' sticks his haid in de do' an' he 'lows, 'ole doman, yo' 'lasses am leakin'.'

"Sho' nuff it wuz leakin' an' had run all down de hall an' out in de yard, but he done pull de stopper out fer meanness so he could laff at mammy when she waded through dat 'lasses. Dey laffs an' laffs while she go steppin' down through de 'lasses lak a turkey walkin' on cockleburs.

"Dem Yankees done a lot of mischief, I knows case I wuz dar. Dey robbed de folkses an' a whole lot of darkies what ain't never been whupped by de master got a whuppin' from de Yankee soldiers.

"De Ku Klux Klan warn't half as bad as dem Yankee robbers what stayed in Raleigh atter de war, robbin', plunderin', an' burnin' up ever'thing. De south had ter have de Ku Klux Klan but dey ain't had no need fer de Yankees.

"De first winter atter de war wuz de worse winter I ever knowed, an' I'se tellin' yo' dat wuz bad. Maybe yo' doan think so but nigh 'bout ever' nigger in de world cussed ole Abraham Lincoln dat winter."

B.N.

N.C. District: No. 2
Worker: T. Pat Matthews
No. Words: 1648
Subject: JOHN SMITH
Story teller: John Smith
Editor: Office force

[HW: 300 slaves raised [TR: illegible], 2 women, some reconstruction material]

John Smith

# JOHN SMITH

**John Smith, a Negro in the Wake County Home, Raleigh, N.C.**
**Interviewed by T. Pat Matthews, May 10, 1937.**

"John Smith is my name, an I wuz borned at Knightdale, right at my marster's house. Yes sir, right in his home. I wuz born right near whar de depot now is. My marster owned de lan', all de lan' dere. I wuz bred an' bawn dere on my marster's plantation. I is, countin' day an' night, 216 years old, not countin' day an' night I is 108 years old.

"My marster's name wuz Haywood Smith an' he wuz one ob de bes' men I ebber seed. He wuz good to all us niggers, he would come round an' talk to us, he lubbed us, and we lubbed him. My marster, Haywood Smith, nebber married but he had a nigger 'oman. She also had a nigger husband. She had two chillun by Marster Haywood Smith, a gal and a boy. Peter Knight owned my marster's lan' at Knightdale atter my marster died. He died de year de war commence.

"Den de gardeen, de gardeen dat wuz appointed for all us slaves, and his name wuz Bat Moore, he carried us slaves to Marster Haywood Smith's brother's chillun in Alabama. He wuz de gardeen. I got dere de month de war commence. Bat Moore carried me to Alabama. Marster Elam Smith's chillun wuz named Frank an' John Elam. Dem boy's mother wuz name' Miss Mary, dere fadder wuz daid. Miss Mary married agin. Her first husband was Elam. Miss Mary moved off, but I staid wid de boys.

"My mother's name wuz Rose Smith, my father's name wuz Powell. He died at Wilmington, N.C. when dey wuz diggin' de trenches roun' de fort dere durin' da war. My mother died in Greene Co. Alabama, at a place called Smithfield. My father belonged to Mack Powell. I made no money before or atter de war. I worked in Alabama until de war close.

"I seed millions of Yankees, just like bees. When de war close I went wid' em. I did not work enny for a year. I wuz so glad when de war ended, and dey tole me I wuz free I did not know what to do. I went wid de Yankees, dey wuz kind to us. Dey said dey wuz shore glad to see us. Dey gib us just what dey wanted us to hab.

"During de war, I had corn bread wid one piece o' meat a day. De meal wuz not sifted. De white folks had sifters made of horse hair but de slaves didn't have no sifters. When I carried a dress off to have it made on Sunday for Mist'ss during de war, when she could not make it herself, she gimme a biskit. We called Sunday, Blue Monday. She gimme de biskit fur workin' on Sunday. Den I got a biskit fur going atter de dress. I got about two biskits a year when de war was going on. I wuz workin' to keep de soldiers fed, dey got de biskits.

"Tom Bridgers wuz marster's overseer. He had 160 chilluns by niggers. Marster Bridgers rode a horse when he went ober de plantation.

"De only game I eber played wuz marbles. I played fer watermelons. We didn't hab eny money so we played fer watermelons.

"In Alabama we got up at 4 o'clock and worked to 9 or 10 o'clock den we had breakfast, en rested till 4 o'clock. Dat wuz when de weather wuz dry and hot. It wud kill de truck to work it den. When it wuz wet we worked longer. In North Carolina we worked from sun to sun, but we rested two hours at noon. You hardly ever heard of a man gittin' sick. If he did, he had de typhoid den Dr. Sewell at Knightdale, atter a while called Jedge Sewell, would come en doctor him. Old man Jedge Sewell was buried near St. Augustine School, other side Tarboro Road.

"I didn' have to pay anthing fer going to Alabama. I wuz carried. Bat Moore carried me, he wuz de gardeen, but I had to pay to come back. Dey went atter me, and I had to work two years to pay it back.

Yes, Sir-ree, two whole years to pay fer coming back. I wuz glad to git back. Sometimes, dey gib us a fofe of de crap to farm. Some years we didn' make much, when it wuz dry. No, we didn' make much. People didn' sociate together, pore whites, free niggers, slaves, and de slave owners. No dey didn' sociate much befo' de war, but dey did atter de war, dey got to mixin' den.

"I et rabbits, an' possums, coons an' fish. I muddied de water an' caught fish. I caught rabbits, coons, an' possums wid dogs. Dey fared but middlin pore chance wid us. We caught rabbits in hollers an' caves; an' possums in trees, but we had a hard time ketchin' squirrels. We niggers had no guns, so we had a hard time ketchin' squirrels. I et rabbits in summer whin dey had kits in 'em. We caught all dese animals wid dogs.

"De white chillun didn' work, but de white folks wuz good to me. Yes, Sir-ree, dey wuz good to me. If dey done anything to me it wuz my fault. I belonged to Elam Smith's chilluns, Frank and John Elam.

"I seed many Yankees during de war in Alabama. When de war ended dey tole me I wuz free. I wuz so glad I didn' know whut to do. De Yankees tole me I wuz free. I went wid 'em. I stayed wid 'em from May till August. Den I slipped away from 'em. I had no clothes and shoes till de Yankees come. Yes, Sir, I went barefooted. Dey gimme clothes and shoes, but I slipped away from 'em because dey wanted me to do things I didn' want to do.

"White folks, if I must tell you, I must. I think Jesus sent you to me so I can tell my story. Dey just wanted me to forage aroun' and git chickens, collards, taters en anybody's hogs I could git. I didn' have no slips or shoes, no unner clothes for 40 years befo' de Yankees come, but I slipped away. I didn' want to do what dey wanted me t'do.

"De pore white folks done tolerable well but de rich slave owners didn' 'low 'em to come on dere plantations. Dey didn' 'low free niggers to come on de plantations if dey could help it, but dey couldn' hep it. Dey slipped in dere at night when de marster didn' know it.

"My marster owned three plantations and 300 slaves. He started out wid 2 'oman slaves and raised 300 slaves. One wuz called short Peggy, and the udder wuz called long Peggy. Long Peggy had 25 chillun. Long Peggy, a black 'oman, wuz boss ob de plantation. Marster freed her atter she had 25 chilluns, just think o' dat, raisin' 300 slaves wid two 'omans. It sho is de truf do'.

"There wuz no jails but dey had whippin' pos' on de plantations. When a nigger done anything he wuz tied and whupped, dare ain't no scars on my back, no nary a one. Dere wuz slave auction blocks at Rolesville, en down to Rosinburg, Harpsborough, below Zebulon, next place, Smithfield.

"White folks didn' hep me to read an' write. If I wuz caught wid a book I had better run an' git in a hole somewhar. Dey didn' low me to hab nothing to do wid books.

"My marster preached to us on Sunday. He wuz a preacher. My marster preached to his slaves. No slaves didn' run away from my marster. He wuz too good to 'em. De slaves from other places run away do', an' when dey caught 'em dey whupped 'em too.

"Yes Sir, my marster gib us Christmas. Sometimes he gib us two weeks befo' we went to work agin Christmas. Licker wuz no mo 'en water. Brandy, de highest price of any of it wuz 40 cts. a gallon. We had a plenty uv licker, but nobody got drunk. Sometimes a white man got drunk en now en den a nigger would git drunk.

"All worked for one an'er den. I tell you dis young bunch ain't right, dey don't do right, dey don't work fer one an'er.

"I never married befo' de war. Nobody married on marster's plantation, but dey had 'omans. My 'oman wuz mighty good to me. I slep' anywhar I could befo' de war ended, in de shuck pen, cotton seed house, an' went barefooted in slavery days. I married Helen Jones atter de war. I had four chilluns by her, 2 gals an' 2 boys. One o' dem boys is livin' now, but I doan know whar he is. I had one child by my 'oman in slavery time. My 'oman died in Greene County Alabama. I been married twice. I married another 'oman named Amy Gumpton in Wake County. She had four chillun by me, one, a boy is in de navy yard, a girl in Brooklyn, New York, one in Wake County, a farmer, an' one died. I lub de southern people, but de debbil got de bes' of 'em; dey wuz good to me.

"I doan think Mr. Abraham Lincoln wuz a good man, no sir-ree, de debbil got him atter he whupped and won all de lan'. He wanted to gib it back agin. De debbil got de bes' o' him. He didn' lib long atter he whupped, did he?"

|                    | No. 2              |
|--------------------|--------------------|
| **N.C. District:** |                    |
| **Worker:**        | T. Pat Matthews    |
| **No. Words:**     | 924                |
| **Subject:**       | JOHN SMITH         |
| **Person Interviewed:** | John Smith    |
| **Editor:**        | G.L. Andrews       |

# JOHN SMITH

10 Pettigrew St., Raleigh, N.C. Age 77.

"My mother was named Charlotte Smith and father was named Richmond Sanders. You know niggers were sold an' traded an' given away just like stock, horses, mules an' de like in slavery time.

"My mother belonged to John Smith and father belonged to Richmond Sanders. I belonged first to John Smith, but was give away when I was a child to Solomon Gardner. John Smith's plantation was in Johnston County near Smithfield. Solomon Gardner's place was in Wake County. All these people are dead an' gone. My uncle, Ben Thomas, died 'bout one month ago in Johnston County. He was the last of the old gang. Mother and father said we got reasonably good food and clothes. The houses were small and poorly furnished but were warm and they got on very well. There was 'bout twenty-five slaves on the place and they worked long hours under overseers.

"The rules were strict about books, goin' visiting an' having meetings of any kind. No slave was allowed to carry guns or hunt without some white man with him unless his marster give him a pass. Dey caught rabbits in gums, birds in traps an' hunted possums wid dogs at night. Dere was not much time for fishin' cept at lay-by time and at de Fourth of July. Den slaves an' whites sometime went fishin' in de Neuse River together. At Christmas de holidays was give slaves and den dey had plenty to eat, shoes, etc.

"Slaves were sold at Smithfield on a auction block but a lot were carried to Richmond, Va. and to Fayetteville, N.C. Children were not made to work till dey got 12 or 14 years old unless it was some light work around de house, mindin' de table, fannin' flies, an' pickin' up chips to start a fire, scratchin' marster's head so he could sleep in de evenings an' washin' missus feet at night 'fore she went to bed. Some of de missus had nigger servants to bathe 'em, wash dere feet an' fix dere hair. When one nigger would wash de missus feet dare would be another slave standin' dere wid a towel to dry 'em for her. Some of dese missus atter de war died poor. Before dey died dey went from place to place livin' on de charity of dere friends.

"I was born 2nd Sunday in May 1860. I remember seein' de Yankees but I know very little 'bout 'em. Guess mos' all dem Yankees are dead now. De ones dat whupped an' de ones dat got whupped are mos' all dead. I lerned to read an' write since slavery. I remember de Yankees. Dey give us chilluns hardtack. Dey had cans on dere backs an' guns, blue clothes an' brass buttons on dere clothes. Dey had covered wagons in front an' dey was walkin'. I remember seein' dem kill a hog and take part of de hog an' carry it off on dere backs.

"De only time I saw anything in de slave situation dat made a big impression on my mind was when Marster Thomas tied my Aunt Anne Thomas to a peach tree and whupped her. I will never forgit how she cried. Another thing I 'members, my uncle teached me to cuss folks. His name was Needum Thomas. I can remember fore I could walk better than I can remember happenings now.

"Atter de war my daddy took mother an' moved to Dr. Leach's in Wake County, next year we went to Mrs. Betsy Jordan's plantation in Johnston County. The fourth year atter the war they put me to work. We stayed with the Jordans several years then we moved to Mr. Thomas' where my aunt was whupped in slavery time an' de marster dat owned some of our people in slavery time. We stayed there a few years. Then we moved to John Avery's near Smithfield. Father bought a place there an' paid for it.

"Father believed in whuppin like de white folks did. He cut de blood out of me wid a switch an' scarred me up an' I left him. When I was twenty-one, a free man, I went back an' paid father for every day I was away from him from de time I ran away at 16 years old till I was twenty-one. I owed him dat 'cause I was his until I was free. I believes dat is why God has allowed me to live such a long time, 'cause I paid a just debt. Daddy said before he died I had done more for him dan de other chilluns. He whupped me too much but atter all he was my father an' I loved him an' paid him all I owed him for de time I was away.

"I married three times in Raleigh. I married Juliva Smith, she lived one and one half years. We had one child dat lived six days. I have no more chilluns. I married Mahalda Rand. She lived a year and three months and the third an' last time I married Maggie Taylor. I lived with her eleven years an' she died. I am single now.

"Haywood Smith was my first father-in-law. He is 'bout 108 years ole. He lives at de County home.

"I am livin' right in dis world tryin' to be ready when God calls me. Slavery was bad. Workin' the colored people over two hundred years without giving 'em anything but dere food an' clothes. Yes slavery was bad."

LE

N.C. District: No. 2
Worker: Mary A. Hicks
No. Words: 568
Subject: JOSEPHINE SMITH
Story teller: Josephine Smith
Editor: Daisy Bailey Waitt

Josephine Smith

# JOSEPHINE SMITH
## Ex-Slave Story

An interview with Josephine Smith, 94 years old of 1010 Mark Street, Raleigh, N.C.

"I wuz borned in Norfolk, Virginia an' I doan know who we belonged to, but I 'members de day we wuz put on de block at Richmond. I wuz jist todlin' roun' den, but me an' my mammy brought a thousand dollars. My daddy, I reckon, belonged ter somebody else, an' we wuz jist sold away from him jist lak de cow is sold away from de bull.

"A preacher by de name of Maynard bought me an' mammy an' carried us ter Franklinton, whar we lived till his daughter married Doctor John Leach of Johnston County; den I wuz give ter her.

"All my white folkses wuz good ter me, an' I reckon dat I ain't got no cause fer complaint. I ain't had much clothes, an' I ain't had so much ter eat, an' a many a whuppin', but nobody ain't nebber been real bad ter me.

"I 'members seein' a heap o' slave sales, wid de niggers in chains, an' de spec'ulators sellin' an' buyin' dem off. I also 'members seein' a drove of slaves wid nothin' on but a rag 'twixt dere legs bein' galloped roun' 'fore de buyers. 'Bout de wust thing dat eber I seed do' wuz a slave 'oman at Louisburg who had been sold off from her three weeks old baby, an' wuz bein' marched ter New Orleans.

"She had walked till she wuz give out, an' she wuz weak enough ter fall in de middle o' de road. She wuz chained wid twenty or thirty other slaves an' dey stopped ter rest in de shade o' a big oak while de speculators et dere dinner. De slaves ain't havin' no dinner. As I pass by dis 'oman begs me in God's name fer a drink o' water, an' I gives it ter her. I ain't neber be so sorry fer nobody.

"Hit wuz in de mont' of August an' de sun wuz bearin' down hot when de slaves an' dere drivers leave de shade. Dey walk fer a little piece an' dis 'oman fall out. She dies dar side o' de road, an' right dar dey buries her, cussin', dey tells me, 'bout losin' money on her.

"Atter de war I comes ter Raleigh an' wucks fer Major Russ den I cooks a year on Hillsboro Street fer somebody who I can' 'member right now, den I goes ter Louisburg ter cook in Mr. Dedman's hotel, an' hearin' 'bout Melissa I fin's dat she am my sister, so I goes ter Mis' Mitchel's an' I gits her.

"A few years atter de war I marries Alex. Dunson wuz a body slave fer Major Fernie Green an' went through all de war. Me an' him lived tergether sixty years, I reckon, an' he died de night 'fore Thanksgivin' in 1923.

"Slavery wuzn't so good, case it divided famblies an' done a heap o' other things dat wuz bad, but de wuck wuz good fer ever'body. It's a pity dat dese youngins nowadays doan know de value o' wuck lak we did. Why when I wuz ten years old I could do any kind o' house wuck an' spin an' weave ter boot. I hope dat dese chilluns will larn somethin' in school an' church. Dats de only way dey can larn it."

AC

| | |
|---|---|
| N.C. District: | No. 2 |
| Worker: | T. Pat Matthews |
| No. Words: | 631 |
| Subject: | NELLIE SMITH |
| Person Interviewed: | Nellie Smith |
| Editor: | Daisy Bailey Waitt |

# NELLIE SMITH

**Main St. Dunn, North Carolina**
**Route 6**

"My name is Nellie Smith. I wus born on a plantation in Harnett County in 1856, near where Linden now stands. I belonged to ole man Jack Williams. His wife wus dead when I wus borned. There were many acres in the plantation; it wus a large one. I don't know exactly how many acres. There were 'bout fifty slaves on the place. The slave houses were on a hill. Marster lived in the big house; and it wus a big one too.

"I do not remember ever goin' hongry when I wus a slave. Father wus the butler and mother wus a house woman, and we got plenty to eat. My mother wus named Rosetta Williams and father wus named Atlas Williams. I do not remember my grandmother and grandfather, but I remember my great grandmother.

"We had good home made clothes and good beds. Jack Williams wus good to his slaves. He wus good to me and my mother and father, I have heard 'em say that he wus always good to 'em. Our livin' with him wus good and we loved him. He thought a lot o' his niggers. He had six children of his own 4 boys and 2 girls; the boys Dr. Jack Williams, Dr. Jim Williams, William Williams, Jim Williams; the girls Mary and Martha.

"I did little work in slavery time. Sometimes I fanned flies off the table at meal times and did other light work. They made children do very little work in slavery time. We children played base, an' hide the switch.

"I saw a jail for slaves in Fayetteville, North Carolina, but I never saw a slave sold. I saw an overseer whup a man once but he certainly didn't hurt him much. He done more talkin' dan whuppin.

"We went to the white folks' church but they would not allow any of us any books. No one taught us to read an' write. My father ran away once because he would not take a whuppin'. When he came back they did not do or say anything to 'im. Jack Williams would not allow a patteroller to whup a nigger on his land. If they could git on his land dey were safe. He had overseers at the plantation. I remember one whose name wus Buck Buckannon. When we got sick Dr. Jack Williams looked after us. When Marster Jim Williams got to be a doctor he looked after us.

"Yes, I remember de Yankees. Dey went to our house one Sunday mornin'. Dey did not fight on our [Pg 288] side of the river; dey fought on de other side o' de river near de Smith House. It wus the battle of Averysboro. De Smith House wus a hospital. Dey came into the house, my sister Irene wus house girl. The Yankees put deir pistols to her head and said, 'You better tell me where dem things are hid. Tell us where de money and silver is hid at.' Sister did not tell. Boss had started off wid de silver dat mornin'. De Yankees caught him, took it, an' his boots, horse and all he had. He come back home barefooted. Dey got mos' everthing at Marster's house. Dey took my mother's shawl, an' a lot of things belongin' to de slaves.

"I have heard o' de Ku Klux Klan, ha! ha! Yes, I have. I heard tell of dey beatin' up people, but I never got into any tangle wid 'em. I just don't know bout all dem old folks Lincoln, Davis, Booker Washington. I think slavery wus a bad thing cause dey sold families apart, fathers from their wives and children, and mothers away from their children. Two of my sisters were fixed up to be sold when the war ended."

LE

| | |
|---|---|
| **N.C. District:** | No. 2 |
| **Worker:** | Mary A. Hicks |
| **No. Words:** | 465 |
| **Subject:** | SARAH ANN SMITH |
| **Person Interviewed:** | Sarah Ann Smith |
| **Editor:** | G.L. Andrews |

[TR: Date stamp: AUG ? 1937]

# SARAH ANN SMITH

**An interview with Sarah Ann Smith of 623 West Lenoir Street, Raleigh, North Carolina.**

"I wus borned January 22, 1858 ter Martha an' Green Womble in Chatham County, near Lockville. My father 'longed ter Mr. John Womble an' mammy 'longed ter Captain Elias Bryant. Dey had six chilluns, I bein' nex' ter de oldes'.

"Father wus a carpenter an' by his havin' a trade he got along better before an' atter de war dan de other niggers. Mammy wus housekeeper an' cook an' she always wus neat as a pin an' as quick as lightnin'. Both families wus good ter dere slaves, givin' dem plenty ter eat an' enough ter wear.

"I stayed wid mammy on Captain Bryant's plantation, an' I doan 'member doin' any wurk at all 'cept lookin' atter de babies onct in a long while.

"When de Yankees come Marse wus off ter de war so dey tuck de place wid out any trouble at all. Dey wusn't as good ter us as our white folkses wus an' somehow we doan feel right 'bout 'em takin' Marse's stuff, but we knows hit ain't no use ter say nothin' 'bout hit.

"At last de war wus ober, de Captain wus too busted ter hire us ter stay on, so we moved over ter Mr. Womble's place den.

"Life wus a heap different from what hit wus 'fore de surrender. We ain't had no fun now case when we has time we is too tired an' when we do have time is soldom. No mo' dances an' parties fer us. We ain't eben got de 'lasses ter have a candy pullin'. We ain't got de 'ligion we had 'fore de war, so prayer meetin' am not hilt often. De Yankees gived us a school but dey ain't give us nothin' ter eat so we's got ter wurk, we ain't got no time fer edgercation.

"I growed up in dis han' mouth way an' when I wus thirteen I seed Henry Smith who wus rentin' a little farm dar near us. He wus young an' slim an' yaller. My folks wanted me ter marry Bill Bunn but he wus thirty-odd, black an' heavy, an' I ain't laked him.

"Me an' Henry we cou'ted jist as we pleased case dey warn't strict on us an' when I tol' him dat I reckin dat I is got ter marry Bill Bunn he gits mad an' he sez dat I ain't nother, case I is gwine ter marry him. Well I did an' I ain't never been sorry yet.

"Henry has been dead now fo'teen years an' de five chilluns what we had am dead too an' I is hopin' ter git my pension soon. I does need hit, bein' all alone in de worl'."

LE

N.C. District: No. 2
Worker: T. Pat Matthews
No. Words: 394
Subject: WILLIAM SMITH
Story teller: William Smith
Editor: Daisy Bailey Waitt

# WILLIAM SMITH

**920 Oberlin Road**

"My full name is William Smith. I was born August 17, eighty years ago, near Neuse River at a place called Wilder's Grove. I belonged to Gaston E. Wiley and my missus was Sarah. Don't remember how many children they had but one or two o' 'em are living in Raleigh now, some place on North Street. I had good food and clothing and a good place to sleep. I was not big enough to work much but they were good to me. I jest done little things aroun' the house.

"I remember seein' the Yankees. I seen 'em take things. Yes, I wus big enough to see 'em shoot hogs, an' cows, an' kill the chickens. They went through the house and took what they wanted. After the war we moved over about the Asylum on the Haywood Place. We went to Bryant Green's from the Haywood place. We lived in Raleigh a long time, then I went to Arkansas. My mother and father died in Raleigh.

"I stayed in Arkansas 40 years, and then came back to Raleigh. I am partly paralyzed. I have had a stroke. I married Anna Regan of Wake County. She went from Wake County to Arkansas and I married her there. Her mother's father and the family all went to Arkansas. She is 71 years old the 8th of last April. She has had two strokes and can't talk any more. We have no boys but two girls, Matilda and Emma Maye Smith. Matilda Parker my daughter lives in Pittsburg, Pa. Emma Maye works to support us. She works as nurse for Mrs. J.H. Hunter but right now is out of work. Charity helps us a little. One half peck meal, 1 pound powdered milk, two cans grape fruit juice, one half pound coffee per week. This amounts to about eighty cents worth rations per week. The charity don't have much to give.

"I have been back from Arkansas nine years the seventh of last April. I was never teached no books. I never saw a patteroller, but daddy told me about 'em. I do not remember much about churches before the surrender. I cannot read and write.

"I don't remember the overseers, and I know nuthin' 'bout dem men Lincoln and the rest of 'em you have asked me bout. Reckon they were all right."

BN

N.C. District:         No. 2
Worker:                Mary A. Hicks
No. Words:             797
Subject:               THE BOUND GIRL
Person Interviewed:    Laura Sorrell
Editor:                G.L. Andrews

[TR: Date stamp: JUL 24 1937]

# THE BOUND GIRL

**An interview with Laura Sorrell, 72 years old, of 207 Battle Street, Raleigh. The story is her mother's.**

"My mammy, Virginia Burns, wus borned in Fayetteville, Cumberland County. She never knowed her parents an' frum de fust she can 'member she is a bound girl.

"Frum de fust she could 'member she wus bound out ter a Mis' Frizelle what beat her, give her scraps lak a dog, an' make her wuck lak a man. Dey eben makes her git on de well sweep an' go down in de well an' clean hit out. She said dat she wus skeerd nigh ter death.

"She wus a grown woman when she 'cided dat she can't stand de treatment no mo'. She has cut wood since she wus big enough ter pick up de axe an' she makes up her min' ter quit.

"Dey wus a-fixin' ter chain her up an' beat her lak dey usually done when she 'cides ter go away. She has ter go den or take de whuppin' an' she ain't got time ter make no plans.

"Fust she runs ter de Marster's bedroom an' slips on a pair of his ole shoes, den she goes out ter de big chicken house back of de barn. She hyars de Marster a-callin' fer her 'fore she gits ter de woods so she runs back an' hides in de chicken house.

"Dey calls an' dey calls, an' de chickens comes ter de roost but she lays low an' doan make no fuss, so dey goes on ter sleep. She hyars de folkses a-callin' her but she lays still, den she sees de torches what dey am usein' ter find her an' she thanks God dat she ain't in de woods. Atter awhile she thinks dat she can sneak out, but she hyars de bayin' of de bloodhoun's in de swamp so she lays still.

"Hit am four o'clock 'fore all gits quiet. She knows dat hit am safe ter go now, case she has done hyard Mister Frizelle an' one of de patterollers a-talkin' as dey goes back ter de house. Dey 'cides ter go home an' start out ag'in de nex' mornin' bright an' early.

"Mammy am skeerd pink but she knows dat unless she am keerful dey am gwine ter ketch her. She lays still till daybreak den she flies fer de woods.

"I'se hyard mammy say dat dem nights she slept in de woods wus awful. She'd find a cave sometimes an' den ag'in she'd sleep in a holler log, but she said dat ever'time de hoot owls holler or de shiverin' owls shiver dat she'd cower down an' bite her tongue ter keep frum screamin'.

"She said dat de woods wus full of snakes an' hit wus near 'bout two weeks 'fore she got ter Guilford County. She had stold what she et on de way dar, an' dat hadn't been much so she wus weak.

"One day she crept outen de woods an' look roun' her an' hit bein' in July, she spies a watermillion patch. She looks roun' an' den flies out dar an' picks up a big million, den she shakes a leg back ter de woods.

"While she wus settin' dar eatin' de watermillion a young white man comes up an' axes her her business an' she, seein' dat he am kind-lookin', tells him her story.

"She fully 'specks him ter turn her ober ter de sheriff but 'stid of dat he tells her dat his name am Daniel Green, an' dat he am a Union sympathizer, an' den he takes her ter some colored folkses house.

"Dese colored folkses am named Berry an' my mammy am stayin' dar when she falls in love wid my paw, Jake Sorrell, an' marries him.

"She ain't never been ter dances an' sich before but now she goes some, an' hit wus at one of dese dances whar she met my paw. When she gits engaged ter him she won't let him kiss her till she axes Marster Daniel iffen she can marry him. Yo' see she wus wuckin' fer Marse Dan.

"Well he give his consent an' dey wus married. Dey had me soon, case I wus eight months old when de Yankees come, an' we wus freed by de law.

"My mammy an' paw had a hard time do' dey ain't had but us two chilluns, but dey manages ter feed us all right. Dey wus superstitious an' paid de witch doctor a right smart ter keep off de witches but jist de same we got along well as most folks eben do' we did have ter eat hard tack an' black molasses fer seberal years atter de war."

LE

| | |
|---|---|
| N.C. District: | No. 2 |
| Worker: | T. Pat Matthews |
| No. Words: | 1414 |
| Subject: | RIA SORRELL |
| Person Interviewed: | Ria Sorrell |
| Editor: | G.L. Andrews |

[TR: Date stamp: AUG 23 1937]

# RIA SORRELL

### 97 years old. 536 E. Edenton Street, Raleigh, N.C.

"I jist lak three years of bein' one hundred years old. I belonged to Jacob Sorrell. His wife wus named Elizabeth. My age wus give to me by Mr. Bob Sorrell, the only one of ole marster's chilluns dat is livin' now.

"Dey had four boys, Marcillers, Bob, Adolphus and Dr. Patrick Sorrell. Dey had three girls, Averada an' two udder ones dat died 'fore dey wus named. I wus born on marster's plantation near Leesville, in Wake County. Dats been a long time ago. I can't git around now lak I could when I wus on de plantation.

"Dere wus 'bout twenty-five slaves on de place an' marster jist wouldn't sell a slave. When he whupped one he didn't whup much, he wus a good man. He seemed to be sorry everytime he had to whup any of de slaves. His wife wus de pure debil, she jist joyed whuppin' Negroes. She wus tall an' spare-made wid black hair an' eyes. Over both her eyes wus a bulge place in her forehead. Her eyes set way back in her head. Her jaws were large lak a man's an' her chin stuck up. Her mouth wus large an' her lips thin an' seemed to be closed lak she had sumptin' in her mouth most all de time.

"When marster come ter town she raised ole scratch wid de slaves. She whupped all she could while marster wus gone.[Pg 301] She tried to boss marster but he wouldn't allow dat. He kept her from whuppin' many a slave. She jist wouldn't feed a slave an' when she had her way our food wus bad. She said underleaves of collards wus good enough for slaves. Marster took feedin' in his hands an' fed us plenty at times. He said people couldn't work widout eatin'.

"Our houses wus good houses, 'case marster seed to it dey wus fixed right. We had good beds an' plenty of kiver. De houses wus called de nigger houses. Dey wus 'bout two hundred yards from de big house. Our houses had two rooms an' marster's had seven rooms.

"We didn't have any overseers, marster said he didn't believe in 'em an' he didn't want any. De oldest slaves on the place woke us up in the morning, an' acted as foreman. Marster hardly ever went to de field. He tole Squire Holman an' Sam Sorrell, two ole slaves, what he wanted done an' dey tole us an' we done it. I worked at de house as nurse an' house girl most of de time.

"Mother an' father worked in de field. Mother wus named Judy an' father wus named Sam. You sees father wus a slave foreman. Marster bought Squire Holman from de Holmans an' let him keep his name. Dats why he wus called dat.

"We worked from sunup till sunset wid a rest spell at 12 o'clock of two hours. He give us holidays to rest in. Dat was Christmas, a week off den, den a day every month, an' all Sundays. He said he wus a Christian an' he believed in givin' us a chance. Marster died of consumption. He give us patches an' all dey made on it. He give slaves days off to work dere patches.

"I shore believes marster went to Heaven, but missus, well I don't know. Don' know 'bout her, she wus so bad. She would hide her baby's cap an' tell me to find it. If I couldn't fin' it, she whupped me. She would call marster, an' I doin' de best I could to please her, an' say come here Jacob an' whup dis nigger, but marster paid no attention to her. He took our part. Many wus de meals he give us unbeknown to his wife. Dere wus no mixin' white an' black on marster's place, no sir, nothin' lak dat. He wus lak a father to us. Sometimes he brought hog haslets an' good things to de nigger house an' tole us to cook it. When it wus done he come an' et all he wanted, got up an' said, 'I'm goin' now,' an' you didn't see him no more till next day.

"We had prayer meetin' anytime an' we went to the white folks church. Dere wus no whiskey on de place, no, no, honey, no whiskey. Now at corn shuckin's dey had a big supper an' all et all dey wanted. I'll tell you Jake Sorrell wus all right. We didn't have any dances no time. Some nights marster would come to our cabins, call us all into one of 'em an pray wid us. He stood up in de floor an' tole us all to be good an pray. I saw him die. I saw him when de breath went out of him. De last word he said wus, 'Lord do your will, not mine.' Den he breathed twice an' wus no mo'.

"Missus died since de surrender, when she got sick she sent for me to go an' wait on her. I went an' cleaned her lak a baby, waited on her till de evenin' she died dat night. I went off dat evenin' late to spend de night an' next mornin' when I got dere she wus dead. I jist couldn't refuse missus when she sent for me even if she had treated me bad.

"My grandmother wus as white as you is. She wus Lottie Sorrell. Marster bought my grandmother. I do not know my grandfather's name. Grandmother wus a cook an' she tole me the reason she was so white wus 'cause she stood over de fire so much. Ha, ha, dats what she tole me. She had long straight hair. I 'members her well.

"Yes I 'members de Yankees. De Southern, our folks, wus in front. Dey come along a road right by our house. Our folks wus goin' on an' de Yankees right behind. You could hear 'em shootin'. Dey called it skirmishin'. It wus rainin' an our folks wus goin' through de mud an' slush. Dey had wagins an' some would say, 'Drive up, drive up, Goddamn it, drive up, de damn Yankees right behind us.' Dey had turkeys an' chickens' on de wagins an' on dere hosses. Dey got things out of de houses an' took de stock. Dey searched de houses an' took de quilts an' sheets an' things.

"De Yankees wus soon dere an' dey done de same thing. Dat wus a time. Dey took all dey could find an' dere want much left when all got through. De Yankees poured out lasses an' stomped down things dey could not carry off. I wus afraid of de Yankees. Dey come up an' said, 'Haint you got some money round here?' I tole 'em I knowed nothin' about money. Dey called me auntie an' said 'Auntie tell us whar de money is, you knows.' I says, 'Dey don't let me see everything around here, no dat dey don't.'

"When dey tole us we wus free we stayed right on wid marster. We got crackers an' meat from de Yankees an' when de crop wus housed in de fall marster give us part of all we made. We come to Raleigh on a ole steer cart to git our crackers an' meat dat wus our 'Lowance. We stayed at marster's till father died. I married there. We finally moved to the Page place 'bout eleven miles north of Raleigh. We been farmin' wid de white folks eber since, till we got so we couldn't work.

"I married Buck Sorrell since de surrender. We had four boys an' two girls, six children in all. Dey are all dead, 'cept one, her name is Bettie. She works at Dr. Rogers'.

"Dr Young looked after us when we wus sick.

"Dere wus one thing dey wouldn't allow, dat wus books an' papers. I can't read an' write. I heard talk of Abraham Lincoln comin' through when talk of de war come 'bout. Dey met, him an' Jeff Davis, in South Carolina. Lincoln said, 'Jeff Davis, let dem niggers go free.' Jeff Davis tole him you can't make[Pg 305] us give up our property.' Den de war started.

"A lot of de niggers in slavery time wurked so hard dey said dey hated to see de sun rise in de mornin'. Slavery wus a bad thing, 'cause some white folks didn't treat dere niggers right."

LE

N.C. District: No. 2
Worker: Mary Hicks
No. Words: 320
Subject: A SLAVERY STORY
Story Teller: CHANEY SPELL
Editor: George L. Andrews

# CHANEY SPELL

**An interview with Chaney Spell, 101 years old, Contena Heights, Wilson, North Carolina.**

"I really doan know who my first marster wus, case I has been sold an' hired so much since den. I reckin dat I wus borned in New Hanover er Beaufort County an' I wus sold fust time in my mammy's arms. We wus sold ter a man in Carteret County and from dar de speculators took me ter Franklin County. I wus sold ter a Mr. McKee an' dat's de fust thing dat I 'members.

"I doan 'member anything 'bout maw 'cept dat dey called her Sal an' dat she died years an' years ago. I reckin dat I once had a pappy, but I ain't neber seed him.

"Marster McKee wus mean to us, an' we ain't had nothin' to eat nor wear half of de time. We wus beat fer ever' little thing. He owned I reckin two er three hundret slaves an' he had four overseers. De overseers wus mean an' dey often beat slaves ter death.

"I worked in de house, sometime 'round de table, but I ain't got so much to eat.

"When word come dat we wus to be sold I wus glad as I could be. Dey tol' me dat de marster has gambled[Pg 308] away his money an' lost ever'thing but a few slaves. Later I learned dat he had lost me to a Mr. Hartman in Nash County.

"Marse Sid Hartman wus good as he could be, sometimes his overseers wusn't but when he foun' it out he let dem go. Marse Sid ain't got but one weakness an' dat am pretty yaller gals. He just can't desist dem at all. Finally Mis' Mary found it out an' it pretty near broke her heart. De ole marster, Marster Sid's daddy, said dat long as he could ride a hoss he could look out fer de plantation so Marse Sid took Mis' Mary to de mountains.

"Soon atter dey went away de war broke an' ole marster wus right busy, not dat de slaves ain't stuck to him but de Yankees won't let dem stick. When Marse Sid an' Mis' Mary come home de war wus closin' an' dey has lost dere slaves. De slaves still loves 'em do' an' dey goes over an' cleans house an' fixes fer de young folks.

"Atter de war I married Lugg Spell an' we had five chilluns. He's been dead dese many years an' I'se worked, worked an' worked to raise de chilluns. I has been on charity a long time now, a long time."

EH

N.C. District: No. 2
Worker: Mary Hicks
No. Words: 432
Subject: A SLAVERY FAMILY
Reference: Tanner Spikes
Editor: George L. Andrews

[TR: Date stamp: AUG 4 1937]

# A SLAVERY FAMILY

**An interview with Tanner Spikes, 77 years of age, of 43 Bragg Street, Raleigh, North Carolina.**

"My mammy had fifteen chilluns which wus all borned on Doctor Fab Haywood's plantation here in Wake County. My mammy 'longed ter him, but my daddy 'longed ter a Mr. Wiggins in Pasquotank County. I think that Dr. Haywood bought him just 'fore de war. Anyhow, we took de name of Wiggins.

"Mammy's name wus Lucinda an' pappy's name wus Osburn. I doan 'member seein' many Yankees on Dr. Haywood's place. I doan reckon many comed dar. Anyhow, we had a gyard.

"I 'members a corn shuckin' what happened 'fore de war wus over, an' what a time dem niggers did have. Dey kisses when dey fin' a red year an' atter dat dey pops some popcorn an' dey dances ter de music of de banjo which Uncle Jed am a-playin'. Dey dances all night de best I can 'member.

"I seed a few Yankees, but dey wus just lookin' fer something ter eat. We ain't knowed nothin' 'bout freedom, but de Yankees tol' us dat we ort ter be free, dey also said dat we ort ter have meat an' stuff in de smokehouse. My mammy sez dat dey ain't got good sense an' she tells marse what dey said.

"De Yankees has done tuck all de rations so dar ain't nothin' lef' fer de niggers ter take but mammy tells Marse Haywood what dey sez anyhow. Marse Haywood sez dat iffen he ketch any niggers in his smokehouse dat he'll skin 'em alive. He also sez dat we ain't free an' dat we ain't never gwine ter be free.

"De nex' year, atter de war, wus a hard year. We ain't had nothin' ter eat but hardtack an' 'lasses an' sometimes not half enough of dat. My pappy still farmed fer Marse Haywood, but hit ain't as good as it is in slavery days.

"Seberal years atter dat, while we wus livin' on Davie Street, I met Frank Spikes an' I married him. I can't tell yo' much 'bout our love-makin' case hit warn't much, but he always called me 'honey gal' an' he axed me ter marry him in de kitchen while I was washin' dishes. He jist puts his arms 'round me an' he sez, 'I wants ter marry yo', honey gal.'

"Well we gits married by de Baptist preacher in Raleigh fifty odd years ago an' we lives tergether till dis past March, when he dies.

"Other boys comed ter see me but I ain't loved none of dem but Frank. He ain't never whupped me but onct an' dat wus fer sassin' him, an' I reckin dat I needed dat.

"We had five chilluns an' I'se stayin' wid my daughter since he died, but I misses him, yes mam, I misses him purty awful."

EH

| | |
|---|---|
| **N.C. District:** | No. 2 |
| **Worker:** | T. Pat Matthews |
| **No. Words:** | 817 |
| **Subject:** | ANNIE STEPHENSON |
| **Person Interviewed:** | Annie Stephenson |
| **Editor:** | G.L. Andrews |

[TR: Date stamp: AUG 6 1937]

# ANNIE STEPHENSON

80 years old
1813 Rosewood Ave.
Richmond, Va.

Now at 717 Saunder's Street
Raleigh, N.C.

"I wus born in Hillsboro, N.C. I 'longed to Charles Holman and my missus wus named Rachel. He owned a plantation near Hillsboro. It wus a mighty big plantation in Orange County, an' he had a good many slaves on dat place. We had tolerable good food an' log cabins and clothes dat you wove in de loom. Home-wove cloth. We had no feather bed. We did not know nuthin' 'bout feather beds. Slaves like dat had bunks an' some slept on de floor. We went barefooted most of the time. Slave shoes had wooden bottoms on 'em. Chilluns wus not give shoes at our place till dey wus big enough to work.

"I 'member seein' de Yankees. Dey wore blue clothes an had brass buttons on 'em. De only work I done wus to sweep yards an' nurse small chilluns. I done very little heavy work. My mother wus named Nicy Oldman an' she worked in de field. My father wus named Billy Briggs, cause he 'longed to the Briggs family. I do not 'member seein' my father but one time. I never seen a slave sold or whupped, but I heard tell of it. My mother tole me 'bout marster whuppin' so severe. We had a rough boss. He had two colored foremen. Dey were slaves who 'longed to marster.

"Dere wus no patches allowed to any of the slaves, an' none of 'em had any money.

"We wus not allowed to have any prayer meetin's. Mother said she never knowed one on de plantation.

"Dere wus a lot of talk 'bout de patterollers but marster done his own sneakin' around. He done a lot of eavesdroppin'. My mother said when dey tho't he wus asleep he wus awake. He wus strict on his slaves an' I didn't know what church wus. No books of any kind wus allowed to slaves an' I can't read an' write.

"They give two days Christmas. Mother said dat had always been marster's rule.

"I 'member de cornshuckin's. Dey lasted two or three days. Dere wus enough slaves to shuck de corn. Dey had plenty of cider at corn shuckin's an' a lot better things to eat den at other times. Marster made corn, peas, an' tobacco on de farm, mostly corn. Dey had plenty hogs an' dat wus a time when dey killed 'em. Dryin' up de fat for lard, trimmin' an' saltin' de meat an' chitlins. De hog guts wus called chitlins. Slaves wus allowed to eat meats as soon as de hogs wus gutted. Dey wus allowed to boil some lean parts of de meat an' eat it at de killin's.

"We played base an' hide an' jumpin' when I wus a chile.

"When we got right smart an' sick we had a doctor. When we wus not mighty sick, we took tea made of catnip, sassafras, an' roots.

"Yes, I 'member when dey tole us we wus free. Mother got up de chilluns to leave. She got just a few clothes. I 'member seein' my uncle come to de house an' put up de horse. He put 'im in de stable an' we all lef' together. We went to my uncle 'bout five miles away on his marster's plantation. His marster wus named Harvey Roundtree. We stayed there three weeks, den we went to a white man's place, Bill Gates. We stayed there several years. Mother had six chilluns. Three wus boun' out for dere victuals an' clothes an' three wus with her.

"We come to Wake County when I wus fully grown. We come in a covered wagon. I saw father one time to 'member him. He died before de war closed, an' mother never married again. We went to Mr. Jeff Upchurch of Wake County an' worked on his farm. We stayed there ten or twelve years an' I married while we wus there. I married Albert Stephenson. We stayed right on there about six years after we married. We then went to Mr. Lonnie Stephen's place, the man who onct owned my husband's father. We stayed there two years workin' as day hands, then we rented a farm from Mr. Joe Smith. Dis wus de fust time any of us had ever farmed for ourselves. We kept it up until old age made us unable to farm an' all de chilluns had got grown an' lef' us.

"We had thirteen chilluns, an' six is livin' yet. My husband died two years ago dis comin' August.

"Slavery from what I knows an' whats been tole me wus a mighty bad thing. Don' see how some of de slaves stood it. I never did min' work but I is unable to work now. I has got a good will but I is worn out. De only way I lives is by goin' 'round 'mong my people. I have no home of my own."

LE

N.C. District:     No. 2
Worker:            Mary A. Hicks
No. Words:         1519
Subject:           SAM T. STEWART, EX-SLAVE
Person Interviewed: Sam T. Stewart
Editor:            Daisy Bailey Waitt

[TR: Date stamp: JUN 1 1937]

Sam T. Stewart

# SAM T. STEWART

[HW: 84 years.]

"My name is Sam T. Stewart. I was born in Wake County, North Carolina Dec. 11, 1853. My father was a slave, A.H. Stewart, belonging to James Arch Stewart, a slave owner, whose plantation was in Wake County near what is now the Harnett County line of Southern Wake. Tiresa was my mother's name. James Arch Stewart, a preacher, raised my father, but my mother was raised by Lorenzo Franks, a Quaker in Wake County. When I was two years old James Arch Stewart sold my father to speculators, and he was shipped to Mississippi. I was too young to know my father.

"The names of the speculators were—Carter Harrison, and—, and a man named Roulhac. I never saw my father again, but I heard from him the second year of the surrender, through his brother and my aunt. My father died in Mississippi.

"The speculators bought up Negroes as a drover would buy up mules. They would get them together by 'Negro drivers', as the white men employed by the speculators were called. Their names were,——Jim Harris of Raleigh, and——yes, Dred Thomas, who lived near Holly Springs in Wake County. Wagon trains carried the rations on the trip to Mississippi. The drivers would not start until they had a large drove. Then the slaves were fastened together with chains. The chain was run between them, when they had been lined up like soldiers in double file. A small chain was attached to a Negro on the left and one to the Negro on the right and fastened to the main chain in the center. Billy Askew was another speculator. He lived on the corner of Salisbury and Carbarrus Street in Raleigh. Sometimes as many as thirty slaves were carried in a drove. They walked to Mississippi.

"My brothers and sisters are dead. Down on the plantations our houses were built of poles daubed with mud, with a rived board (split board). I had good beds, good clothes, and plenty to eat. We made it and we ate it. When a slave owner treated his slaves unusually good some other slave owner would tell him that he was raising slaves who would rise against him. Lorenzo Franks, who owned me and my mother, was a Quaker. He treated his slaves unusually well. He would not sell any of them. His brother was an Iron Side Baptist preacher, and he would tell his brother he was raising slaves who would rise against him. Franks owned seventeen slaves, I don't know how many Stewart owned."

[HW: m p. 6] [TR: Editor indicated three paragraphs on page 6 (page 322 of the volume) should have been moved here.]

"I did farm work in slavery time. I earned no money except what we made on patches. These patches were given to my mother by my master. We caught birds and[Pg 319] game, sent it to town, and sold it for money. We caught birds and partridges in traps. Our master would bring them to town, sell them for us, and give us the money. We had a lot of possums and other game to eat. We got our food out of the big garden planted for the whole shebang. My master overseered his plantation.

"We didn't think much of the poor white man. He was down on us. He was driven to it, by the rich slave owner. The rich slave owner wouldn' let his Negroes sociate with poor white folks. Some of the slave owners, when a poor white man's land joined theirs and they wanted his place would have their Negroes steal things and carry them to the poor white man, and sell them to him. Then the slave owner, knowing where the stuff was, (Of course the slave had to do what his master told him.) would go and find his things at the poor white man's house. Then he would claim it, and take out a writ for him, but he would give him a chance. He would tell him to sell out to him, and leave, or take the consequences. That's the way some of the slave owners got such large tracks of lands.

"The free Negro was a child by a white man and a colored woman, or a white woman and a Negro slave. A child by a white man and a Negro woman was set free when the man got ready. Sometimes he gave the free Negro slaves. Oscar Austin, an issue, was set free and given slaves by his master and daddy. Old man Oscar Austin lived by the depot in Raleigh. He is dead now.

"When a child by a Negro man slave and a white woman arrived he could not be made a slave, but he was bound out until he was 21 years old. The man, who ever wanted him, had him bound to him by the courts and was his gardeen until he was 21 years old. He could not be made a slave if he was born of a free woman. There were jails for slaves called dungeons; the windows were small. Slaves were put into jail for misdemeanors until court was held, but a white man could not be kept there over 30 days without giving bond. Whites and slaves were kept in the same jail house, but in separate rooms.

"They never taught me to read and write; and most slaves who got any reading and writing certainly stole it. There were rules against slaves having books. If the patterollers caught us with books they would whip us. There were whipping posts on the plantation but patterollers tied Negroes across fences to whip them. There was no church on the plantation. We had prayer meetings in the cabins. We had big times at corn shuckings and dances. We all had plenty of apple and peach brandy but very few got drunk. I never saw a nigger drunk until after the surrender. We went to the white folks' church. We were partitioned off in the church.

"The patterollers visited our house every Saturday night, generally. We set traps to catch the patterollers. The patterollers were poor white men. We stretched grape vines across the roads, then we would run from them. They would follow, and get knocked off their horses. I knew many of the patterollers. They are mostly dead. Their children, who are living now in Wake County and Raleigh, are my best friends, and I will therefore not tell who they were. I was caught by the patterollers in Raleigh.

"I would have been whipped to pieces if it hadn't been for a white boy about my age by the name of Thomas Wilson. He told them I was his nigger, and they let me go. We had brought a load of lightwood splints in bundles to town on a steer cart. This was near the close of the war. We had sold out one load of splints had had been paid for them in Confederate money. We had several bills. We went into a bar and bought a drink, each paying one dollar a drink, or two dollars for two small drinks. The bar was in the house where the Globe Clothing Store is now located on the corner of Wilmington and Exchange Streets. Just as I swallowed my drink a constable grabbed me by the back of the neck, and started with me to the guard house, where they done their whippin'. Down at the guard house Nick Denton, the bar tender, told Thomas Wilson 'Go, tell the constable that is your nigger'. Thomas came running up crying, and told the constable I was his nigger. The constable told him to take me and carry me on home or he would whip both of us. We then hitched our ox to the cart and went home."

[TR: The editor indicated with lines that the following three paragraphs should be moved to page 2 of this interview (page 318 of the volume).]

"When I was a child I played marbles, 'Hail over', and bandy, a game played like golf. In striking the ball we knocked it at each other. Before we hit the ball we would cry, 'Shins, I cry', then we would knock the ball at our playmates. Sometime we used rocks for balls.

"We got Christmas holidays from Christmas to New Years day. This was also a time when slaves were hired out or sold. You were often put on the auction block at Christmas. There was a whipping post, an auction block, and jail located on Court House Square where the news stand is now located on Fayetteville Street. There was a well in the yard.

"We were treated by doctors when sick. We were given lots of herbs.

"I do not believe in ghosts.

"I did not feel much elated over hearing I was free, I was afraid of Yankee soldiers. Our mistress told us we were free. I farmed first year after the war. We had no horses, the Yankees had taken the horses, and some of us made a crap with grubbing hoes.

"I think Abraham Lincoln was a man who aimed to do good, but a man who never got to it. I cannot say anymore than that his intentions were good, and if he had lived he would have done more good."

[HW: —— Insert from p. 6.]

N.C. District:      No. 2
Worker:             Mary A. Hicks
No. Words:          326
Subject:            Ex-slave recollections
Person Interviewed: Emma Stone
Editor:             Daisy Bailey Waitt

[TR: Date stamp: JUN 7 1937]

# Ex-Slave Recollections

**An interview with Emma Stone, 77 of Heck's-Town, Durham, Durham County. May 21, 1937.**

"My mammy wuz a Free Issue an' my pappy belonged ter de Bells in Chatham County. Pappy wuz named Edmund Bell, mammy wuz named Polly Mitchel. My sisters wuz Fanny, Jane, Ann, Josephine, Narcissus, and Cressie. My brothers wuz Lizah, Hilliard an' another one, but I doan 'member his name.

"Yo' knows dat I doan 'member much, but I does know dat days on de plantation wuz happy. When my mammy married pappy she moved ter de Bell's plantation so we chilluns, long wid her, wuz lak de udder slaves.

"De missus gib us her old hoop skirts ter play in an' we played nigh 'bout all de time. We wuz doin' dis when de Yankees comed by. Dey drives dere hosses up ter de gate an' dey says dat dey is lookin' fer Wheeler's Cavalry. We knows dat it done pass dar de day 'fore, but we is too skeered ter say a thing.

"De Yankees stays 'round dar fer a little while, an' dey gathers rations, den dey goes on atter Wheeler. We uster sing a song 'bout Wheeler's Cavalry but I only 'members dat it went lak dis:

"'Wheeler's Wheeler's Cav—al—ry,Marchin' on de battlefieldWheeler's Wheeler's Cav—al—ryMarchin' on de battlefield.'

"It wuz really a game we played, while we marched an' pranced an' beat on tin pans. De missus ain't carin' case we is bein' true ter de south she thinks. Shucks we doan care nothin' 'bout Wheeler 'cept what we hyar, an dat ain't so good. We doan keer 'bout de Yankees nother, case we is skeered of dem.

"I hyard grown folkses praisen' Lincoln but I doan know much 'bout him. I doan know nothin' much 'bout none of it, but I does know dat it wuz on a Sunday dat de picket wuz lookin' fer Wheeler an' dat we wuz playin' hide an' seek."

N.C. District: No. 2
Worker: Mary A. Hicks
No. Words: 848
Subject: WILLIAM SYKES
Person Interviewed: William Sykes
Editor: Daisy Bailey Waitt

William Sykes

# WILLIAM SYKES
Ex-Slave Story

**An interview with William Sykes 78, of State prison, Raleigh, N.C.**

"My mammy Martha an' me we 'longed ter Mister Joshua Long in Martin County, an' my paw, Henry 'longed ter Squire Ben Sykes in Tyrell County. Squire Sykes lived in what wus called Gum Neck, an' he owned a hundert slaves or more an' a whole passel of lan'.

"I lived wid my mammy in Martin County from de fust dat I could 'member, me an' my brothers, Henry, Benjamin an' Columbus, an' my sisters Hester, Margaret, Lucy an' Susan.

"I doan 'member so much what happen 'fore de war, of course, but I does 'member a heap of little things. I knows dat Mister Long an' Mis' Catherine wus good ter us an' I 'members dat de food an' de clothes wus good an' dat dar wus a heap o' fun on holidays.

"Most o' de holidays wus celebrated by eatin' candy, drinkin' wine an 'brandy. Dar wus a heap o' dancin' ter de music of banjoes an' han' slappin'.

"We had co'n shuckin's, an' prayer meetin's, an' sociables an' singin's. I went swimmin' in de crick, went wid ole Joe Brown, a-possum huntin', an' coon huntin', an' I sometimes went a-fishin'.

"When de Yankees comed dey come a tearin'. Dey ain't done so bad in our neighborhood, case hit warn't so full of de 'infernal Rebs', as de Yankees said. Dey tooked de bes' o' eber'thing do' but dey ain't doin' so much deruction. Dey eben buyed terbacker from my mammy, an' dey paid her a dollar an' fifty cents a pound, stim an' all.

"Dey paid her wid shin plasters, which wus green paper money, an' de fust dat eber I seed.

"We slaves wus skeerd o' de Yankees, an' fer some reason I got sent ter paw at Squire Sykes' house in Tyrell County.

"Squire Sykes come stompin' in one day an' he says ter my paw, 'Henry, dem damm Yankees am comin' ter take my niggers 'way from me, an' I ain't gwine ter stan' fer hit nother. Le's you an' me take dese niggers an' march straight ter de Blue Ridge mountains, an' up dar in dem mountains dar won't be no trouble, case dey won't dare come up dar atter us.'

"Wal, we got on de march fer de mountains an' we march on ter Judge Clayton Moore's grandfather's place in Mitchell County, whar we camps fer seberal days.

"While we wus dar one day, an' while Mr. Jim Moore, de Jedge's daddy am in town de missus axes my cousin Jane ter do de washin'.

"Jane says dat she has got ter do her own washin' an dat she'll wash fer de missus termorrer. De missus says 'you ain't free yit, I wants you ter know.'

"'I knows dat I's not but I is gwine ter be free', Jane says.

"De missus ain't said a word den, but late Sadday night Mr. Jim he comes back from town an' she tells him 'bout hit.

"Mr. Jim am some mad an' he takes Jane out on Sunday mornin' an' he beats her till de blood runs down her back.

"De patterollers wus thick dem days, Mr. Joe Jones wus our regular patteroller an' he gibe us de very debil.

"A few days atter Jane got her beatin' we marches away. De wimen am left at Jamesville but us mens an' boys, we marches on ter Buncombe County an' we ain't seed no mo' Yankees.

"Atter de war my paw an' mammy went ter live on Mr. Moore's plantation an' we had a hard time. A whole heap o' times I has had nothin' ter eat but one cupful o' peas an' a hunk of co'nbread all day long. A white lady, Mis' Douglas give me a quart of milk eber Sunday, but I had ter walk three miles fer hit.

"We ain't wucked none in slavery days ter what we done atter de war, an' I wisht dat de good ole slave days wus back.

"Dar's one thing, we ole niggers wus raised right an' de young niggers ain't. Iffen I had my say-so dey'd burn down de nigger schools, gibe dem pickanninies a good spankin' an' put 'em in de patch ter wuck, ain't no nigger got no business wid no edgercation nohow.

"Yes'um, dey says dat I is a murderer". Uncle William stroked his long white beard. "I runned from dis young nigger seberal times, an' I wus tryin' ter run wid my knife what I had been whittlin' wid open in my han'. I wus skeerd nigh ter death, so when he grabs me I throw up my han's an' in a minute he falls. I breshes de blood offen my coat, thinkin' dat he has hurt me, an' I sees de blood pourin' from de jugular vein.

"I has sarved ten months o' my sentence which dey gived me, three ter five years fer manslaughter; what could I do? I stood up an' I said, 'Thank you, Jedge.'"

L.E.

N.C. District:        No. 2
Worker:               Mary A. Hicks
No. Words:            503
Subject:              ANNIE TATE
Person Interviewed:   Annie Tate
Editor:               Daisy Bailey Waitt

# ANNIE TATE
# Ex-Slave Story

**An interview with Annie Tate 73 of 624 S. Harrington Street, Raleigh, N.C.**

"I wuz a year old when de war wuz ober but of course I ain't knowin' nothin' 'bout slavery 'cept what my mammy said, an' dat ain't so much.

"I reckon dat it wuz a brother of Calvin Jones dat my mammy belonged ter, anyhow, it wuz at Wake Forest. My mammy wuz Rosa Jones till she married Phil Perry, my pappy.

"My mammy's mammy, who also belonged ter de Jones family killed herself 'cause dey sold her husban'. Mammy said dat she wuz eight or ten years old at de time.

"Old marster wuz very fond of my grandpaw an' he wouldn't 'low de oberseer ter beat him, but ole marster went off on a trip an' he left young marster in charge of de big farm an' de whole slue o' slaves dat he owns.

"One day atter ole marster wuz gone de oberseer tried ter run de hawg over gran'paw an' wuz cussin' him scan'lous. Gran'paw cussed back at him an' den de oberseer started ter beat him. Gran'paw drawed de hoe back ober his haid an' tells him dat if'en he comes a step closter dat he am gwine ter bust his haid open. De oberseer comes on an' de hoe 'cends on his haid choppin' hit wide open.

"Ole marster ain't dar so young marster makes seberal of de slaves hold him while he lashes him wid de cowhide. He cuts his back all ter pieces an' den he throws him in de barn, chained down ter de flo'.

"Gran'mammy snuke out ter see him an' whisper ter him through de cracks, but one night she goes out dar ter de barn an' he am gone. She runs ter young marster an' axes him whar am gran'paw an' he tells her dat he am sold ter a man from Mississippi an' dat if'en she whimpers 'bout him sellin' de black bastard dat he will whup her, den wash her down wid vinegar, red pepper an' salt.

"Pore gran'maw am nigh 'bout crazy so she walks off'en de plantation. Down on de aidge of de plantation runs de Neuse so gran'maw gits dar, an' jumps in.

"My mammy am little an' she ain't got no brothers an' sisters so de missus takes her in de house wid her. Dey said dat de ole marster had a fit most when he fin's out 'bout what been done dar while he am gone, so he am extra good ter mammy.

"At de surrender he calls his niggers in an' he says dat he will give 'em permission ter libe on de riber plantation, dey can build deir shacks dar an' live dar durin' dere life time. Some of dem does dis, an' fer seberal years dey stays on dar. Mammy said dat he tol' de Ku Kluxes ter stay off'en his lan' too, dat he could manage his own niggers."

L.E.

N.C. District: No. 2
Worker: T. Pat Matthews
No. Words: 1258
Subject: R.S. TAYLOR
Story teller: R.S. Taylor
Editor: Daisy Bailey Waitt

# R.S. TAYLOR

**710 South McDowell Street**

"My name is Ransom Sidney Taylor. I was borned in slavery the 5th day of January, 1857. Adam Taylor was my father and Mary Taylor my mother. My brothers were: William H., Jesse, and Louis; sisters: Virginia, Annie, and Isabella; all born in slavery. We all belonged to John Cane. He owned a plantation on Ramkatte Road[5] near Yates Mill, between Yates Mill and Penny's Mill. There was a whiskey still at Penny's Mill.

"There were sixty slaves in all, but Marster only kept seven on the plantation with him at Yates Mill. Marster's sister Mary was our missus after he died. He died before the surrender. The war was going on when he died. He was a Northern man. His sister came down to the funeral from New York and then went back, then she came back to settle up the estate. She stayed here a long time then. She told all the slaves they were free. That was about the close of the war.

"Marster John Cane was buried in the Catholic Graveyard in Raleigh. His wife had died in the North, so my mother told me. We had plenty of something to eat, beans, peas, butter milk and butter and molasses and plenty o' flour.[6] We made the wheat on the plantation and other things to eat. We didn't have clothes like they have now but we had plenty o' good and warm wove clothes. Our shoes had wooden bottoms, but were all right.

"We had prayer meetings on the plantation and at times we went to the white folks' church. Marster was a Catholic, but we went to the Methodist Church[7], Edenton Street Methodist Church. My marster would not allow anyone to whip his Negroes. If they were to be whipped he did it himself and the licks he gave them would not hurt a flea. He was good to all of us and we all loved him.

"We called our parents pappy and mammy most o' the time. My marster looked like you, jes' the same complection and about your size. He weighed around 200 pounds had curly hair like yours and was almost always smiling like you. My marster was an Irishman from the North. Mother and father said he was one o' the best white men that ever lived. I remember seein' him settin' on the porch in his large arm chair. He called me 'Lonnie', a nickname. He called me a lot to brush off his shoes. I loved him he was so good.

"Our overseer was named John H. Whitelaw. He got killed at the Rock Quarry near the Federal Cemetery when they were carrying a boiler to the Rock Quarry a long time after the surrender about 14 or 15 years ago. He and John were standing on the side of the boiler and the boiler turned over and killed both of 'em. Marster's overseer was bad to us after marster died. Nothing we could do would suit him, and he whipped the Negroes. We never heard the word Negroes until we moved to Raleigh after the surrender. They called us niggers and colored folks.

"We were darin' to have a book to study. It was against the Confederates' rules at dat time, but marster called us in to have prayer meeting on Sunday mornings.

"I have seen patterollers. Dey had' em but not when my marster was living. Dey didn't come around den, but when he died dey come around every night; we never knowed when dey was comin', you know.

"I never saw a slave really whipped. Marster would switch a slave sometime, but it was a matter o' nothing 'cause he didn't hurt much.

"We had good houses and plenty o' good places to sleep, and we fared fine in slavery time. We called marster's house with its long porch the 'dwelling house'. When the Yankees came through they told us we were free and we didn't have to work for the Johnnies no more.

"We got everything all right on the plantation near Yates Mill, then we moved to Raleigh.

"My mammy belonged to old Captain Hunter before she was married to pappy. When she got married the Taylors bought her, and she and pappy stayed with the Taylors. As soon as we got the plantation fixed up, we moved to Raleigh and mammy and pappy went back to her white folks, the Hunters. My father was a carpenter by trade, and a preacher. He preached at St. Paul's Church on the corner of Harrington and Edenton Streets. We lived in Raleigh all our lives except Annie. She went to Brooklyn, New York and died there about four years ago.

"I thinned corn, and turned potato vines, and helped look after and feed the stock. Our marsters gave us some money, five and ten cents at a time. That's the only way we got any money.

"We caught rabbits, hunting in the day time, and possums, hunting at night. We hunted on holidays. We had holidays at lay-by time, and the 4th of July. When we caught up with the work we had nothing to do. We got Christmas holidays.

"I never saw a slave sold and none never ran away. We went fishing in Swift Creek. I never saw a jail for slaves and never saw any in chains. We played push and spin on the plantation.

"My mother looked after most of us when we were sick. She used roots, herbs, and grease, and medicine the overseer got in town. When my mother got through rubbin' you, you would soon be well.

"When I first saw the Yankees I was afraid of 'em. It was a curiosity to see 'em comin' through the fields with dem guns and things. They come down and talked with us and told us we were free and then I was not so scared of 'em.

"I married Francis [HW: corrected to Frances] Lipton in 1885. We were married at the end of McDowell Street at Mr. Chester's home. Just a quiet wedding with about 30 friends present. I didn't think a thing about slavery while we fared mighty well; but it was bad on other plantations.

"I don't know anything about Booker T. Washington, nor Jefferson Davis, but I know Jim Young. He was a Negro politician. I do not know much about Lincoln or Roosevelt.

"De[8] Yankees jes' shot hogs and cows and took everything on de plantation dey wanted. I can see 'em now runnin' chickens. Dere was an old rooster, he said, 'Cluck, cluck, cluck cluck,' as he run. Dey shot his head off and he turned somersets awhile, and rolled over dead. Jes' seemed lak if dem Yankees pointed a gun at a chicken or hog dey would roll over dead. Dey had live geese tied on their hosses. One ole gander would say, 'Quack, quack, quack,' as the hoss stepped along and jarred him. Some o' de Yankee soldiers were carrying hams of hogs on deir bayonets. Dat wus a time, Lawsy, Lawsy, a time.

One ole hen, she had sense. When de Yankees were killin' de res' o' de chickens she ran for de piney woods and hid dere and stayed till de Yankees left Raleigh; den she come home. Mammy caught her and raised about forty chickens off her in Raleigh."

BN

## FOOTNOTES:

[5] [HW: Ramsgate Road—nicknamed Ramcat or Rhamkatte in derision of Governor Tryon.]

[6] Yates Mill was a flour mill.

[7] [HW: St. Paul's A.M.E. Methodist Church moved to Edenton St. site in 1853, formerly old Christ Church building.]

[8] The Negroes interviewed frequently speak fairly correctly at first but when they begin to talk of old times lapse into dialect.

N.C. District: No. 2
Worker: T. Pat Matthews
No. Words: 1177
Subject: ELIAS THOMAS
Person Interviewed: Elias Thomas
Editor: G.L. Andrews

[TR: Date stamp: AUG 6 1937]

# ELIAS THOMAS

**84 years of age**
**521 Cannon Ave., Raleigh, N.C.**

"I was here when the Civil war was goin' on an' I am 84 years old. I was born in Chatham County on a plantation near Moncure, February 1853.

"My marster was named Baxter Thomas and missus was named Katie. She was his wife. I don't know my father's name, but my mother was named Phillis Thomas.

"It took a smart nigger to know who his father was in slavery time. I just can remember my mother. I was about four or five years old when she died.

"My marster's plantation was fust the 'Thomas Place'. There was about two hundred acres in it with about one hundred acres cleared land. He had six slaves on it.

"When I was eight years old he bought the Boylan place about two miles from his first home and he moved there. There was about one thousand acres of land of it all with about three hundred acres cleared for farming. On the Thomas place his house had six rooms, on the Boylan place the house had eight rooms. He brought in more slaves and took over all the slaves after John Boylan died.

"John Boylan never married. He was a mighty hard man to git along with, an' Marster Baxter Thomas was about the only one who could do anything with him when he had one of his mad spells. They were no blood relation but marster got possession of his property when he died. It was fixed that way.

"We called the slave houses 'quarters'. They were arranged like streets about two hundred yards on the northside of the great house.

"Our food was purty good. Our white folks used slaves, especially the children, as they did themselves about eatin'. We all had the same kind of food. All had plenty of clothes but only one pair of shoes a year. People went barefooted a lot then more than they do now. We had good places to sleep, straw mattresses and chickenfeather beds and feather bolsters. A bolster reached clear across the head of the bed.

"We worked from sun to sun with one hour and a half to rest at noon or dinner time. I was so small I did not do much heavy work. I chopped corn and cotton mostly. The old slaves had patches they tended, and sold what they made and had the money it brought. Everybody eat out of the big garden, both white and black alike. Ole missus wouldn't allow us to eat rabbits but she let us catch and eat possums. Missus didn't have any use for a rabbit.

"Sometimes we caught fish with hooks in Haw River, Deep River, and the Cape Fear, and when it was a dry time and the water got low we caught fish in seines.

"My marster only had two children, both boys, Fred, and John. John was about my age and Fred was about two years older. They are both dead. My marster never had any overseers, he made boss men out of his oldest slaves.

"We thought well of the poor white neighbors. We colored children took them as regular playmates. Marster's boys played with 'em too and marster gave them all the work he could. He hired both men an women of the poor white class to work on the plantation. We all worked together. We had a good time. We worked and sang together and everybody seemed happy. In harvest time a lot of help was hired and such laughing, working and singing. Just a good time in general. We sang the songs 'Crossin' over Jordan' and 'Bound for the Promised Land'.

"I never saw a jail for slaves but I have seen slaves whipped. I saw Crayton Abernathy, a overseer, whip a woman in the cotton patch on Doc. Smith's farm, a mile from our plantation. I also saw ole man William Crump, a owner, whip a man and some children. He waited till Sunday morning to whip his slaves. He would git ready to go to church, have his horse hitched up to the buggy and then call his slaves out and whip them before he left for church. He generally whipped about five children every Sunday morning. Willis Crump, a slave was tied up by his thumbs and whipped. His thumbs was in such a bad fix after that they rose and had to be cut open. Willis was whipped after the war closed for asking for his wages and having words with ole man Crump because he would not pay him. They fell out and he called his friends in and they took and tied him and whipped him.

"No books were allowed to slaves in slavery time. I never went to school a minute in my life. I cannot read and write. We had prayermeetings on the plantation about once or twice a week. We went to the white folks church on Sunday. We went to both the Methodist and Presbyterian. The preacher told us to obey our marsters. I remember the baptizings. They baptized in Shattucks Creek and Haw River. I saw a lot of colored folks baptized.

"I do not remember any slaves running away from our plantation but they ran away from ole man Crump's and Richard Faucett's plantations near our plantation. Jacob Faucette ran away from Faucette and Tom Crump ran away from ole man Crump. They ran away to keep from getting a whippin'.

"Colored folks are afraid of bears so one of the slaves who saw Tom Crump at night told him he saw a bear in the woods where he was stayin'. Tom was so scared he came home next morning and took his whippin'. Both came home on account of that bear business and both were whipped.

"When we got sick Dr. Hews, Dr. Wych and Dr. Tom Buckhannan looked after us. A lot of the slaves wore rabbit feet, the front feet, for good luck. They also carried buckeyes.

"I remember the Yankees. I will remember seein' them till I die. I will never forget it. I thought it was the last of me. The white folks had told me the Yankees would kill me or carry me off, so I thought when I saw them coming it was the last of me. I hid in the woods while they were there. They tore up some things but they did not do much damage. They camped from Holly Springs to Avant's Ferry on Cape Fear River. William Cross' plantation was about half the distance. The camp was about thirty miles long. General Logan,[9] who was an old man, was in charge.

"I married Martha Sears when I was 23 years old. I married in Raleigh. My wife died in 1912. We had fourteen children, five are living now.

"When the war closed I stayed on eight years with my marster. I then went to the N.C. State Hospital for the Insane. I stayed there 28 years. That's where I learned to talk like a white man."

LE

**FOOTNOTES:**

[9] HW: Maj.-Gen. John A. Logan, Fifteenth Army Corps (Union.)

N.C. District: 2
Worker: Mary Hicks
No. Words: 260
Subject: MR. BELL'S PLANTATION
Reference: Jacob Thomas
Editor: George L. Andrews

[TR: Date stamp: AUG 6 1937]

# MR. BELL'S PLANTATION

**An interview with Jacob Thomas, 97 years of age, of 1300 South Bloodworth Street, Raleigh, North Carolina.**

"I wus borned in Elberton County, Georgia, on de plantation of Marse Tom Bell. My mammy, Isobel, uster live in North Carolina, but she wus sold from her husban' an' baby an' carried ter Marse Tom's place in Georgia. Atter she got dar she wus married agin an' had me. Dat is I reckin dat she wus married. I never did know my pappy.

"Mammy wus sold in Smithfield on de slave block an' carried off, chained 'hind a wagin. She turn' roun' an' looks back at her husban' who cries an' de oberseer's lash cuts his back, 'case dey ain't 'lowed ter cry at a sale.

"From de time I can fust 'member I wucked on de farm. We planted cane, cotton, corn, an' rice in de low groun's. We ain't had ter wuck so powerful hard an' we am 'lowed a heap of pleasures, but some of us boys wus mean an' we had ter be whupped, lak de time we tied tin cans on de tail of Jinks, marster's fine huntin' dog. De dog near run hisself ter death an' Marse Tom had us whupped fer hit.

"He raised fine hosses too, an' he ain't 'lowed us boys ter git clost ter dem, but one Sunday when Uncle Amos went ter sleep in de shade of de trees roun' de pasture I gits on Lady, one of de fines' young mares, an' I flies away on her.

"She ain't used ter nobody ridin' her bareback so she kicks up quite a rucus but I sets on. Down cross de pasture she goes an' I enjoys hit fine till she steps in a hole an' falls.

"De mare am crippled but I leads her back an' tries ter git away widout anybody seein' me. Ole Amos has woked up dis time an' of course he tells Marse Tom.

"Dat's de wust whuppin' I'se eber had, I'se tellin' yo'. Dey streaked me all ober den dey makes me lay down, chained han' an' foot all de day long. Dat ain't done no good do 'case I rid dem hosses eber'time I got de chance.

"I got married ter Pheobe de year dat de war begun. She wus a slim little brown-skinned gal what look so puny dat yo' jist natu'ally wants ter take care of her. I ain't courted her fer long 'case de marster gives his permission 'fore I axes fer hit. We is married 'fore de magistrate in June 'fore de war begun.

"Near 'bout at de start of de war I wus took ter Atlanta ter he'p buil' de fort an' dar I stays till de Yankees comes a-rippin' an' a-tarin'. Dey shoots de fort ter pieces an' den marches in an' hangs up de ole Stars an' Stripes.

"We had four chilluns den Pheobe died an' lef' me. Atter dis I moves ter Star, South Carolina, an' I marries Rebecca White who also died five years ago an' so I comed ter live wid Roberta.

"I doan know whether slavery am better er not. Most of de niggers claims dat all of de slaves wus good, but I knows better. I done a heap of meanness. An' once atter I done so mean an' got a whuppin' I runned away. Comes night an' I comes back home an' de nex' day I done somethin' er other ter git another whuppin' fer.

"Dar's dis much we ain't worried 'bout livin' den lak we does now, an' dar's dis much fer bein' free, I has got thirteen great-gran'chilluns an' I knows whar dey everyone am. In slavery times dey'd have been on de block long time ago.

"I always thought a lot of Lincoln 'cause he had a heap of faith in de nigger ter think dat he could live on nothin' at all."

EH

N.C. District:     No. 2
Worker:            Mary A. Hicks
No. Words:         397
Subject:           MARGARET THORNTON
Person Interviewed: Margaret Thornton
Editor:            G.L. Andrews

[TR: Date stamp: SEP 10 1937]

# MARGARET THORNTON

**An interview with Margaret Thornton, 77 years old, of Hayti, Four Oaks, North Carolina.**

"I wus borned an' raised on de plantation of Jake Thornton of Harnett County. My mammy, Lula, my pappy, Frank, an' my brother an' sisters an' me all wus dere slaves. De man I finally marries, Tom, am also a slave on de plantation.

"I wus jist five years ole when de Yankees come, jist a few of dem to our settlement. I doan know de number of de slaves, but I does 'member dat dey herded us tergether an' make us sing a heap of songs an' dance, den dey clap dere han's an' dey sez dat we is good. One black boy won't dance, he sez, so dey puts him barefooted on a hot piece of tin an' believe me he did dance.

"I know dat my white folks hated de Yankees like pizen but dey had ter put up wid dere sass jist de same. Dey also had to put up wid de stealin' of dere property what dey had made dere slaves work an' make. De white folks didn't loose dere temper much do', an' dey avoids de Yankees. Now when dey went protrudin' in de house dat am a different matter entirely.

"I wus brung up ter nurse an' I'se did my share of dat, too honey, let me tell you. I has nursed 'bout two thousand babies I reckins. I has nursed gran'maws an' den dere gran' chiles. I reckin dat I has closed as many eyes as de nex' one.

"Atter de war we stayed on, case Marse wus good ter us an' 'cided dat we ain't got nowhar ter go. I stayed on till I wus thirteen or fourteen an' den me an' Tom married. He had a job at a sawmill near Dunn, so dar we went ter live in a new shanty.

"Tom never did want me ter work hard while he wus able ter work, but I nursed babies off an' on all de time he lived. When he wus in his death sickness he uster cry case I had ter take in washin'. Since he's daid I nurses mostly, but sometimes I ain't able ter do nothin'. I hopes ter git my pension pretty soon an' dat'll help a heap when I'm laid up, not able ter turn my han' at nothin'."

LE

N.C. District:   No. II
Worker:          Mrs. W.N. Harriss
Words:           550
Edited:          Mrs. W.N. Harriss
Subject:         Tillie, Daughter of a Slave
Interviewed:     Tillie, Caretaker,
                 Cornwallis Headquarters, corner Third and Market Sts, Wilmington.

## TILLIE, DAUGHTER OF A SLAVE

**Caretaker, Cornwallis Headquarters**
**Corner Third and Market Streets**
**Wilmington, N.C.**

"La, Miss Fannie, what you mean askin' me what I knows about slavery! Why I was bawn yeah's after freedom!" With a sweeping, upward wave of a slender, shriveled brown arm to indicate the wide lapse of time between her advent and the passing of those long ago days. The frail, little body might have been any age between sixty and a hundred; but feminine vanity rose in excited protest against the implication of age suggested by the question.

Tillie is one of the landmarks of Wilmington. She was one of the servants in the house of which she is now caretaker, at the time of the owner's death, and the heirs have kept her on allowing her to live in the old slave quarters in the back garden. She sits in the sun on the coping of the brick wall, or across the street on the low wall of the grounds around St. James Church. Children and their nurses gather there on the lawn, and Tillie holds forth at length on any topic from religion and politics to the cutting or losing of teeth. She makes the bold statement that she can tell you something about everybody in Wilmington. That is "eve'body _we_ knows." There is a general uneasiness that perhaps she can. Little escapes the large, keen, brown eyes, and the ears are perpetually cocked.

After several conversations in passing, memory was coaxed to the time when as a _very_ young child she remembered incidents of slave times which she had heard from her mother.

"My mother belonged to the Bellamys, an' lived on their plantation across the river in Brunswick. It was the bigges' place anywhere hereabouts. I was raised on it too. Of co'se it was in the country, but it was so big we was a town all to ourselves.

"Did any of the colored people leave after freedom? Of co'se they did'n'. Were'nt no place to go to. None of us was 'customed to anybody but rich folks, an' of co'se their money was gone. I've heard Mis' Bellamy tell how her child'en made enough out of potatoes to buy their clo'es right on that plantation. So we all stayed right there. My mother brought us all up right there on the plot she'd been livin' on all the time. When I come along we had plenty to eat. She had a whole pa'cel of us, and we always had plenty of collards, an' po'k an' corn bread. Plenty of fish.

"O, yes, stuff was sold. I can remember timber bein' cut, an' our folks got some wages to buy clo'es. We did'n have no school, but we had a church. Soon as I was big enough I came to Wilmin'ton to work. I never has lived with none but [TR: duplicate "but" crossed out] the bes'. My mother always said 'Tillie, always tie to the bes' white folks. Them that has inflooence, 'cause if you gits into trouble they can git you out'. I've stuck to that. I've never had any traffic wid any but the blue bloods, an' now look at me. I'm not able to work, but I got a home an' plenty to eat. An' I ain't on no relief, an' Tillie can sho' hold her head up."

N.C. District:     No. 2
Worker:            T. Pat Matthews
No. Words:         740
Subject:           ELLEN TRELL
Person Interviewed: Ellen Trell
Editor:            G.L. Andrews

[TR: Date stamp: SEP 10 1937]

# ELLEN TRELL

Age 73
20 McKee St., Raleigh, North Carolina.

"Needham Price owned about fifty slaves, and mother an' I were among that number. He was a very rich man, and owned a large plantation in Wake County, N.C., near the town of Knightdale.

"My father belonged to Tom Bodie way down in Edgecombe County, and mother and I went by the name of Bodie. My father's given name was Haywood. Mother's name was Caroline. The fare was bad in regard to food and clothing, but the slave quarters, though small and shanty-like in appearance, were warm an' dry. The rules were strick and the privileges few. Mother was whipped and scarred by the lash so bad the scars were on her when she died. I have seen them many times.

"There were no books of any kind allowed the slaves and no social gatherings tolerated. Slaves were allowed to go to the white folks church and at times all slaves were carried to services at the church. The preacher told them to obey their marsters and missuses, that the Bible said obey.

"Marster lived in a large house with fourteen rooms, which the slaves called the big house. He had four house servants to do his and missus bidding. They were 'specially trained as Marster did a lot of entertaining in slavery time. Marster and missus had a lot of parties where they served a lot of good[Pg 361] food and various kinds of liquors to their guests. When marster was in his cups he was mighty rough, and any of the slaves who displeased him at these times were liable to get a beating.

"I have heard a lot of talk about ghosts and witches among the colored folks. I have seen a few who had spells put on them by witches. My mother had a spell put on her and she lay in bed talking to herself and sweating draps of sweat as big as the end of my finger. She would groan and say, 'go away evil spirit, go away,' but the spell would not leave her until she went to a white witch-doctor and got cured.

"After the surrender father came up from Edgecombe County and he and mother went and worked with Mr. Ruth Dunn of Wake County. They stayed close, never going out of the county. Mother, after a year of [HW: circle around "of"] two at Mr. Dunn's, began to think about goin' back home. She was free and though her ole marster had treated her rough she loved the missus and said she rather stay with marster Price than anyone else. Father went to see Mr. Price. He told him to tell Caroline to come on back home and that he shure better bring her back. Mother said when she got back home they all had a general good time cooking, eating, and laughing. Marster tole her he never wanted her to leave him again. Mother said she was so full of gladness she could not reply so she just stood there and cried.

Marster walked off. Mother took charge of the house and father jist about took[Pg 362] possession of the farm. He looked after the stock, all the farm tools, kept plenty of wood on the wood pile all the year roun'.

"Father and mother carried the keys and acted like the place belonged to them. They got most of the slaves who were agreeable to come back. Marster gave them work and he loafed and prospered. Because he trusted the Negroes so much they felt the responsibility put upon them, and they worked for his interests.

"Mother and father stayed there until they died. I stayed with father and mother until I married Badger Farrell then we stayed in a cabin on the plantation several years. Most of my life was spent near Knightdale, Wake County, until my husband died fifteen years ago. I had eight children, four girls and four boys. They are all dead except one, a boy, whom I have lived with in Raleigh since my husband died.

"I think slavery was a bad thing. This story is the things my mother and father told me of slavery and my own observations since I became old enough to remember the general happenings. Mother said the place which had been a place of torture in slavery days turned out to be a haven of rest after slavery, a home where peace, plenty and contentment reigned supreme."

LE

N.C. District:     No. 2
Worker:            T. Pat Matthews
No. Words:         760
Subject:           HENRY JAMES TRENTHAM
Person Interviewed: Henry James Trentham
Editor:            G.L. Andrews

## HENRY JAMES TRENTHAM

**Raleigh, N.C. Rt. 2**
**Age 92 years**

"I wus born de second day of December 1845. Dat would make me 92 years of age. I wus born on a plantation near Camden, S.C. I belonged to Dr. Trentham and my missus wus named Elizabeth. My father wus named James Trentham and mother wus named Lorie. I had two brothers and one sister. We all belonged to Dr. Trentham.

"Marster's plantation wus a awful big plantation with 'bout four hundred slaves on it. It wus a short distance from the Wateree River. The slave houses looked like a small town and dere wus grist mills for corn, cotton gin, shoe shops, tanning yards, and lots of looms for weavin' cloth. Most of de slaves cooked at dere own houses, dat dey called shacks. Dey wus give a 'lowance of rations every week. De rations wus tolerably good, jest bout like people eat now. Dere wus a jail on de place for to put slaves in, an in de jail dere wus a place to put your hands in called stocks. Slaves wus put dere for punishment.

"I seed lots of slaves whupped by de overseers. Marster had four overseers on de place an' dey drove us from sunup till sunset. Some of de women plowed barefooted most all de time, an' had to carry dat row an' keep up wid de men, an' den do dere cookin' at night.

"We hated to see de sun rise in slavery time cause it meant anudder hard day, but den we was glad to see it go down.

"Marster lived in a large two story house wid 'bout twelve rooms in it. We called it de plantation house. Dere wus a church on de plantation an' both white an' black went to preachin' dere. Dere wus Sunday School dere too. De preacher tole us to obey our missus an' marster. He tole us we must be obedient to 'em. Yes sir, dat's what he tole us. Some of de slaves run away. When dey wus caught dey wus whupped and put in de stocks in de jail. Some of de slaves dat run away never did come back. De overseers tole us dey got killed reason dey never come back.

"De patterollers come round ever now an' den an' if you wus off de plantation an' had no pass dey tore you up wid de lash.

"Marster an' missus rode around in a carriage drawn by two horses and driven by a driver. Dey had four women to work in de house as cooks, maids, an' de like.

"No huntin' wus allowed a slave if no white man wus wid 'im, an' dey wus not allowed to carry guns.

"De corn shuckin's was a great time. Marster give good licker to everybody den. When anybody shucked a red ear he got a extra drink of whiskey. We had big suppers den an' a good time at corn shuckin's. Atter de shuckin' at nite [HW: night] dere would be a wrastlin' match to see who was bes' on de plantation. We got a week holliday at Xmas. Den wus de time shoes wus give to[Pg 366] de slaves, an' de good times generally lasted a week. At lay-by time wus another big time. Dat wus 'bout de Fourth of July. Dey give a big dinner an' everbody et all de barbecue an' cake dey wanted.

"I saw slaves sold at Camden. Marster carried some slaves dere an' put 'em on de auction block an' sold 'em. I wus carried but I wus not sold. I went with the old doctor. I wus his pet. Dey carried slaves away from de plantation in chains. Dey carried five or six at a time. If a nigger didn't suit him he sold him.

"Missus didn't like for him to beat 'em so much no how. De old doctor had three boys, William, Sidney and Henry and two girls, Missie and Carrie.

"Dey would not allow slaves no books an' I can't read an' write. I did not git any learnin.

"When a slave died dere wus only a few to go to de buryin. Dey didn't have time to go, dey wus so busy workin'. De slaves wus burried in plain wood boxes which wus made by slave men on de plantation. Our marster looked atter us when we got sick.

"I married Ella Davis 31 years ago in South Carolina, near Camden. We had twelve chilluns, six boys and six girls.

"Slavery wus pretty rough and I am glad it is all over."

N.C. District:       No. 2
Worker:              T. Pat Matthews
No. Words:           631
Subject:             JANE ANNE PRIVETTE UPPERMAN
Person Interviewed:  Jane Anne Privette Upperman
Editor:              G.L. Andrews

[TR: Date stamp: AUG 4 1937]

## JANE ANN PRIVETTE UPPERMAN

**74 years old, of 330 West South Street.**

"I wusn't livin in Raleigh when my mother wus freed from slavery. We wus livin' in Nash County right near the border of Wake County. We belonged to Shirley Brantly. Our missus wus named Penina.

"I wus born a slave, but I wus only 'bout two years old at de time of de surrender. I am 74 now. I wus born in April. I had my age in a Bible, but de book got tore to pieces an' my age got lost.

"We lived on Marster Brantly's plantation an' de slave quarters wus near de great house. Mother said she wurked in de fiel's from sun to sun. Dey did not eat breakfast in de mornin' fore dey went to wurk. It wus cooked an' put on a shelf an' dey had breakfas' at about eleven o'clock in de day. Mother said sometimes de flies got to de meat an' blowed it fore dey could come in to eat it. Mother said de food wus bad an' not fixed right.

"Dere wus a lot of de slaves divided among marsters chillun. I can't remember how many.

"Marster wus a soldier an' when he come an' tole mother she wus free, Missus Penina tole her, 'No, you aint free, you'se got to stay here an' wurk right on.' Marster tole her if she had been through wid what he been through wid she could give mother up as free as takin' a drink of water.

"When de war ended father come an' got ma an' took her on to his marsters plantation. My father wus named Carroll Privette an' my mother wus Cherry Brantly, but after she wus free she begun to call herself by my fathers name, Privette. Father belonged to Jimmie Privette across Tar River from whar ma lived. He lived near a little place named Cascade. We lived there at father's marster's place till most of de chillun wus 'bout grown, den father bought a place in Franklin County from Mr. Jack Griffin. He stayed there long enough to pay for de place; den he sold it an' we moved to Clayton.

"At this time all de older chillun wus married, an' dats what dissatisfied my father. He had nobody to help him wurk. Arch, Frank, an' Dennis wus married. Mary wus married. Two girls an' one boy wus lef' single. Dere wus seben of de chillun. We moved from Clayton to Raleigh. I wus married in Raleigh. I married William Upperman.

"Mother an' faather died in Raleigh. Mother died right here in dis house. My mother an' father couldn't do no writin', but father could read a little. He could read hymns an' de Bible.

"I aint remember nothin' 'bout slavery 'ceptin' what I've heard 'em say. Some said dey had a good time an' liked slavery. Dat wus when dey had good marsters. Den some says dey had a hard time an' didn't like it. Dat wus when dey had bad marsters. Slavery wus good an' bad accordin' to de kind of marster you had.

"My husban' died September 6, 1925. I am unable to wurk. I've had a stroke on one side. I'se jest hangin' 'round home.

"My daughter wurks for de WPA an' supports me but now she has been laid off. My chillun, some of 'em live in Harlem, New York, but dey has to have so much to live on dey can't help me. Dey sends me a Christmas present most of de time, an' dey remembers me on mother's day sometime.

"I aint signed up wid any of de places to get money yet. Don't see what I is goin' to do. I aint got 'nough money to pay bus fare to de registerin' place other side of town."

LE

N.C. District:       No. 2
Worker:              Mary A. Hicks
No. Words:           901
Subject:             EX-SLAVE STORIES
Person Interviewed:  Ophelia Whitley
Editor:              Daisy Bailey Waitt

# EX-SLAVE STORIES

**An Interview by Mary A. Hicks with Ophelia Whitley of Zebulon, (Wake Co.) N.C. May 12, 1937.**

"I wuz borned at Wakefield in 1841, here in Wake County. My mammy wuz named Eliza an' my pappy wuz named Thomas. Dar wuz eleben uv us chilluns, Frances, Sally Ann, Jane, Pattie, Louisa, Alice, Firginia, Sam, Haywood, Boobie and me. We belonged to Mr. Agustus Foster an' he wuz right good to us even do' he had a hundred or so other slaves.

"I 'members one whuppin' I got when I wuz little 'bout a big matter dat looked little at de time. Mens would come by in kivered wagons, (we called dem speckled wagons) an' steal Marse Gus' nigger chilluns. He had lost a heap of money dat way, so he forbids us of goin' out ter de road an' he orders us ter stay 'way back in de rear uv de house. One day we sees a drove uv dese wagons comin' an' we flies down ter de road. De marster ketches us an' I flies, but he hobbles ter our cabin on his crutches an' he pinches me, pokes me wid de crutch an' slaps my face.

"His son Billy wuz de overseer an' he wuz good ter git along wid, but he shore made dem darkies wuck. De wimmen plowed an' grubbed, an' I'se known dem ter leave de field, go ter de house an' find a baby an' be back at wuck de next day. Dat ain't happen often do', mostly dey done light wuck fer a week or so. De babies wuz carried to Ant Hannah's house an' she raised 'em all so's dat de other wimmen could wuck. De mammies ain't even 'member which wuz dere chilluns half de time, so dar wuz no mo'nin' when somebody got sold.

"I 'members a slave sale an' hyarin' de marster tell Cindy an' Bruce ter act up fer de benefit of de buyers. Cindy said dat she could do ever'thing, so she brung a good price, but Bruce, atter sayin' dat he could do it all, wuz tole ter hitch up a hoss in a hurry. He got de hoss an' turned his head ter de spatter board an' tried to hook de hoss up hind part befo'. De marster can't find no buyer, so he whups Bruce awful atter he gits him home, but dat black boy says, 'Marse, Yo' can kill me, but I'd ruther stay on hyar.' I'se seed niggers in chains, but dey wuz travelin', or wuz mighty bad niggers.

"We had log cabins to live in an' dey wuz comfortable but we ain't had much jubilees, de marster not believin' in such things. We warn't teached nothin', not even religion an' we got whupped if we wuz ketched wid a piece uv paper or a slate. De white folks warn't teached nothin' den, an' you know dey won't gwine ter take no trouble wid de niggers. De niggers had a doctor[Pg 374] do' when dey got sick same as de white folks, an' dey got a lot of spring tonic an' such, made out of barks an' roots.

"When de slaves got married dey done it dis way: de marster hilt a broom an' dey solemnly steps over it twict den dey kissed an' dey wuz married, 'course dar wuz something dat de marster said, but I done forgot whut it wuz.

"When we hyard dat de Yankees wuz comin' some of de niggers went fer de woods an' stayed till atter de surrender, but most uv us stayed on an' wucked jist de same.

"My marstar made his own brandy an' whiskey an' when de Yankees come he wuz a rich man. His smoke house wuz ful o' hams an' he hid 'em in de ceilin' of my mammy's shack, an' he buried dem barrels of brandy, but de Yankees done found it all an' dey ain't left nothin'.

"I 'members how some of dem Yankee officers cussed in front of my mussus an' how I tole' em dat dey mought be Yankees but dey won't half raised at dat.

"Atter de surrender my marster had ter make de slaves leave, but he moved my papy's cabin furder an' we jist stayed on same as always till he died. I 'members moughty well when my mammy an' papy got married case I seed it two years atter de surrender.

"Dar wuz two witches lived in our neighborhood. Dey wuz sisters named Miss Quinnie an' Miss Tilda an'[Pg 375] I'se seed dem brewin' coffee a many a time an' pourin' it out in a long neck goard. Dey done a powerful lot of things which I can't recollect right dis minute, anyhow dey wuz witches.

"I uster see ghosts on dis very road nigh 'bout ever' night. Dey wuz white an' spongy lookin' an' dey set under de bushes an' holler an' holler an' holler. I'se poured water on 'em many a time but it ain't done no good.

"Do you know chile, slavery wuz a good thing, but folks has improved a lot since den, an' de Yankees warn't half as good ter us as our ole marster an missus wuz, even if'n dey did put a stop ter de Ku Klux Klan beatin' sorry niggers dat had ort ter be hung."

MH/LE

N.C. District: No. 2
Worker: Mary A. Hicks
No. Words: 614
Subject: EX-SLAVE STORY
Story teller: Tom Wilcox
Editor: Daisy Bailey Waitt

# EX-SLAVE STORY

[HW: 81 years]

### An Interview on May 19, 1937, with Tom Wilcox of Method.

"I wuz borned on March 18th, 1856 durin' de biggest snow dat eber hit Eastern Carolina; dey says dat hit wuz up ter de roof. De place whar I wuz borned wuz in Warren County; jist acrost de Halifax County line. My mammy's marster wuz Mr. B. Osco Harris an' his wife wuz named Martha.

"My mammy's name wuz Alice an' my pappie's name wuz Camelin. I had three brothers, Little Berry, Cornelius James, an' C.J. Dar wuz four gals, Anne, Pattie, Pennie, an' Mary Frances.

"De white folks wuz good ter us an' we loved 'em, but we wanted ter be free, case de Lawd done make us all free.

"My missus wuz a religious woman an' I can't tell yo' de number uv times she has beat me case I done some kind uv wuck on a Sunday. We went ter church ever Sunday an' we wusn't 'lowed ter cuss an' sich things.

"I wuz nine when de war commence. Durin' de war an' I wuz workin' in de fiel', long wid de fifty or[Pg 378] sixty other slaves. Dar wuzn't nary a Yankee track made in our section, an' we ain't knowed much 'bout de war.

"As I done tell yo' onct we wuz fed an' clothed good an' we lived fer each other, but my pappy belonged ter one man an' my mammy ter another one an' so we wanted ter be all together. Atter de war we stayed on till '69, den we come ter Raleigh. Most uv de wimmens an' chilluns wuz sent by de train, but me an' pappy an' Berry, we walked all de way by Louisburg, an' driv' pappy's thirteen heads of cattle.

"In 1871 we buyed ten acres uv lan' at Method fer three dollars a' acre an' moved out hyar.

"No mam, we ain't liked Jeff Davis, but we did like Mr. Lincoln. I 'members a verse uv a song dat we sung durin' de first uv de war. It goes dis way.

"'Jeff Davis is a rich man,Lincoln is a fool,Davis rides a big fat horse,Lincoln rides a mule.Knick knack dey sayWalk ole Georgia row.'

"Dar wuz another song I 'members but I can't think uv no games, case we ain't neber played none. Yo' has hyard dat atter a dog gits so full uv fleas he can't tote no mo'. Well, dat's de way I is. I peddles my peanuts, but I barely makes a livin'.

"Hyar's de song do' de best I 'members it an' it wuz sung atter de war.

"'Ole Confederate has done played out,Shrew ball, shrew ball,Ole Confederate has done played outShrew ball say I,An' ole Gen'l. Lee can't fight no mo';We'll all drink stone blindJohnnies go marchin' home.
"'I bought me a chicken fur fifty cents,Shrew ball, Shrew ball,I bought me a chicken fur fifty centsShrew ball say I,I bought me a chicken fur fifty centsAn' de son uv a bitch done jump de fence,We'll all drink stone blindJohnnies go marchin' home.
"'Eighteen hundret an' sixty oneShrew ball, shrew ball,Eighteen hundret an' sixty oneShrew ball say I,Eighteen hundret an' sixty oneAn' dat's de year de war begunWe'll all drink stone blindJohnnies go marchin' home.
"'Eighteen hundret an' sixty-fiveShrew ball, Shrew ball,Eighteen hundret an' sixty-fiveShrew ball say I,Eighteen hundret an' sixty-fiveDe Yankees et ole Lee alive;We'll all drink stone blindJohnnies go marchin' home.'"

| | |
|---|---|
| N.C. District: | No. 2 |
| Worker: | T. Pat Matthews |
| No. Words: | 723 |
| Subject: | CATHARINE WILLIAMS |
| Person Interviewed: | Catherine Williams |
| Editor: | Daisy Bailey Waitt |

# [CATHARINE WILLIAMS

**2214 Barker Street**

"My name is Catharine Williams. I was born December twenty fifth, 1851. I remember my mother, but I do not know anything about my father. My mother's name was Adeline Williams. Mother baked ash cakes, but my children would not eat 'em. She died fifty years ago. I had four children when she died, but I had three boys and two girls. I was born in Virginia but I cannot tell what part. I was four years old when my mother brought me to North Carolina. Our old master, Dabney Cosby,[10] moved from Virginia to North Carolina then. We came straight into Raleigh, North Carolina and have been living in Raleigh ever since.

"We were Williams when owned by Cosby and we were never sold again, but remained in the same family till we were set free after the surrender. We had good food, fair clothing and comfortable sleeping places. I know what a pallet is. All slep' on 'em a lot in slavery days, especially when it was hot weather. I makes 'em now sometimes.

"My missus wus named Fannie. I do not know how many slaves they owned, but Marster did not have a plantation, he lived in town. He was a brick mason, and he made brick. He had two brick kilns.

"Our missus and marster were kind to us but they did not teach us to read and write. I learned to read and write since the surrender. I went to church and Sunday school. There were no Negro preachers, but we attended the white folks's church. We did not have any prayer meetings because our homes were in the white folks's yard.

"I was never whupped, and mother and myself were well treated, so I have no complaint to make against our white folks.

"The first work I done was nursing the children in the home, next I waited on the table, then general house [HW: work].

"At the last days of the war Wheeler's Calvary camped around my house at night. They tole us the Yankees would be in Raleigh the next morning and shore 'nough they came in next morning. If the citizens had not gone out and surrendered Raleigh to the Yankees they would have torn Raleigh to pieces. We were living on the corner of Hargett and Dawson Streets. The Yankees done us no harm. They done all right in Raleigh. They did not[Pg 383] take nothing around home. They put out guards around the homes by the time they got in. We were not afraid of 'em, none of us children, neither white nor colored; they played such purty music and was dressed so fine. We run after the band to hear 'em play.

"I heard talk of the patterollers, but never saw any. I knew very little about the jail in Raleigh for slaves. I never saw any slaves sold or any in chains. I never knew of any slaves running away to the North. We children both white and colored enjoyed the Christmas holidays together. We played running and jumping and hide and seek.

"We had doctors when we got sick. Dr. Johnson was one of them. After the war we stayed on with Marster and Missus until they died. I have been on Oberlin Road about twenty-five years.

"No Sir, what you talkin' 'bout? No, there were no Negro schools in Raleigh at the time of the surrender, but I have had a good time all my life as far as bein' treated right is concerned.

"I have never married. I will have to find that man yet, and at this age I don't expect to find him. Ha! ha! never found that man yet. I am staying with my niece.

"I know nothing about Abraham Lincoln. He helped us to be free. I knew nothing about Jefferson Davis, Booker T. Washington or Roosevelt. I know very little about Jim Young, only he was a polititian."

LE

## FOOTNOTES:

[10] Dabney Cosby, a practical architect and contractor, came to Raleigh from Halifax County, Virginia, and did a good deal of building in the city between 1850 and 1860. The original Yarborough House (1852) was built by him. The Heart house, corner Hargett and Dawson Streets, Cosby's home, and another stucco house, corner Hargett and Harrington Streets are still standing in the locality mentioned in the story.

N.C. District: No. 2
Worker: T. Pat Matthews
No. Words: 755
Subject: REV. HANDY WILLIAMS
Person Interviewed: Rev. Handy Williams
Editor: Daisy Bailey Waitt

# REV. HANDY WILLIAMS

**Dunn, North Carolina.**

"My name is Handy H. Williams. When de war went up I wus twelve years old, 12th of March. I belonged to Blaney Williams, and his wife wus named Polly. My mother wus named Margaret Williams, and my father wus named Sam Williams. I do not remember my grandmother and grandfather; can't remember 'em.

"My father lived in Greene County. De plantation wus in Greene County. Dere were about 190 acres in de farm and dere wus about 25 slaves on it.

"We lived in Greene County till the war went up. We had plenty to eat, good clothes and a nice place to sleep. Marster wus not good to us, but he gave us plenty to eat and wear. He worked us from light till dark and then my mother had to do house work after workin' in de fields all day, an' father had to do de feedin' or pick cotton at night.

"We had no holidays. Prayer meetings were not allowed in de quarters and a slave darsent to be caught wid a book in his han'.

"De patterollers come by often an' dey caught and whupped de slaves many times. Marster whupped slaves for mos' anything. Sometimes he would get mad, an' whup us when he hardly had an excuse. Yes sir, he would get drunk and whup somebody jest 'cause he was mad. Some of de slaves run away. My Uncle Needham Williams run away. When he come back he wus whupped an' then put up and sold. Aunt Chaney, my mother's sister, wus put up and sold. She wus sold away from her children. When de war went up, she come back home. My Aunt Beadie wus sold on de block in Fayetteville. I remember her well, but we have never heard from her since. She never come back after the surrender. God only knows what become o' her.

"When de war went up we went to Harnett County to Mr. Jim Surles' place, about three miles from whur this town now stands. Dunn wus not here then.

"We stayed there five years, and then moved to Mingo in what is now Sampson County on the Louis Martin Tew Place, and my father bought a place. The deed called for 199 acres more or less. Dat's what de deed called for. We paid for de place, but my father mortgaged de place. He didn't lose it, cause it wus fixed so dat no one could sell or mortgage it while any of de heirs wus livin'. All are dead 'cept Pink Williams and myself, and de lan' fell back to us. Mammy and daddy are both dead long time ago, 'bout twenty-five years.

"Dey had overseers on marster's farm in Greene County and dey were mean to de slaves. I wus not big enough to work much, but dey had me feedin' stock and helpin' around de house.

"We children didn't play any games we wus afraid to play around de white folks. Marster wus a rip snorter and he would get you if you got in his way. He lived in de great house not far distant from de quarters, but we did not go dere unless we had to go dere to work.

"Yes sir, you know how children is when dey hear wagins coomin', and a big crowd marchin' together. Yes sir, I remember de Yankees. Dey rode dere horses against de fences and tore em down. Dey comed in de yard and turned over de bee gums. Dey shot de chickens. Dey would say 'Dere he goes, shoot him, shoot him', and den de guns would go 'bam, bam, bam, an' de chickens would fall dead'. Dey shot de dogs in de yard. Course, to Heben, I am tellin' de truth. Dey took de meat and destroyed mos' everything at Marster's. After dey lef', if you could get a few beans or peas dey wus mighty good. People et tater peelings an' some come near starvin'.

"I wus mighty lucky an' what I got I got it from de Southern white folks; dey been mighty good to me since de war. I have worked for de town 'bout 35 years and I work for it now. I ain't able to do much now, but[Pg 389] I have a section of de Courthouse. I keeps it might clean.

"I know nothin' much bout de great men you ax me 'bout; don't remember much about 'em. I think slavery wus a bad thing, yes sir, I shore does."

LE

N.C. District:   No. 2
Worker:          T. Pat Matthews
No. Words:       544
Subject:         JOHN THOMAS WILLIAMS
Person Interviewed: John Thomas Williams
Editor:          G.L. Andrews

[TR: Date stamp: SEP 10 1937]

# JOHN THOMAS WILLIAMS

### 77 years old. 1272 Pettigrew Street, Raleigh, North Carolina.

"I don't know who I am nor what my true name is. I wus born December 25, 1860 on a plantation in New Hanover County. The plantation belonged to John Williams, whose wife wus named Isabella and the farm wus on land which is now in the corporate limits of Wilmington, N.C.

"The reason I don't know who I am is that I don't remember my father and mother or any of my people. When I got so I could remember anything I wus with the Williams family. Marster an' missus, an' their family are the only ones I ever looked upon as my people. They never told me who I wus.

"After the war I stayed with them a long time and helped them on the farm. They run a truck farm. I got along all right while I wus with the Williams family, but when I got grown I left them. I loved them but I realized I wus a nigger and knew that I could never be like them, and that I wus one to myself.

"When I left I went to Little Washington, N.C. Then to Plymouth. I stayed at these places several years working as a hand on truck farms. From there I went to Charlotte, Greensboro, and Norfolk. I then went North an' stayed eight years in New York City as a waitman for a white man and his family. I then went to Plymouth, N.C.

"I married Maggie Swain, a former sweetheart, as soon as I got back to Plymouth. We had two children. She lived six years. I then married Mary Davenport of Little Washington. We had seven children. She died and I come to Raleigh and married Maggie Towel. We had no children by our marriage.

"I own no home and have never owned one. Excepting the eight years I spent in New York City my life has been spent in farming. I farm some now and do little jobs for the white folks.

"I don't know much about slavery, as I wus too young to know much about it. There wus other slaves belonging to Marster Williams but I don't remember any of them because when I got so I could know what it wus all about they were free and gone from the plantation.

"I have asked thousands of questions trying to find out who my people are but no one has ever told me who I am or who my people are. If I have any brothers and sisters, I don't know it.

"I have nothing to say about being partly white, I leave that to your imagination. I have thought about it a lot. I don't know.

"I have been blessed with good health, I am breaking now but I am still able to do light jobs.

"I am a good fiddler. The white folks have taught me to do lots of different things. I have had very few advantages and I cannot read and write.[Pg 393]

"I have never been in jail in my life. I can give good references from dozens of white folks. I try to live right, be honest and above all give my fellow man a square deal."

LE

# Interview with LIZZIE WILLIAMS, Ex-slave,

35 Max Street,
Asheville, N.C.

**By Marjorie Jones, Aug. 24, 1937.**

"I's bo'n in Selma, Alabam', I can't mind how long ago, but jes 'bout ninety yeahs. I come to dis country 'bout 1882. Yes, I's purty porely des days an' I's gettin' homesick for my ol' home.

"I's bo'n and lib on ol' man Billy Johnson's plantation—thousan's acres of groun' and plenty of niggahs. My pappy he allus b'long to ol' man Billy. He not sich a bad man but de Lawd knows I's seed bettah ones. When I's right sma't size Missy Mixon, she was Marse Billy's wife sistah, she get Marse Billy to let her hab me. She war a good woman. She took me to town to lib and make a little white girl outten me. Y'all knows what I means; I got treated moh like de white folks den de res' of de' niggahs.

"But 'twarn't long afore Missy send me to New 'Leans to nurse de sick chile of her sistah. I never war satisfi' down dar. Evverbody so differen'. But de nex' year we go back to Alabam'.

"I went to Marse Ellis Mixon's, he tubble mean to his niggahs. But I belong to de Missus, she allus treat me good. All de little niggahs have to learn to work when dey little; get out'n pull weeds; dey neber had no time to play. Most dem niggahs was scared to death, jes like de ones on Billy Johnson's plantation. Dey know dey get whupped jes like a mule iffen dey act like dey don' wanna wurk. Dey neber get much to eat, jes side meat, co'n bread and 'lasses. Ol' Billy he had overseers whut was mean to de pore niggahs. Sometime dey ties dem up an' dey strip dem and dey whups dem wif cow hide, else dey lets other niggahs do it.

"All de niggahs have to go to church, jes lik' de white fokes. Dey have a part of de church for demselfs. After de wah we hab a church of our own. All de niggahs love to go to church an' sing. I mind a lot of de songs we used ter sing in de fiel's. I mind my pappy used ter sing in de fiel'. 'Git on bo'd, little chillun, git on bo'd.' Sometimes day babtiz in de ribber. Den dey sing:

"'I wanna be readyI wanna be readyI wanna be ready good Lawd to walk in Jarusalem jes like John.John say de city was jes four square,To walk in Jarusalem jes like John.But I'll meet my mothah and fathah dar,To walk in Jarusalem, jes like John.'

"I 'members 'bout de paddyrollers. De niggahs hab' to get a pass from de massa or de missus if dey go ennywhar. De paddyrollers jes lik' police. 'Bout dozen of dem ride 'long togedder. Fus thing dey say: 'Whar yo' pass?' Den iffen yo' hab one dey lets you go but iffen you don' hab one dey strips yo' to de waist and dey lams yo' good till de blood comes.[Pg 396] Sometime dey rolls you over a barrel and lams you while de barrel rolls.

"I mind a tale my pappy tell 'bout one time he see de paddyrollers comin'. He scared to death cas he did'n hab no pass. He kno' iffen dey finds him whut dey do. So pappy he gets down in de ditch an' throw sand an' grunts jes like a hawg. Sho' nuf dey thinks he a hawg and dey pass on, cept one who was behin' de others. He say: 'Dat am de gruntin'es ol' hawg I ebber hear. I think I go see him.' But de udders day say: 'Jes let dat ol' hawg lone an' min' yo own business.' So day pass on. Pappy he laff 'bout dat for long time.

"I mind ol' Mose, he hab monthly pass from de massa but he forgit it one day and de paddyrollers whup him and throw him in de callaboose. In de mawnin' when de massa wake and fin no fresh water and no fire in de stove and de cows not milk, he say: 'I know Mose in de callaboose,' and he hab to go atter Mose.

"Lots of de pore niggahs run away, but 'twarn't no use. Der wa'nt no place to go. Day was allus lookin' for you and den you had to work harder den ebber, 'sides all kin's of punishment you got. Den dey nearly sta've you to def, jes feed you on bread and water for long time.

"De niggahs nebber kno' nothin' 'bout learnin', jes wuk' all dey's fit for. De only thing I ebber do wif a book is jes to dust it off. I mind two little niggahs whose missy teach dem to read. Emily, she look lik' a white gal. She was treated jes like she white. Her daddy was a white man. Emily was a sma't gal. She belong to one of de Johnson mens. She do all de sewin' for her missy. When de missy go to buy clothes for de chillun she allus take Emily along. Her pappy pay no more 'tention to her den to de res' of de niggahs. But de missy she was good to her. She never stay in de quarters, she stay in de house with de white fokes. But Emily have de saddes' look on her yaller face cas' de other niggahs whisper 'bout her pappy.

"Many de pore niggah women hab chillun for de massa, dat is iffen de massa a mean man. Dey jes tell de niggahs whut to do and dey know better den to fuss.

"Ol' missus she good to me. I mind one time I got tubble mad an' say some ugly words. Marse Ellis he come up ahin' me and he say: "Lizabeth I gwina wallup yo' good for dat.' I 'mense cryin' and run to de missus and she say: 'Look heah Ellis Mixon, y'all mind yo' own business an' look atter yo' own niggahs. Dis one b'longs to me.' Jes same when de missus went upstairs Marse Ellis take me in de smoke house and sta't to hit me. I yell for de missus an' when she come she plenty mad. Marse say he nebber ment to whup me, jes scare me little.

"I mind 'bout de wah. We niggahs neber know whut it 'bout. We jes go on an' work. Nebber see nothin', nebber hear nothin', nebber say nothin', but de wah all 'roun'. Evah day we heah dat de Yankee sojers comin'. De plantations was gittin' robbed. Evabody kep' a hidin' things. It was a tubble time. I mind plain when dey comes to Selma. All de fokes was at church when de Yankees come. Day warn't no fightin' much, dey didn' hab time. Dey jes march in an' take de town. But O,[Pg 398] Lawdy, dat night dey burn de stores an' houses an' take all de things dey want. Cannons and guns all 'round, it war tubble sight.

"Marse Ellis' plantation 'bout 15 mile from Selma on Pea Ridge. I mind one night Marse come home from town and he say: 'Lizabeth.' I say, 'Yes, suh.' He say: 'Bring me some fresh watah from de spring.' I run as fas' as I kin an' bring de watah an' gib it to him, den he say: 'Lizabeth, de Yankees am comin' soon, an' I knows yo'se gwin to tell 'em where I hide all my 'longings, guns an' ebberthing.'

"'No' I says, 'jes why would I tell whar yo' hide yo' guns an' things?' Missy come in den and she say: 'Go on an' let Lizzie 'lone, bettah be feared dem niggahs you done so mean to gwine tell, dats all you got to be feared of. But you, let Lizzie 'lone, she b'long to me.'

"Marse Ellis he go out an' hide some mo' stuff. Dat night de sojers burn Selma. Dat war on Sunday. Next night we wake up in de middle of de night an' de house what we keep de bes' carriage an' horse was a'burnin'. De pore ho'se done break outten de barn an' was a runnin' roun' all over de place a'screamin' wif her poor back bu:nt tubble. We nebber find out iffen de Yankees set de barn fire or not. Guess dey did. Dey done set Marse Hyde's house afire an' burn it to de groun' with Marse Hyde in it. Marse Hyde he had plantation in New 'Leans and when de Yankees take de town Marse Hyde he promise not to leave but when de sojers [HW: know] he 'scape and come to his house on Pea Ridge, so when de Yankees fin' him here dey burn him in de house wif all his 'longings.

"On de Tuesday mawnin' after dey burn Selma I wake up to see Marse Ellis' plantation all surroun' wif Yankee sojers. I war nigh scared to death. I so 'fraid dey hurt me an' Missy but dey didden, dey jes march through de house an' when dey see Marse Ellis dey ask him for he guns an' things dey want. Marse Ellis show dem whar de things war. 'Twarn't no use to do anything else. I take Marse Frank's 'backer an' hide it in de Missus' trunk. Den when de sojers git what dey want dey laugh and ma'ch 'way on de hill.

"After de surren'er all de niggahs jes lost. Nowhar to go, nothin' to do, 'less dey stay wif de massa. Nobuddy hab anything but 'federate money and it no good. My pappy had 'bout three hunner dolla's but 'twarn't no good 'tall.

"All some of de white fokes think of war killin' de pore niggahs what worked for dem for yeahs. Dey jes scour de country and shoot dem, 'specially de young men. One day dey come down de road to'ards my pappy. Dey start askin' questions 'bout what he gwine to do now he free. 'What I gwin to do?' says pappy. 'What can I do? I jes stay on de plantation an' help ol' Massa iffen I can get an ol' mule an' a piece of an ol' plow.'

"One of de boys look at pappy an' say: 'I like take yo' head for a target,' but de ol' man wif dem say no so dey leave my pappy 'lone. Dey hab de commissary whar de fokes git food; it b'long to de Yankee sojers. Food scarce lik' ebberthing. Folks say now dey hab hard times; dey don' know nothin' 'bout hard times less day lib in war time and be slave to white fokes.[Pg 400]

"Den dey was de Ku Klux Klan. Dey war frightful lookin' critters. My pappy say dey go out in de country an' tie pore niggahs to de tree and beat 'em to death. Dey dress all kin's of fashions. Most of dem look like ghosts. Dey nebber go lik' de paddyrollers, dey jes sneak 'round at night when de poor niggahs in bed. Den 'bout twelve 'clock dey tie up all de niggahs dey ketch and atter dey through beatin' dem dey leaves dem wif dey han's tied in de air and de blood astreamin' outten dey backs.

"Atter freedeom I come heah to live wif my fokes de Williams's, dats how I come to be Williams. Nebber had no chillun of my own. Dey calls me 'Lizbeth Johnson 'fore I went to live with de Mixons, den I be one of de Mixon niggahs, den later I be a Williams; don' guess names matter much no way."

N.C. District: No. 2
Worker: Mary A. Hicks
No. Words: 801
Subject: PENNY WILLIAMS
Story teller: Penny Williams
Editor: Daisy Bailey Waitt

# PENNY WILLIAMS
## Ex-Slave Story

**An interview with Penny Williams 76, of 716 S. East Street, Raleigh, N.C.**

"I wus borned at de Hinton place 'bout three miles south of Raleigh, an' course we 'longed ter Mr. Lawrence Hinton.

"My mammy wus named Harriet Moore an' my pappy wus named Mack Moore, dat wus cause dey 'longed fust ter a Mr. Moore I 'specks. I had ten bruders an' sisters, an' we all done putty good.

"De marster owned 'round two hundert slaves an' 'bout four hundert acres o' lan' an' dey had ter wuck peart, dey sez.

"We had 'nough ter eat, sich as it wus, but dat ain't braggin', I reckins. An' we wus punished putty bad iffen we complains, sasses or 'fuses ter wuck lak we should. Nat Whitaker wus de oberseer an' patteroller an' he wus strick, I'se tellin' you. I'se seed him beat slaves till de blood run.

"Dar wus some nigger mens what 'ud go coutin' spite of de debil, an' as de marster ain't gibin' dem no passes dey goes widout 'em. Mr. Whitaker, he whups, an' whups, but dat ain't stop 'em. At las' Marster Lawrence 'cides ter hang cowbells on dere necks so's he can hyar dem if'en[Pg 403] dey leabes de place atter night.

"I'se tellin' you chile, dem niggers am gwin' anyway. Dey ain't got sense nuff ter put dere han's in de bell ter keep de clapper from ringin', but dey does stuff de bell wid leaves an' it doan ring none, 'sides dat dey tears deir shirts, or steals sheets from missus clothes line an' fold dem ter make a scarf. Dey ties dese 'roun' deir necks ter hide de bell an' goes on a-courtin'.

"Dey ain't got no pins ter pin de scarf on, but dey uses thornes from de locust tree or de crabapple; an' dey hol's fine.

"Dey warn't no spoons, knives, an' forks dem days, but de smart slave cut him some outen hickory an' dey wus jist as good as de other kin'.

"Dey also ain't go no matches dem days so flint rocks wus rubbed tergether.

"I 'members mostly 'bout de rear en' o' de war, 'specially 'bout de Yankees comin'. I 'members dat marster an' his fambly done moved ter town, case dey can't git no 'tection dar. Dar wusn't a soul on de place but de slaves dar when de Yankees comed a-takin' an' a-killin'.

"I 'members dat I wus drawin' water at de well, when de Yankees comed. I looks up de road an' dar am a gang o' 'em comin'. I draps de bucket back in de well an' I flies in de big house.

"Well sir, dey kills de chickens, hogs, geese, an' eber' thing as dey comes, eben ter marster's collie, an' when dey gits ter de big house dey swears dat dey'll burn hit down. Dey stan's dar fur a minute, an' den one o' 'em sez dat hit am too putty ter burn, another one sez dat hit am too putty ter belong ter a damm Reb, but dey doan burn it. I hyars hit all from de winder in de big house, an' I shore is glad dat dey ain't burn hit.

"Dey tears up all dey wants to, den dey robs de smokehouse; an' dey goes on 'bout dere business.

"Atter de surrender our white folkses comes back an' we stays on five or six years I reckon, den we moves ter Mis' Emma Greens' place five miles furder in de country. We shore ain't got 'long good atter de war. De Yankees what 'ud die ter free us ain't carin' iffen we starves nother."

Suddenly Aunt Penny was attracted by a hummingbird flitting around the pomegranate bush near the doorstep.

"Does you know which am de bes' way ter ketch a hummin' bird chile?" After a negative answer she smiled. "When you sees him 'roun' de flowers den you soaks two er three in whiskey, dey bird will suck till he gits drunk an' can't fly 'way, dat's how you ketch him.

"I hates de town sparrers an' de cowbirds what ain't got nuff sense ter leave de floods. You read 'bout hit in de papers I reckon. You knows dey am bout de size of a[Pg 405] peckerwood.

"Yesum, one witch tried ter ride me onct. I wus in de bed, an' she thought dat I wus 'sleep. I feels her when she crawls up on my lef' leg an' stops de circulation. I knows how ter fix her do' so I gits up an' puts a knife under my pillow.

"I has slep' wid dat knife dar ever' since dat time an' I ain't had no mo' trouble wid witches ner circulation nother. So I reckons dat I fixed her good an' plenty."

N.C. District: No. 2
Worker: Mary A. Hicks
No. Words: 471
Subject: AUNT PLAZ
Source: Plaz Williams
Editor: Geo. L. Andrews

# AUNT PLAZ

**An interview with Plaz Williams of Four Oaks who says that she is around 90 years of age.**

"Margaret Thornton sez dat she has got de world record beat on nussin' but dat's whar she's wrong. She ain't a day over seventy, yit she sez dat she has nussed more dan I has an' me ninety. Right now I'se a nussin' of a 'oman what has jist got back from de hospital. Yes, mam, a heap of people sez dat dey'd rather have me dan de doctor.

"I wus borned in Mississippi, so dey tells me, den I wus sold ter Mr. Moses Mordecai of Raleigh, atter dat I 'longed ter a Mr. Henry Lane who lived in Wake County. Dar wus two er three of dem Lane's named Henry, course dis one wus de youngest.

"I worked in de fiel's like a man an' I liked it too. Marse Moses had oberseers what beat you fer nothin' but Marse Henry ain't dat sort of a person at all. Marse Moses an' Marse Henry both drunk whiskey an' such but dey wus different when dey wus drunk. Marse Moses 'ud beat you an' cuss you, but Marse Henry 'ud laugh at you an' play wid you.

"I know one time Marse Moses comed ter see Marse Henry an' atter dey had drunk awhile Marse Henry seed me in de yard. Hit bein' on Sunday he calls me ter come to his library. When I gits in he axes me iffen I'se ever been drunk an' I tells him no. Den he pours me a glassful an' sez for me ter drink it. I begs at fust, den I sez dat I won't drink de brandy. Marse Henry laugh an' would have let me go but dat debil, Marse Moses, sez, 'Le's hol' her an' pour it down her guzzle, Henry.' Dat's what dey done an' dey pours down seberal drinks. Terreckly Marse Henry axes me ter fetch him some water but when I starts my laigs am too weak to go so I sets down on de floor. Marse Henry laugh an' laugh but Marse Moses sez, 'Whup de shameless hussy what ain't got no mo' raisin' dan ter git dog drunk.' He would have whupped me too but Marse Henry won't let him do it. 'Stid of beatin' me he sez ter git in de corner an' sleep it off.

"I doan know nothin' 'bout de Yankees comin' case we wus sent 'way back in de country ter stay. Marse Henry comes out dar an' tells us dat we is free. Marse Henry has told Jack Williams dat he can't have me 'fore dis, so I axes, 'Can I marry Jack now, Marse Henry.' He sez yes, so 'fore night I is at Jack's cabin. I thought dat dar ain't got ter be no preacher, but a week er two atter dis a preacher comes by an' marries us.

"We moved here case hit am better farmin' land. We worked hard ter make anything do', an' fer awhile I thought dat we'd starve ter death.

"Dar ain't so much ter tell about atter de war. Our chilluns died fast as we had 'em. We worked hard an' 'bout twenty years ago Jack died. I'se been on de charity some but I hope dat when I gits my pension I won't have ter trouble dem no more."

N.C. District: No. 2
Worker: Mary A. Hicks
No. Words: 652
Subject: MELISSA WILLIAMSON
Story teller: Melissa Williamson
Editor: Daisy Bailey Waitt

# MELISSA WILLIAMSON
# Ex-Slave Story

**An interview with Melissa Williamson 77 of Bledsoe Avenue, Raleigh, N.C.**

"Dis June fifteenth sebenty-eight years ago I wuz borned in Franklin County near Louisburg.

"My mammy an' me belonged ter Mr. Billy Mitchell [HW: Mitchell (?)] 'fore she died, which wuz one of de fust things dat I 'members, an' den Mis' Mitchel tuck me in her house an' raise me. Dat wuz de fust year of de war, I believes.

"De Mitchels [HW: Mitchells (?)] wuz good ter us in a way, an' dey doan spare de rod when it am needed, nor does dey think dat a picaninny can't go barefooted in de hot summertime. Dey believes in a heap of wuck do' an' no play at all, an' very little rations.

"De men slaves 'ud wuck in de fiel's an' at dinnertime dey ain't had nothin' 'cept a quart of buttermilk, an' a ash cake. I got a whole heap better dan dey did, but youngin'-like I begged dem fer some of dere dinner.

"I neber thought dat Mis' Mitchel wuz hard till I seed her whup Aunt Pidea. Aunt Pidea wuz a good soul an' she wuz good ter we youngins, an' we loved her. She got ter[Pg 412] gittin' frantic do', an' she'd put on her dinner on de stove, den she'd go ter de woods an' run an' romp lak a chile.

"Mis Mitchel had loved her too, but atter awhile she got mad an' she wuz mad bad too. She tuck Aunt Pidea out ter a tree, stripped off her waist, tied her ter de tree an' whup her wid a cowhide till de blood runs down her back.

"We wuz told dat de Yankees would kill us an' we wuz skeered of dem too, an' I wuz always runnin' fer fear de Yankees would git me. When dey did come I wuz out at de well, drawin' water wid de windlass an' I wuz so short dat I had ter jump up ter grap de handle. I looked up de road an' de Yankees wuz comin' up de road as thick as fleas on a dog's back. I gives a yell, turns de windlass a loose, an' flies roun' de house ter my missus. Hit's a wonder dat windlass ain't turn ober an break my haid in.

"I had hyard 'bout my sister what wuz sold 'fore I wuz borned, an' I ain't knowin' whar she is, but atter de war had been ober fer two years she comed ter Mis' Mitchel's an' got me. She carried me ter Louisburg an' sont me ter de Yankee school dar. I 'member a song dat de Yankees teached us, or at least a part o' one.

"'How often we think o' childhood joysAnd tricks we used to playUpon each other while at schoolTo while the time away.'"
Chorus

"'They often wished me with them But they always wished in vain I'd rather be with Rosenell A-swinging in the lane.'"

"I won't talk ter my chilluns 'bout slavery days, case I doan want 'em ter git stirred up 'bout it. I'se told 'em dat we ain't paid no mo' dan de white folkses fer our freedom, case some of dem sold dereselbes ter git hyar an' dey fought in wars dat de nigger doan know nothin' 'bout.

"I know dat Mis' Mitchel done wrong when she ain't give us enough ter eat, an' when she whup Aunt Pidea 'bout bein' crazy, but I 'members somethin' else dat make me tender towards her an' other white folkses.

"I 'members dat Mis' Mitchel used ter take me visitin' ter white folkses houses an' some o' dem hates niggers an' won't give me no place ter sleep, 'cept on de floor by missus bed. Sometimes I can feel her now, kiverin' me up wid her own clothes durin' de night or feelin' me to see if I'm chilly or too hot."

AC

N.C. District: No. 2
Worker: T. Pat Matthews
No. Words: 1108
Subject: ALEX WOODS
Story teller: Alex Woods
Editor: Daisy Bailey Waitt

# ALEX WOODS
# Ex-Slave Story

**8 Ford Alley—end of Martin Street, Raleigh, N.C.**

"My name is Alex Woods. I wus born May 15, 1858. In slavery time, I belonged to Jim Woods o' Orange County. De plantation wus between Durham and Hillsboro near de edge o' Granville County. My missus name wus Polly Woods. Dey treated us tolerable fair, tolerable fair to a fellow. Our food wus well cooked. We were fed from de kitchen o' the great house.

"We called marster's house de 'great house' in dem times. We called de porch de piazza. We were fed from de kitchen o' his house during de week. We cooked and et at our homes Saturday nights and Sundays. We wove our clothes; children had only one piece, a long shirt. We went barefooted, an' in our shirt tails; we youngins' did.

"We did not have any shoes winter nor summer, but mother and father had shoes with wooden bottoms an' leather tops. Dr. Tupper, de man who was principal of de Shaw School, de man who started de school and de church on Blount St., gave me my first pair o' shoes. Dis wus the second year after de surrender. I wus nine years ole den. Dey were boots wid brass on de toes, solid leather shoes, made in Raleigh on Fayetteville Street in de basement o' Tucker's Dry Goods Store, 'bove de Masonic Temple as you go up. Ole man Jim Jones, a colored shoe maker, worked in dis shop.

"I can read, but I cannot write, 'cause I've been run over three times by automobiles. Once my buggy wus torn to pieces, an' I wus knocked high in de air. De first time dey run into me dey killed my hoss. De third time dey paralized my arm and busted the linin' o' my stomach.

"I learned to read an' write since de surrender by studying in spare time. Dey wouldn't let any slaves have books in slavery time. Mother had a book she kep' hid. Dey would whup a slave if dey caught him wid a book.

"Dere were between twenty-five and thirty slaves on de plantation but dere wus no church. Dey would not allow us to have prayer meetings in our houses, but we would gather late in de night and turn pots upside down inside de door to kill de sound and sing and pray for freedom. No one could hear unless dey eaves-drapped.

"The patteroller rode around to see after de slaves and whipped 'em when dey caught' em away from home. I have seen slaves whipped. Dey took them into the barn and corn crib and whipped 'em wid a leather strap, called de cat-o'nine tails. Dey hit 'em ninety-nine licks sometimes. Dey wouldn't allow 'em to call on de Lord when dey were whippin' 'em, but dey let 'em say 'Oh! pray, Oh! pray, marster'.

Dey would say, 'Are you goin' to work? Are you goin' visitin' widout a pass? Are you goin' to run away?' Dese is de things dey would ax him, when dey wus whuppin' him.

"My old marster's brother John wus a slave speculator. I 'member seein' him bringin' slaves in chains to de plantation when he wus carryin' 'em to Richmond to put 'em on de auction block to be sold. Dey were handcuffed wid a small chain to a large chain between 'em, two men side by side; dere wus 'bout thirty in a drove. Dere wus 'bout three or four white men on horses. Dey wus called slave drivers; some went before, an' some behind. Dey carried pistols on dere sides. De distance wus so fur, dey camped out at night. De slaves set by de fire, and slept on dese trips wid de chains on 'em. Evertime de mens come to our house I wus afraid my mother and father would be sold away from me. If a woman wus a good breeder she sold high, sometimes bringin' five hundred to a thousand dollars. De man who wus doin' de buyin' would inspect dem. Dey would look in dere mouthes, and look 'em over just like buyin' hosses. There were no jails on de plantation.

"Sometimes we went to the white folkses church. De preacher would tell us to obey our missus and master. Dat's what de preacher tole us. Dey would take us back home and give us plenty to eat after preachin' was over, and tell us to do what de preacher said. Dey tasked us Saturday mornings, and if we got it done we could go to de branch on a flat rock and wash our clothes.

"Dey 'lowed my father to hunt wid a gun. He wus a good hunter an' he brought a lot o' game to de plantation. Dey cooked it at de great house and divided it up. My father killed deer and turkey. All had plenty o' rabbits, possums, coons, an' squirrels.

"My father's first wife wus sold from him, an' I am de chile o' de second wife. I had five brothers, Greene, Isom, Nupez, den Sam Woods, who wus no slave, den Spencer Woods, he wus no slave. I had five sisters: Mollie, Rasella, who were slaves, an' Nancy, Catharine, an' Fanny who were not slaves. My father wus named Major Woods, and mother wus named Betty Woods.

"Yes Sir, I 'member gettin' sick before de surrender, an' dey bled me and gave me blue mass pills. Dey wouldn't tell me what wus de matter. Missus chewed our food for us, when we wus small. De babies wus fed wid sugar tits, and the food missus chewed. Deir suckled mothers suckled dem at dinner, an' den stayed in de field till night. I remember missus chewin' fer me, an' de first whippin' I got. Missus whipped me for pushin' my sister in de fire. Sister called me a lie and I pushed her in de fire an' burned her hand. Missus whipped me. We never did fight nor push one another after dat.

"Marster used colored overseers when he did not work his men hisself.

"I wus very much afraid o' de Ku Klux. Dey wore masks and dey could make you think dey could drink a whole bucket of water and walk widout noise, like a ghost. Colored folks wus afraid of 'em. Dey wus de fear o' de niggers.

"I married Addie Shaw in 1888 first, den in 1918 I married agin. I think Abraham Lincoln wus all right. He caused us to be free. Franklin D. Roosevelt is all right; he kept a lot of people from perishing to death."

BN

District:       No. 2
Worker:         Mary Hicks
No. Words:      580
Subject:        A SLAVE STORY, ANNA WRIGHT
Person Interviewed:   ANNA WRIGHT
Editor:         George L. Andrews

[TR: Date stamp: AUG 17 1937]

# ANNA WRIGHT

**An interview with Anna Wright, 72 years of age, of Wendell, North Carolina.**

"I wus borned de year de war ended so I can't tell nothin' dat I seed, only what my mammy tol' me. We lived dar on Marse James Ellis' plantation till I wus five or six years old, so I 'members de slave cabins an' de big house.

"De plantation wus in Scotland County an' de big house set on a little knoll. Back of de big house set de rows of slave cabins an' back of dem wus de apple orchard an' de bee orchard. Hit wus a purty place sho' nuff, an' dey tells me dat dey wus happy 'fore de war, 'case Marse James wus good ter dem.

"Dere must of been 'bout two hundret slaves, 'cordin' ter de number of cabins. De slaves wurked hard in de fiel's but unless de wurk wus pushin' dey had Sadday evenin' off ter go a-fishin' er do anything de wanted ter do. Two or three times a year Marse James let dem have a dance an' invite in all de neighborhood slaves. Dey had corn shuckin's ever' fall an' de other slaves 'ud come ter dem.

"De candy pullin's wus a big affair wid de niggers. Dey'd come from all over de neighborhood ter cook de lasses[Pg 422] an' pull de candy. While de candy cooled dey'd play drappin' de handkerchief an' a heap of other games. De courtin' couples liked dese games 'case dey could set out or play an' court all dey pleased. Dey often made up dere min's ter ax de marster iffen dey could narry [TR: marry] too, at dese parties.

"De weddin's wus somethin' fine, believe me. De niggers dressed lak a white folks weddin' an' de circuit parson married dem in de big house parlour. De marster an' de missus wus dere, an' dey always gived presents ter de bride too. Atter de ceremony wus over dar'd be a feas' an' a dance. Most likely dar'd be a heap of noise. I've heard mammy tell of seberal big weddin's.

"Mammy tol' me dat Marse James wus a very religious man, an' dat wus why de preacher married de slaves, an' why he made all of de slaves go ter church on Sunday an' say de blessin' at meal times.

"My pappy wus named Tom, an' he wurked in de fiel's fer Marse James. Hit wus pappy dat haul up de waremelons in de wagin body atter I could 'member, an' dey said dat he haul dem up in slavery times too. Marse James raise a plenty melons fer all of de slaves an' he raise plenty of hogs ter eat de rines. De slaves uster have a watermelon slicin' 'bout once a week an' sometimes dey'd invite de neighbors in.

"You wants ter know 'bout some ole slavery foods, well I'll tell you what I knows. Did you ever hear of kush? Kush was cornbread, cooked in de big griddle on de fireplace, mashed up with raw onions an' ham gravy poured over hit. You mought think dat hit ain't good but hit am.

"Fried chicken wus seasoned, drapped in flour an' den simmered in a big pan of ham gravy wid a lid on hit till hit wus tender, den de lid wus tuck off an' de chicken wus fried a golden brown as quick as possible.

"Does you know de old southern way of makin' baked chicken dressin'? Well, it wus made from soft corn bread wid bacon grease, onions, black pepper an' boiled eggs. Some of de folks used cheese too in dis dressin'.

"De griddle cakes wus flour an' meal mixed, put on a big ole iron griddle on de fireplace an' flipped over two times. Ashe cake wus made of either meal or flour, wrapped in a damp cloth an' cooked in de hot ashes on de h'ath. Taters wus cooked in de ashes too an' dey wus good like dat. I'se heard mammy say dat de slave chilluns uster bake onions dat way.

"Fish, dem days, wus dipped in meal, 'fore dey wus cooked, 'cept cat fish; an' dey wus stewed wid onions.

"Cornmeal dumplin's wus biled in de turnip greens, collards, cabbages, an' so on, even ter snap beans, an' at supper de pot licker wus eat wid de dumplin's. Dat's why de folks wus so healthy.

"Speakin' 'bout sweets, de blackberry or other kind of pie wus cooked in a big pan wid two crusts. Dat made more an' wus better ter boot. Cakes wus mostly plain or had jelly fillin', 'cept fer special company.

"From the first I could 'member de white folks an' niggers alike ain't had much ter eat. A heap of our rations wus vege'ables, squirrels, rabbits, possums an' coons. We drunk parched meal water fer coffee an' we done widout a heap of things, but atter awhile we got richer, an' Marse James got some money for something from de No'th, so dey got 'long all right.

"When I wus twelve we moved ter Wake County, out near Wendell an' when I wus thirteen I married Sam Wright, an' we got along fine till he dies 'bout ten years ago. We ain't had but three chilluns but we lived through a heap of bad depressions.

"What we needs mostly am law an' justice. Why hit wus better when de Ku Kluxes had law, dey tells me. Now-a-days de nigger fights on de streets like dogs. Back den de bossman seed to hit dat dar wus law an' order in de town an' in de country too fer dat matter, an' dem wus de good ole days."

EH

N.C. District: No. 2
Worker:       T. Pat Matthews
No. Words:    1,017
Subject:      **DILLY YELLADAY** [TR: or YELLADY?]
Story teller: **Dilly Yelladay**
Editor:       **Geo. L. Andrews**

[TR: Date stamp: JUL 24 1937]

# DILLY YELLADY

[TR: or YELLADAY?]

**909 Mark Street**

"Yes sir, I 'members 'bout what my mammy tole me 'bout Abraham Lincoln, Grant, an' a lot of dem Yankees comin' down ere 'fore de surrender. Frum what dey tole me Sherman knowed de south like a book 'fore he come thro' last time. Dat he did. Yankees come thro' dressed like tramps an' dey wus always lookin' fur some of dere people. Dat wus dere scuse. Dey wus at big shindigs de southern white folks had 'fore de war.

"Mammy an' dad dey said de niggers would git in de slave quarters at night an' pray fer freedom an' laf 'bout what de Yankees wus doin' 'bout Lincoln an' Grant foolin' deir marsters so.

"Ole Jeff Davis said he wus goin' to fight de Yankees till hell wus so full of 'em dat dere legs wus hangin' over de sides, but when dey got 'im in a close place he dres in 'omans clothes an' tried to git away frum 'em but dey seed his boots when he started to git in dat thing dey rode in den, a carriage. Yes dats what it wus a carriage. Dey seed his boots an' knowed who it wus. Dey jus laffed an' pointed at 'im an' said you hol' on dere we got you, we knows who you is an' den dey took 'im. He wus mighty brave till dey got 'im in a close place den he quit barkin' so loud. Mammy an' dad dey said dere wus a lot of de white folks didn't keer much 'bout Jeff Davis. Dey said he wus jus de bragginest man in de worl', always a-blowin'. Dat bird flew mighty high but he had to come back to de groun' an' course when he lit de Yankees wus waitin' for 'im an' ketched 'im.

"I wus born May 2nd, two years after de surrender. I is 70 years old. My mammy belonged to Autsy Pool. When he died she fell to his son Billy Pool. There wus six of the chillun, an' they wus given out to the Pool chillun. Dey went like lan' does now; dey went to de heirs. Ole man Autsy loved likker so good he would steal it from hisself. He'd take a drink an' den blow his breath an' keep wife from smellin' it."

[HW margin: (following paragraph) to p. 7]

"My uncle, Parker Pool, tole me de Yankees made a slave of him. His Marster wus so good to him he wus as happy as he could be 'fore de Yankees come.

"I wus born on the Harper Whitaker place near Swift Creek. Simon Yellady wus my father. He wus born in Mississippi an' he belonged to Dr. Yelladay.

"My father an' his brothers run away an' went to de Yankees. I heard daddy tell 'bout it. He got sick an' dey shipped him back home to North Carolina. Dey shifted niggers from place to place to keep de Yankees frum takin' 'em. When dere got to be too many Yankees in a place de slaves wus sent out to keep' em from bein' set free.

"Mother said onct when she wus carrying the cows to de pasture dey looked down de railroad an' everything wus blue. A nigger girl by the name of Susan wus with her. My mother wus named Rilla Pool. Dey said dey jus fell down an' de Yankees commenced sayin' 'Hello Dinah,' 'Hello Susie.' Mother an' Susan run. Dey just went flyin'. When dey crossed a creek my mother lost her shoe in de mud, but she just kept runnin'. When she got home she tole her missus de Yankees were ridin' up de railroad just as thick as flies. Den my great-grandmother said, 'Well I has been prayin' long enough for 'em now dey is here.' My great-grandmother wus named Nancy Pool an' she wus not afraid of nothin'. I wus a little teency thing when she died.

"My mother tole we all about dem times dey rode de horses up to de smoke house an' got de meat. De Yankees went to de clothes line an' got de clothes an'[Pg 429] filled de legs an' arms wid corn an' slung it over dere saddles an' rode away. Yes, de Yankees freed us but dey lef' nuthin' for us to live on. Dey give us freedom but dey took mos' everything an' lef' us nuthin' to eat, nuthin' to live on.

"We lived in Wake County all de time. I did not git only to the third grade in school. Sister Mary Eliza got to de second grade. Father could write a little, mother couldn't. Couldn't go to school 'cept when it wus too wet to work. Work, work, work, thirty acres in cotton an' cawn, cawn plowed till de 15th of August, plow, plow, plow hard ground, bad ground. Nine girls an' one boy workin' from sun to sun. My mother had twenty-three chillun. She wus just as smart as she could be, worked in de field till just awhile before she died. She been dead 'bout twenty years. My father been dead 'bout ten years. He died right here in Raleigh with me, at 121 corner Mark an' Bledsoe Street.

"I've had a hard time workin' all my life. I ain't able to work now but I does all I can. I have places to work a little every day for my white folks. I am gwine to work long as I kin. My mother an' father said dey had good marsters an' dey were crazy 'bout 'em. Sometimes[Pg 430] dey sold slaves an' den de patterollers whupped 'em now an' den, but dey had nuthin' to say against dere white folks.

"Well, I los' my home. I have worked mos' uv my life since I come to Raleigh, buyin' a home, but I got ole an' couldn't keep up de payments an' dey come down ere an' took my home. 'Twas the wurst thing dats come to me in my whole life. Less you tried it yo' can't 'magine how bad it makes you feel to have to give up yer home."

AC

N.C. District: No. 2
Worker: T. Pat Matthews
No. Words: 398
Subject: HILLIARD YELLERDAY (A SLAVE STORY)
Reference: Hilliard Yellerday
Editor: George L. Andrews

# HILLIARD YELLERDAY

**1112 Oakwood Avenue, Raleigh North Carolina.**

"My mother and father told me many interesting stories of slavery and of its joys and sorrows. From what they told me there was two sides to the picture. One was extremely bad and the other was good.

"These features of slavery were also dependent on the phases of human attitude and temperment which also was good or bad. If the master was broadminded, with a love in his heart for his fellowman, his slaves were at no disadvantage because of their low social standing and their lack of a voice in the civil affairs of the community, state, and nation. On the other hand if the master was narrowminded, overbearing and cruel the case was reversed and the situation the slaves were placed in caused a condition to exist concerning their general welfare that was bad and the slave was as low socially as the swine or other animals on the plantation.

"Some owners gave their slaves the same kind of food served on their own tables and allowed the slaves the same privileges enjoyed by their own children. Other masters fed their slave children from troughs made very much like those from which the hogs of the plantation were fed. There were many instances where they were given water in which the crumbs and refuse from the masters table had been placed. They gathered around this food with gourds and muscle shells from the fresh-water creeks and ate from this trough. Such a condition was very bad indeed."

[HW: begin]

"My mother was named Maggie Yellerday, and my father was named Sam Yellerday. They belonged to Dr. Jonathan Yellerday, who owned a large plantation and over a hundred slaves. His plantation looked like a small town. He had blacksmith shops, shoe shops, looms for weaving cloth, a corn mill, and a liquor distillery. There was a tanyard covering more than a quarter of an acre where he tanned the hides of animals to use in making shoes. There was a large bell they used to wake the slaves, in the morning, and to call them to their meals during the day. He had carriages and horses, stable men and carriage men. The carriage master and his family rode in was called a coach by the slaves on the plantation. His house had eighteen rooms, a large hall, and four large porches. The house set in a large grove about one mile square and the slave quarters were arranged in rows at the back of master's great house. The nearest cabins were about one hundred yards from it.

"Dr. Jonathan Yellerday looked after slaves' health and the food was fair, but the slaves were worked by overseers who made it hard for them, as he allowed them to whip a slave at will. He had so many slaves he did not know all their names. His fortune was his slaves. He did not sell slaves and he did not buy many, the last ten years preceding the war. He resorted to raising his own slaves.

"When a girl became a woman she was required to go to a man and become a mother. There was generally a form of marriage. The master read a paper to them telling them they were man and wife. Some were married by the master laying down a broom and the two slaves, man and woman would jump over it. The master would then tell them they were man and wife and they could go to bed together. Master would sometimes go and get a large hale hearty Negro man from some other plantation to go to his Negro woman. He would ask the other master to let this man come over to his place to go to his slave girls. A slave girl was expected to have children as soon as she became a woman. Some of them had children at the age of twelve and thirteen years old. Negro men six feet tall went to some of these children.

"Mother said there were cases where these young girls loved someone else and would have to receive the attentions of men of the master's choice. This was a general custom. This state of affairs tended to loosen the morals of the Negro race and they have never fully recovered from its effect. Some slave women would have dozens of men during their life. Negro women who had had a half dozen mock husbands in slavery time were plentiful. The holy bonds of matrimony did not mean much to a slave. The masters called themselves Christians, went to church worship regularly and yet allowed this condition to exist. Mother, father, sister and I were sent as refugees from Mississippi to N.C. They were afraid the Yankees would get us in Mississippi. I was only four years old when the war ended as I was born April 6, 1861 so I do not remember the trip. We were sent to Warren County to the Brownloe's plantation where we stayed until the war ended.

"There was a question as to just what Mississippi would do and then mother said the Doctor feared we would be taken by the Yankees there so he sent us to N.C. to the above named County. Mother was sent to stay with Mrs. Green Parrish and she took me with her. Mr. Green Parrish was gone to the war. In the last of the war, he was wounded and sent home. While he was recovering I fanned the flies off him. That's the first thing I remember about the war. When he got well he went back and then the war soon ended. After the war ended father and the family moved to Halifax County and worked on a farm belonging to Mr. Sterling Johnston. I was in Warren County when I first began to remember anything and I do not have any specific remembrance of the Yankees. We stayed in Halifax County eighteen years, going from one plantation to another, but we made no money. The landlords got all we made except what we ate and wore. They would always tell us we ate ours up. Sometimes we would be almost naked, barefooted and hungry when the crop was housed and then the landlord would make us leave. We would go to another with about the same results.

"There was a story going that each slave would get forty acres of land and a mule at the end of the war. The Yankees started this story but the mule and land was never given and slaves were turned out without anything and with nowhere to go.

"We moved to Wake County and I farmed until 1903. I had not gotten one hundred dollars ahead in all this time so I got a job with the railroad, S.A.L. Shops in Raleigh, N.C. and that is the only place I ever made any money.

"Father died in 1900 and mother in 1923. I worked from 1903 until 1920 with the S.A.L. Railroad as flunkey. I worked as box packer and machinist's helper. Mother and father died without ever owning a house but I saved my money while working for the Railroad Company and bought this lot 157 X 52-1/2 and had this house built on it. The house has five rooms and cost about one thousand dollars. I've been so of late years I could not pay my taxes. I am partially blind and unable to work anymore."

EH

www.ingramcontent.com/pod-product-compliance
Lightning Source LLC
LaVergne TN
LVHW061309060426
835507LV00019B/2071